TURNING
POINTE

CHLOE ANGYAL

TURNING POINTE

How a New Generation *of* Dancers
Is Saving Ballet *from* Itself

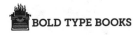
BOLD TYPE BOOKS

New York

Bold Type Books
116 East 16th Street, 8th Floor New York, NY 10003
www.boldtypebooks.org
@BoldTypeBooks

Printed in the United States of America

First Edition: May 2021

Published by Bold Type Books, an imprint of Perseus Books, LLC, a subsidiary of Hachette Book Group, Inc. Bold Type Books is a co-publishing venture of the Type Media Center and Perseus Books.

The Hachette Speakers Bureau provides a wide range of authors for speaking events. To find out more, go to www.hachettespeakersbureau.com or call (866) 376-6591.

The publisher is not responsible for websites (or their content) that are not owned by the publisher.

Print book interior design by Amy Quinn

Library of Congress Cataloging-in-Publication Data
Names: Angyal, Chloe, author.
Title: Turning pointe : how a new generation of dancers is saving ballet from itself / Chloe Angyal.
Description: New York, NY : Bold Type Books, [2021] | Includes bibliographical references and index.
Identifiers: LCCN 2020046028 | ISBN 9781645036708 (hardcover) | ISBN 9781645036722 (ebook)
Subjects: LCSH: Ballet. | Dance—Sex differences.
Classification: LCC GV1787 .A54 2021 | DDC 792.8—dc23
LC record available at https://lccn.loc.gov/2020046028

ISBNs: 978-1-64503-670-8 (hardcover), 978-1-64503-672-2 (ebook)

LSC-C

Printing 1, 2021

For Belle, who longed for ballet lessons, and for Abby, who made sure I had them

This was the dichotomy—the achievement of fragility and delicacy meant a core of strength. Butterflies are not weak.

—ALLEGRA KENT, *ONCE A DANCER: AN AUTOBIOGRAPHY*

CONTENTS

Contents

INTRODUCTION

THE FIGHT FOR THE FUTURE OF BALLET

Every day, in dance studios all across America, legions of children line up at the barre and take a ballet class. This book is about what they learn there, not just about dance, but about gender, race, and power, about the value of their bodies and minds. About their place in the world both in and outside of dance.

The vast majority of those who take ballet classes in the United States are girls, many of whom aspire to grow up to become the ultimate in femininity, the epitome of a very particular kind of womanhood: a ballerina.[1] Very, very few of them—an infinitesimally small number—will achieve that goal. This book is also about what awaits those who do: what the select few who make it to the top of the ballet world experience and endure in order to live their dream of dancing professionally.

Despite its widespread popularity in the United States, despite its central place in American childhood, ballet can seem a world apart—a place governed by different rules than the larger culture of the country, isolated from its most pressing problems and its overlapping crises.

Certainly the nature of ballet—its association with the economic and cultural elite, its cultivated glamour and opacity, its inescapable Frenchness and fanciness, and the almost nunlike lives that so many of its professional practitioners lead—all contribute to this sense that ballet is another world entirely.

1

And it's true that ballet does have some very odd rules. For example, a ballet class doesn't end until the students bow (or curtsy) to the teacher and he or she bows back. Sometimes the bows are performed as an elaborate choreographed sequence, completed, like every ballet exercise, first on the right side and then on the left. It's both an odd rule and a reinforcement of the sense that ballet is a separate world, governed by a different set of laws than the world where most people live.

But as the dance scholar Brenda Dixon Gottschild wrote in her landmark book *The Black Dancing Body*, "Dance is a measure of society, not something apart from it."[2] And ballet—just like American society—is cracking under the weight of multiple interlocking crises, some of them of its own making.

Given the millions of children whose early lives are shaped by ballet, the art form demands our attention. And perhaps the crises rocking American society can be seen with greater, necessary clarity by examining ballet. Because ballet, like the larger society in which it sits, finds itself at a turning point: Will it remain mired in its old traditions and entrenched prejudices, or will it remake itself into something less broken and more beautiful?

While I was reporting this book, I met and interviewed dozens and dozens of inhabitants of the ballet world—dancers, teachers, choreographers, artistic directors, parents, health care providers—who told me stories that demonstrated just how badly ballet needs to be saved from itself.

What I found was an ecosystem in crisis, made fragile and brittle by years of inequality and rendered dysfunctional by sexism, racism, elitism, and a stubborn disregard for the physical and mental well-being of the dancers who make the art form possible.

I interviewed a gifted gender nonconforming dancer who was pushed out of ballet because their teachers refused to imagine what the art form might look like without its rigid gender binary. I interviewed a Black ballet mom whose biracial daughter was subject to racist treatment at the hands of a white ballet mom. A professional dancer who injured himself onstage and continued performing through excruciating pain because his company did not offer adequate health insurance and he could not afford to miss a show. A dancer who was kept offstage because she wasn't thin enough for her artistic director's taste, and an artistic director who described firing dancers for being "out of shape." A Black choreographer who watched his white classmates get handed opportunities he was denied despite his comparable talent and potential. A former elite ballet student who remembered the creepy requests her teachers had made of her and her teenage classmates—and another former elite ballet student who sued one of the world's most revered ballet institutions for creating what she called a "fraternity-like atmosphere," a fertile environment for sexualized abuse of women by men.[3]

Each of these stories suggested that some essential part of the ballet world was breaking down. Together, they revealed that the ecosystem was perhaps already broken, and that, in turn, it was breaking people.

Inhabitants of the American ballet world—people who loved ballet and needed it to love them back—warned me that unless something changed, unless ballet's gatekeepers could radically reimagine what the art form could be and whom it could serve, it would die: death by irrelevance, death by inaccessibility, death by excluding the very dancers and creators and audience members who could keep it alive and carry it into the future.

For some observers the die-off might have been difficult to detect, but the more marginalized members of the ballet world, made prophetic by their exclusion, could see it happening. They could feel it. It was a slow-motion extinction happening one ballet dancer and one ballet dream at a time.

And then the flood came.

⌒

By April 2020, just a few months after I finished the bulk of the reporting for this book, the coronavirus pandemic had swept over the ballet world, wiping away familiar structures and leaving others in a desperate state.

Theaters and dance studios sat empty. Spring recitals were called off. Emerging choreographers had their debuts postponed, and retiring dancers had their farewell performances canceled. Ballet schools pivoted to Zoom classes and then to drastically reduced class sizes, and students staged digital performances and recorded video competition entries. Ballet companies pivoted to digital offerings, emergency fund appeals, and dance pods after canceling their spring seasons.

Around the country, professional ballet dancers kept dancing as best they could in their cramped apartments, using kitchen counters and balcony railings as makeshift barres as they tried to stay in shape through furloughs. Footage of dancers making do in their homes went viral, supposedly inspirational videos of dancers jumping on shin splint–inducing hardwood floors and attempting grand battements in their living rooms as their confused cats dodged their swinging legs.

Some dancers had company contracts to go back to but no idea when they'd be able to go back to them; others were still employed but were barely being paid. Still others saw their freelance dance performance opportunities disappear overnight but remained hopeful that the second half of the year could be salvaged.

By May, it was clear that wasn't going to happen, as theaters stayed dark and companies that had canceled their spring seasons canceled their summer intensives and residencies. Then their fall seasons, then their *Nutcracker*s. *The Nutcracker* is to an American ballet company what the fall football season is to a state school: an essential source of revenue that funds the rest of the year's operations.[4] At some ballet companies, *Nutcracker* takings account for close to 50 percent of the year's ticket sales.[5]

As was the case for so many parts of American life, the pandemic exposed the fragility and dysfunction of a system that had been working well enough for enough privileged people that its failings could be papered over and explained away. And as is the case for so many parts of American life, ballet is never going back to how it was before the flood.

Nor should it: as I learned in my reporting, what was normal for some had already been a crisis for too many others. In the words of Sean Aaron Carmon, a Black contemporary dancer and choreographer who performed with Alvin Ailey American Dance Theater before joining the touring cast of Disney's *The Lion King*, "Your normal was our oppression."

Take, for example, the racial segregation of the American ballet world, where dancers of color and especially Black dancers have had to struggle for generations to get access to elite ballet training and achieve even a token presence in the nation's most prestigious predominately white ballet institutions. There are still American ballet companies—high-profile ones in large and racially diverse cities, with big budgets and large feeder schools—that have just one or two Black dancers in their ranks.

It took two simultaneous crises—a global pandemic and a global mainstreaming of the Black Lives Matter movement—for a large number of American ballet companies to finally make meaningful public commitments to racial justice. In the spring of 2020, under pressure from dancers of color and amid a national reckoning with police brutality against Black people that prompted parallel outrage about employment discrimination in a range of fields, many American ballet companies and schools participated in well-publicized social media actions pronouncing their intention to become more diverse and inclusive.

Schools and companies pledged to do better at recruiting, hiring, and retaining dancers and faculty members of color, especially Black artists and teachers. Companies promised to commission and perform more works by choreographers of color and to remove offensive depictions of racial and ethnic minorities from their existing productions (for example, the "Chinese" tea segment of *The Nutcracker*, which is often performed in yellowface). White dancers committed to speaking out about racial injustices in their field. And in the months that followed, there were some signs of progress: dance schools and companies around the country introduced new rules permitting dancers of color to wear tights and shoes that matched their skin tone, and two of the nation's most prestigious companies commissioned several new ballets by choreographers of color. What began in the summer of 2020 has the potential to prompt a genuine reckoning with the art form's overwhelming and closely guarded whiteness.

Such a reckoning isn't just long overdue; it's essential, and those of us who care about the future of ballet should welcome it. If ballet survives, it will be because of the individuals and institutions who are demanding that it do better, who have long loved ballet and are now insisting that it, finally, love them back.

I caught my first glimpse of the future of ballet before the pandemic, in the spring of 2018. It came to me in the dark, as so many moments of revelation do, at the very end of a performance of *Giselle*, one of the most beloved ballets in the classical canon, with a title role that women in ballet dream of dancing.

The story of *Giselle* is classic fairy tale fare—the old kind of fairy tale, unsweetened and un-Disneyfied. A peasant girl, Giselle, falls for Albrecht, a duke in disguise. She doesn't know that Albrecht, who appears to be a peasant, is in fact engaged to a noblewoman. When Albrecht's deception is revealed by the jealous gamekeeper who also loves Giselle, she goes mad and dies of despair. In death, she joins the Wilis, forest spirits—all women, all victims of masculine betrayal—who trap men in the woods and force them to dance to their deaths. But when the Wilis descend on a grieving Albrecht, Giselle—in an act of love and forgiveness—saves his life. The two are reunited for a brief moment before she returns to her woodland grave and he returns to his castle on the hill.

Like many beloved story ballets, *Giselle* is a tragedy, a tale of love, betrayal, and forgiveness. And as in many beloved story ballets, the heroine dies (or stays dead) at the end. That's the way the story has been told since the ballet was first staged in Paris in 1841, with choreography by two men and a libretto by two men, based on source material by two other men.

In almost three decades of watching ballet, I had only ever seen this version, the men's version, of the story—until the evening at the Joyce Theater in New York City when I saw Dada Masilo's version of *Giselle*.

Masilo, a Black South African choreographer, took the familiar music of Adolphe Adam and the choreography of Jules Perrot and Marius Petipa and remixed them, adding South African rhythms and steps to create something recognizable but radical. Masilo made other changes, too. For example, in the first act, she highlighted the sexualized shame that Giselle feels when she discovers that her lover has lied about his identity. In traditional productions, Giselle pulls down her hair in the famous "mad scene," her change in appearance indicating to the audience that she, too, is coming undone. In Masilo's production, Giselle is stripped of some of her clothing, left vulnerable, humiliated, and exposed by Albrecht's deception.

And in the second act of Masilo's *Giselle*, when Giselle is given the chance to save Albrecht from the deadly revenge of her ghost sisters, she does something I'd never seen her do before: she lets him die. He begs her for forgiveness, but she does not grant it. Instead, she lets the man who betrayed her die, and in the final moments of the music, she steps over his dead body and walks off the stage into a bright light.

This "cold-blooded" interpretation of *Giselle*, wrote the Undefeated's Soraya Nadia McDonald in a beaming review, allowed the character to feel something I hadn't seen in any other production: "untapped feminine rage."[6]

McDonald compared the ballet's final scene to the iconic moment in the movie *Waiting to Exhale* when Angela Bassett's Bernadine, her face eloquent with rage and her nails impeccable, sets her cheating husband's car alight. "Darkness cannot drive out darkness," McDonald wrote, "but Masilo's Giselle doesn't need her love for Albrecht to serve as her guiding light. Choosing herself will suffice."

When the curtain came down at the Joyce that night, I sat in my seat, mouth open, for quite a while. I was not just moved; I was flabbergasted. It had never occurred to me that Giselle had always had this option, that she could choose something else for herself and for the man who wronged her. That she could do something different with the strange power death had brought her.

In all those years of watching this ballet, I had never asked, Why *does* Giselle forgive the man who got her killed? What if she didn't? What if he didn't deserve her clemency? I did not think it was a coincidence that the first production to ask these questions, the first version of *Giselle* to truly reckon with the damage Albrecht's lies do to Giselle's spirit, was also the first version I'd ever seen that was choreographed by a woman of color.

Masilo's production was an intoxicating taste of what this old art form might look like in the hands of the people it has long excluded.

I had had glimpses of this kind of revelation before, mostly by observing other people who were experiencing it. A year earlier, in the spring of 2017, I'd gone to Lincoln Center with the HuffPost Video team to interview audience members at a weekday matinee performance of American Ballet Theatre's *Swan Lake*, starring Misty Copeland. Copeland had been promoted to principal dancer two years before, the first—and to date the only—Black woman to dance at that rank in the company's eighty-one-year history (its closest domestic rival, New York City Ballet, which performs across Lincoln Center's plaza, has never had a Black woman principal in its seventy-two-year history).

That day, we interviewed six-year-old girls and sixty-something-year-old women, many of whom had come to the ballet for the very first time specifically to see Misty. One had come as part of a group of Black women who had chartered a bus from Delaware. One teenage dance student said she hadn't realized Black girls could do ballet until she learned about Copeland. And a trio of Black women said that before Copeland had been promoted to dancing principal roles at ABT, they had traveled the country to see her perform as a guest artist with other companies that would put her in principal roles.

I stood outside the Metropolitan Opera House that baking June day, watching a huge and racially diverse audience line up for a sold-out performance. They were buzzing with excitement, and so was I. It felt

like we were standing at the culmination of a long struggle and the beginning of a thrilling new era.

While writing this book, I experienced that spark of hope over and
over again, the sense that ballet can be saved from its own narrow, exclusive, and self-defeating understanding of who gets to dance and how,
of who belongs in this art form and how they deserve to be treated. Of
whose ballet dreams matter.

~

As I was writing this book, there were two questions I was asked over
and over again. First, was I ever a professional ballet dancer? I was not.

I started ballet lessons almost as soon as I could walk, and my parents' photo albums are full of proof of how much I loved dancing. There
are photos of me in ballet class in a cold and dusty church hall in Sydney, Australia, photos of me backstage in a recital costume and garish
early-90s makeup, photos of me under the Christmas tree in a bathing
suit and ballet slippers, because what is a bathing suit if not a leotard
you can swim in?

Was I the most talented or skilled dancer on that recital stage?
Grainy VHS evidence suggests I wasn't. But I was the most committed
dancer, the most delighted to be out there, the most *extra*. I just loved
to dance.

I took ballet lessons on and off throughout my childhood, taking
some time away for a detour into gymnastics, which reshaped my body
in a way that I was told was incompatible with serious ballet training.
Once I quit gymnastics and hit puberty, it became clear that in addition
to lacking the rigorous training and exceptional talent a girl needs to
make it as a ballet dancer, I really didn't have the body for it—or rather,
I had *too much* body for it.

But even as I moved into other styles of dance, like lyrical jazz and
Broadway-style jazz, I never stopped trying to be good at ballet, and I
never stopped loving it. I joined a mixed-style dance company in college, and after graduation I moved to New York City to begin a career
in journalism. Eventually, at HuffPost, where I had originally been

hired to cover breaking news, I carved out a mini beat for myself: the ballet beat.

My knowledge of the lives of professional ballet dancers comes not from experience but from five years of reporting. From this vantage point, as a white journalist, there are surely some intimate details I have missed, especially of the experiences of dancers of color, but there are certainly some large patterns that I have been able to identify.

The other question I was asked as I wrote this book was, Is *Turning Pointe* a history of ballet? It is not. There are already dozens of rigorously researched, beautifully written histories of ballet. I depended on many of them in order to write this book, and I'm quite sure historians are at work on even more of them as I write this sentence.

I am not a historian. I am a sociologist and media researcher by training, and a journalist and writer by trade. And so this book is not about ballet's history. Instead, it is about ballet's present and, most crucially, its future.

This book is also not a scandalized exposé, a revelation that a world defined by beauty and refinement has a secret, seedy underbelly. Because ballet's secret, seedy underbelly isn't a secret at all; it's fodder for a steady supply of movies and television shows. Ballet's unusual blend of glamour and repression makes it easy to fathom a twisted dark truth behind the upright glittering beauty we see onstage.

I almost wish I had written that kind of book: people love a good scandal. But instead, I wrote a book about an art form that I love, and the ways in which that art form is broken, and how that brokenness endangers its survival.

It's true that some of that brokenness involves scandals, the kind of bleed-and-lead stories that make the papers. More often, though, it involves the kind of systemic and cultural exclusion—by race, by class, by gender—that shapes the rest of American life.

In fact, even the bleeding-and-leading stories, stories about sexual harassment, gruesome injury, and suicide, can be traced to those systemic problems and to the ballet world's skewed power dynamics.

Those power dynamics leave certain groups of people extraordinarily vulnerable to exploitation, and that exploitation can result in physical injury, mental illness, and obvious violations of bodily autonomy, workers' rights, and basic human dignity.

And although I am not a historian, I believe that imagining ballet's just and equitable future requires a full reckoning with its unjust and inequitable past. To give just one example, that means being honest about the Great Men who made great contributions to the art form, and how their shortcomings also contributed to ballet's current brokenness.

It means talking about George Balanchine's revolutionary choreography *and* his reactionary gender politics. It means quoting his inspirational aphorisms about art—"First comes the sweat, then comes the beauty"—without forgetting the appalling things he said to his dancers—"Now, Allegra, no more babies. Enough is enough. Babies are for Puerto Ricans."[7]

It means admiring Jerome Robbins's work—his groundbreaking *The Cage* and his gorgeous *Dances at a Gathering*—and acknowledging that he treated the dancers who performed those ballets with abusive cruelty.[8]

And it means noticing the ways in which the history of ballet, and thus our current understanding of the art form, have been shaped by the failure to be honest, the failure to recognize abuse as abuse, and the entrenched tendency to privilege excellent work over the experience of workers. That these workers are also artists is no excuse, even though it has long been used as one. For decades, the men—and they are almost all men—who have wielded power in ballet have been described in terms that accept the abuse of dancers as the cost of great dancing.

Historians have long written about "fiery" and "choleric" teachers, about "tyrannical" but "visionary" choreographers who worked their dancers "to the point of fainting"—before swiftly moving on to praise those men for their contributions to the art form. Consider historian Carol Lee's description of Charles-Louis Didelot, a Swedish- and French-trained Frenchman who taught in Russia in the early 1800s:

Accounts of Didelot's tempestuous classroom demeanor were legendary in their time and rank high among the most colorful stories to come down from thirteen generations of dancers. . . . A dynamo of energy and impatience, for up to five hours he would cajole, demand, slap, and rage at his youthful charges. He spared neither his foot nor his stick to elicit the proper execution of exercises and steps of the *danse d'ecole*. The more gifted the dancer, the harsher the blows. The students feared him and dreaded his classes. At the same time Didelot's ferocious artistic integrity inspired his pupils and they worshipped their terrifying teacher.[9]

Or consider dance journalist Joseph Mazo's 1974 account of New York City Ballet under cofounders Balanchine and Lincoln Kirstein: "Lincoln knows perfectly well why dancers become injured; he knows the stresses that weary and erode them, but a dancer who gets hurt is 'an idiot'—because the resulting injury prevents him from performing [Balanchine's] ballets. Still, there is an undertone to the calling of names, 'idiot . . . fool . . . bitch . . . cow . . . stupid,' the sound of a mother badmouthing children she loves, wishing them stronger, safer, more secure and more obedient."[10]

Just as it is not somehow anti-ballet to take full account of the art form's brokenness, it is not disrespectful to these men to be honest about their shortcomings. Rather, it is disrespectful to ballet, to the dancers who suffered at the hands of these men, and to the next generation of ballet dancers to ignore those shortcomings or to make excuses for them.

If ballet is going to survive in the twenty-first century, if it is going to chart a path into a more socially just future, this reckoning is due, too. In fact, it is long overdue.

~

The reporting for this book included approximately one hundred interviews with members of the dance world—dancers and former dancers, teachers, choreographers, artistic directors, health care providers, students, parents—most conducted in late 2019 and early 2020. Not all of these people are quoted in the pages that follow, but many are. All but a few interviews were recorded and transcribed, in which cases I have removed verbal tics and filler words ("um," "uh," "like," "you know") unless they seemed essential to the tone of the quote. A handful of interviews were reconstructed from notes I took during the conversation. Some people are quoted anonymously or using a pseudonym so they could speak freely about institutions they once or still belonged to. When I interviewed people under eighteen, it was with a parent's or guardian's permission, and I have used pseudonyms for minors unless a parent gave me permission to use the minor's real name.

Ballet is a global phenomenon. It began in France and Italy, but now you can learn or watch ballet everywhere from Sydney, Australia, where I grew up, to the suburbs of Iowa City, where I now live. With very few exceptions, this book is about the United States, mostly for practical reasons: that is where I live, and a book that reported on the experiences of ballet dancers in other countries would have required a travel budget and language proficiencies that I did not possess.

In choosing whom to interview for this book, I prioritized racial and geographical diversity, with mixed success; my sources were scattered all over the country, but because New York is the center of gravity in American ballet, many of the people I interviewed were based there, even if they'd begun their dance training elsewhere. Similarly, about 35 percent of my sources were people of color, with a concentration among dancers; this reflected a block in the pipeline that carries artists from dancing to positions of greater artistic and administrative power, like choreographing and running ballet companies.

Finally, everyone's experience in the ballet world is different, and you may or may not find yours represented in this book—though I certainly hope that you do. If you find yourself reading about hardships that you have not personally experienced, or pain that you have not personally felt, I urge you not to imagine that just because it hasn't happened to you, it does not happen at all.

In the wake of the coronavirus pandemic, rebuilding ballet for a more just and equitable future isn't simply a matter of remixing ballet's old fairy tales into more contemporary narratives. If only it were that simple. Saving ballet from itself will take radical creativity and an unwavering commitment to justice.

Yes, it will mean telling new stories and installing new storytellers to bring them to life. But more than that, it will mean reimagining what kinds of bodies are worth putting onstage, which women are allowed to be seen as beautiful and graceful, whose childhood dreams are worth nurturing and subsidizing. The work will be hard and complicated, but the choice is simple: evolve or die.

Imagining a more just future for ballet is the only thing that will ensure its survival. Marginalized members of the ballet world have been saying as much for years, decades even, and it is time—past time—for the rest of the ballet world to listen.

Ballet is at a turning point. Whether it heads backward, enthralled by a narrow vision of a broken past, or finds the courage to imagine a more just and beautiful future, is the question of this book.

CHAPTER 1

THE HIDDEN CURRICULUM

By virtue of its physical challenges, [ballet] demands young bodies, and by virtue of its musical and allusive complexities, it demands old wisdom.

MINDY ALOFF

Let's begin where ballet does: at the barre. Picture a ballet barre somewhere in America. Perhaps it's bolted to the wall of a sunlit state-of-the-art studio in midtown Manhattan, where the students have come from all over the nation to devote as many hours as they can to this centuries-old art form, living in residential dorms and taking their academic classes online. Maybe it's a wobbly freestanding barre that's been pulled out into the middle of a multipurpose room in a community center or a church hall in the rural-ish suburbs of Iowa, where students take a mix of tap, jazz, hip-hop, and ballet, scheduled around softball practice or rehearsals for the school play.

Wherever it is in the country—in the world, in fact—and at every level of difficulty, ballet class begins here. Left hand on the barre, feet fanned out in first position, shoulders down, chin up. A deep breath, and the music begins. Perhaps it's from a piano played by a trained ballet class accompanist; more likely, it's a recorded track on a made-for-ballet-class CD or playlist. Pliés, then tendus. Right leg, then left. Depending on whom you ask, the repetition and reliability are either confining or comforting—or both.

Every day, all over the United States, ballet classes unfold this way. Lots of them. Ballet has been a staple of American childhood for several generations, and in the last decade, the popularity of televised dance competitions like *So You Think You Can Dance* and *Dancing with the Stars* have helped create a growing market for private dance education. By one industry estimate, there were about fifty-three thousand dance schools in the US in 2019.[1]

Schools make up the largest part of ballet's ecosystem, an enormous, teeming foundation layer on which the rest of the ballet world depends. Even so, these schools are where most inhabitants of the ballet world—most dancers, most teachers, most parents—will remain. Some students will continue dancing seriously after they graduate from high school, spending their college years in university dance programs and graduating with degrees or minors in dance. However, this route frequently forecloses the chance of joining a professional company, as the years between eighteen and twenty-two are prime dancing years.

A tiny number of America's many ballet students will be deemed to have enough talent, the right training, and the "correct" body to become professionals. The nation's largest ballet companies have between fifty and ninety dancers, and turnover can be slow, especially at the top. Smaller companies tend to have faster turnover but fewer members. Many companies have a strong preference for dancers who have been trained in part or in full by the private feeder schools that are associated with the company. For example, New York City Ballet hires many of its dancers as they graduate from its feeder school, the School of American Ballet, where, in the final years of high school, students are dancing almost full-time.

To increase their chances of getting into feeder schools (and, by extension, their associated companies), students may supplement their regular training with summer intensive programs, which are multiweek residential ballet camps open to students starting at about age twelve and are usually hosted by feeder schools. The lucky few might be offered an invitation to train at the school year-round.

Then there is the ballet competition scene, which was a rapidly growing industry before the pandemic made live ballet competitions impossible. As the ballet competition industry grew, it became more common for dancers to enter these contests, which offer them practice performing and might also put them in front of representatives of feeder schools and the companies they feed. At some competitions, entry to those schools *is* the prize. Some competitions do offer scholarship money for ballet training. But like summer intensives, dance competitions can be very expensive—there's the cost of registration, costumes, private coaching, travel—and can heap an additional financial burden on already-stretched parents.

It's true that not all the millions of girls who take dance classes are taking ballet, but a lot of them are, especially because many girls begin with ballet before branching out into other styles of dance. (As we'll see later, it often goes the other way for boys, who can be convinced to take tap or hip-hop but have to be cajoled and incentivized into taking ballet classes.) In ballet classes, girls outnumber boys twenty to one.[2] And many studios require dance students focused on jazz, modern, or lyrical styles to keep taking ballet, since most dance teachers believe that ballet technique is the foundation on which many other dance styles are built.

As Melissa Klapper painstakingly details in her cultural history of ballet in America, *Ballet Class: An American History*, over the course of the twentieth century, ballet education went from barely existing in the United States to being central to American childhood, and specifically to American girlhood.[3] And so, it is not only the stories of the lucky and talented few who become professional ballet dancers that matter. The stories of all ballet's dancers—the whole vast ecosystem—deserve our attention. Because it's in ballet class, no matter how long they stick with it, that so many girls learn what it means to be a woman.

One reason dancers often move on to other styles of dance after starting in ballet is that ballet classes can seem slow and unrewarding. At the beginning of ballet training, there is a large emphasis on small movements. A battement tendu, where the dancer stands on one foot and stretches the other foot away, knee straight and toes pointed, is a small and simple movement, one that a dancer will repeat dozens of times in a single class. Tendu to the front, to the side, to the back, to the side, all while tethered to the barre, as classical music plays.

As dancers grow stronger and more flexible, those small movements eventually become larger. A battement tendu becomes a grand battement, a big, flashy movement that impresses onlookers. And a grand battement can become a soaring jump, a grand jeté that flies across a studio or a stage such that, for a few thrilling seconds, the dancer defies gravity.

But building that technique takes time and endless repetition. "It may be difficult for those who have never watched a ballet class," wrote Lincoln Kirstein, the cofounder of the New York City Ballet, "to appreciate the tedious practice and relentless correction, even of experienced performers, at the core of this vocation." Ballet rewards those who start early in life, and its emphasis on slow, small movements performed dozens of times means it demands focus and discipline from very young children. Many of the professional dancers I interviewed remembered feeling bored and stifled by their early ballet classes.

Ballet class as we know it today dates from the 1830s, when Carlo Blasis, the director of the ballet school at La Scala in Milan—which still houses one of the world's premier ballet schools and one of its finest ballet companies—codified a three-part class based on his devoted study of Leonardo da Vinci's work on the human body. Blasis "pored over Leonardo . . . in an attempt to uncover the precise mechanics of an expressive body," writes ballet historian Jennifer Homans, and "charted the weights and balances and contemplated the physics of moving thus and so without compromising balance and line."[4] Then he took what he'd learned and fashioned it into a ballet class. It began at the barre, then moved into the center of the room, and finally culminated with jumps and turns that crossed the whole length of the studio. And it lasted three hours.

Today, most ballet classes run between forty-five minutes for young students and ninety minutes for the oldest and most advanced. The first section, barre, is designed to warm up the body. Barre is a combination of stretching and strengthening that allows the dancer to practice, with a little extra support, the movements she'll repeat in the center with nothing but her own body for balance. As the legendary ballerina and teacher Alexandra Danilova put it, "The barre gives you a third leg— you begin class with three legs and you finish with two."[5]

It's in the second and third parts of class, the two-legged parts, that students do something that outsiders might recognize as dancing. But this is deceptive, because barre is dancing too. Even though the dancer appears to be moving only one leg at a time or one side of her body at a time, make no mistake: her entire body is working hard, even with a third leg to help support her. By the end of barre, when the more advanced dancers often change out of their soft canvas ballet slippers and into their pointe shoes, they have also shed all their warm-up gear. One of my ballet teachers used to admonish us that if we weren't sweating halfway through barre, we weren't working hard enough.

For ballet students, class, as the name suggests, is a place for learning. It's where they learn and perfect new skills. For the few students who go on to join professional ballet companies, class will become less about learning and more about daily body maintenance.

In a company, everyone—from the entry-level dancers (apprentices) to the established stars (principals)—takes a morning class together, in most companies five days a week. After a ninety-minute class and a short break, most of the company goes on to complete between four and six hours of rehearsals, either for the ballet they'll perform that night or for some other production entirely. Then another break, a meal, hair and makeup, and then another, shorter class to get their bodies warm for the performance. Then it's showtime. They leave the theater after a performance between 9 and 11 p.m. and come back twelve hours later for another company class.

Even ballet dancers who are paid to perform several nights a week spend vastly more time in class and rehearsal than they do onstage. And for students, whose performance opportunities are usually limited to twice-yearly recitals and, for some, competitions, it's not even close: class is where they spend most of their ballet lives.

New steps and ballet technique aren't the only things young ballet students learn in class. Like every educational space, ballet has an official curriculum—how to lift the leg properly in a grand battement, for example, without hiking up the hip or bending the supporting leg—but it also has a hidden curriculum. The hidden curriculum consists of the unofficial and sometimes unintended lessons students pick up from the way the class is structured or conducted, and the way students are treated. It's from the hidden curriculum, whether in biology class or ballet class, that students absorb assumptions, norms, and values.

So as they're learning the proper way to lift their legs at the barre or how to spot to keep from getting dizzy in a pirouette (another of Carlo Blasis's innovations), ballet students simultaneously learn a set of norms about how to be students and, in many ways, how to be girls and then women.

"In most dance technique classes," writes feminist dance educator Susan Stinson, "the teacher is the authority and the only recognized source of knowledge. . . . The teacher's voice is expected to be the only one heard, except in the case of a well-focused question. The teacher tells and shows the students what to do and, in some classes, how to do it. Students attempt to replicate the movement done by the teacher."[6] Then the teacher gives verbal—and often physical—corrections, instructing the students on what the movement should look like and how to get it closer to the ideal.

Ballet students are rarely permitted to talk to or interact with each other in the studio; instead, they are supposed to watch the teacher or look at themselves in the mirror. I did not realize how ingrained this habit was until I began sitting in on ballet classes to do research for this book and found that, by sheer force of habit, my eyes continually drifted to the teacher, even when I was there to observe the students.

"Some teachers give directions and corrections that refer to internal sensation and artistic qualities, not just the mechanics of the movement," Stinson concedes. "But in reality, most dance training consists of learning how to follow directions and how to follow them well." Stinson notes that although many ballet teachers are women, because of the way classes are structured and run, "the model for traditional dance pedagogy seems to be the authoritarian father."[7]

Students learn that the ideal ballet dancer is silent, observant, and obedient. They also learn that she is white: the pink tights that almost every American girl is required to wear to ballet class were originally designed to mimic the color of white women's skin, and today, girls wear them with matching pink slippers.[8] And they learn that the ideal ballet dancer carries herself with an unruffled, effortless grace and perfect posture, her spine held straight and her neck long no matter how wildly her arms and legs might be moving. Slumping is frowned upon in ballet class, even between exercises. It is an expectation of patrician carriage that reflects ballet's roots as an aristocratic art form.

The ideal dancer should also be pleasing and pleased, her face never conveying how hard she is working or how much pain she is in. "Dance itself is the enactment of an energy which must seem, in all respects, untrammeled, effortless, at every moment fully mastered," Susan Sontag writes. "The dancer's performance smile is not so much a smile as simply a categorical denial of what he or she is actually experiencing."[9]

As puberty approaches, the hidden curriculum has yet more lessons for girls. As dance diversity consultant Theresa Ruth Howard explains it, at "an age when most girls are taught to be hypervigilant about the privacy and protection of their bodies, ballet requires that not only . . . the hands of their instructors, but those of their classmates [are allowed to] touch them in places only certain doctors and lovers should be familiar with. Should a girl be squeamish about being touched or handled, she is told she is in the wrong business."[10]

It's then that adolescent girls in ballet are taught to do three things, Howard says: "to physically submit, to disregard their feelings, and most injuriously to be silent about the first two."

Ballet students learn from these unwritten rules that the perfect dancer is obedient and obliging. She is white, and if she is not wealthy, then she at least moves as if she is. And she adheres to ballet's strict gender binary, which determines what training gear and costumes girls and boys and men and women wear, what shoes they put on their feet, what roles they are cast in, and what steps they perform.

～

Katy Pyle, a white ballet teacher who was a ballet student in Texas and North Carolina in the 1990s, ran up against that gender binary often. They remember that from a young age, the way their body moved, as well as the way it looked, was surveilled and policed by their ballet teachers.

Pyle started serious ballet training at about age eleven, moving from their local dance school in their Texas hometown to a rigorous ballet program in Austin where they took classes five or six times a week. At the beginning, Pyle, who identified as a girl at the time, was excited about the opportunity to master new skills and advance their technique, and their teachers "were just really positive and excited." But after about a year in the program, they remember, "I started to get more messaging about my body in terms of the need to be thin and small." Pyle went to Russia on a performing trip and came home ill, having picked up several parasites while they were abroad.

"So I was super skinny and green, I remember being green, but my teacher was like, 'Oh, looks like Russia really did you good. You look great in your unitard today.'" When the parasites started to die, Pyle started gaining back the weight they'd lost, and that's when they developed an eating disorder, restricting their food intake in search of those positive comments about their body. They were thirteen years old.

It wasn't just a question of how their body looked but how it moved, too. When it came time to cast performances, Pyle noticed that they were being cast in roles that called for big jumps and turns, not the roles that included delicate, feminine choreography. They had wanted to play a bird in a production of *Peter and the Wolf* but were cast as a cat instead. "I wasn't birdlike. . . . I was heavier and more powerful and had more attack, and I was always jumping the highest."

Later, when Pyle joined a ballet company as an apprentice, they looked up the ranks and noticed that there was a clear dichotomy in casting: the artistic leadership of the company cast the more petite, willowy women in the lead roles, while the more muscular and athletic-looking women were cast as understudies or sidekicks.

"There were women that were more muscular and strong and powerful, and they would never get lead roles," Pyle remembers. "There was this one woman who was amazing. I think she was the best technician in that whole group, but she never got a leading role because she was too muscle-y and they didn't like her body, so she was always the understudy for everything."

Because they feared being relegated to the athletic understudy category, Pyle kept starving themself. "I was seeing I was going on that track, and that kind of encouraged me further into my eating disorder and trying to control my body so it didn't end up that way," they remember.

Pyle, who is now forty, remembers that their gender presentation was policed in less-obvious ways, too. In ballet, teachers traditionally refer to students as "girls and boys" or "ladies and gentlemen"—as in, *Let's begin in fifth position, ladies and gentlemen*—though some teachers and company ballet teachers (often referred to as ballet masters and mistresses) have lately switched to the gender-neutral term "dancers."

Pyle consistently got the message that they weren't fitting properly into the "ladies" category; something about the way they danced was *off* in a way that their ballet teachers were constantly noticing and correcting. "Things would be too strong or too powerful, and I knew that I should be trying to appear weaker," they remember, "that I should not look at something directly and move towards it, and that I should tilt my head softly and look at it sideways, and let myself be led instead of leading."

This is what ballet's hidden curriculum teaches girls: that the way to succeed is to be silent, pliant, and, in Pyle's words, "sweet and pretty." To not look at things head on but softly and from the side. To be led and looked at. Girls and women who fail to conform to the art form's rigid gender binary are penalized or pushed out, or they punish their own bodies with starvation or other dangerous, disordered behavior.

"Dance training teaches them to be silent and do as they are told, reinforcing cultural expectations for both young children and women," Stinson writes. "'Finding one's voice' is a metaphor that appears frequently when women describe their own journeys from silence to critical thinking; for women, learning to think means learning to speak with their own voices. Traditional dance pedagogy, with its emphasis on silent conformity, does not facilitate such a journey. Dancers typically learn to reproduce what they receive, not to critique or create."[11]

⌒

The vast majority of ballet students in America are girls. Every single male ballet dancer I interviewed reported that when they were young students, they were the only boy in their ballet class. And every woman dancer I spoke to remembered that in their earliest classes there were just one or two boys, if that. Several men said they had been the only boy who took ballet in their entire dance *school*, and it was rare for parents of boys who currently dance to report multiple boys in their son's class.

But boys do exist in ballet, and the hidden curriculum has a different set of lessons to teach them. Because boys are scarce, they are often treated as precious commodities in a dance school and are held to lower standards of talent, skill, and behavior than their female classmates.

Stinson argues that while boys and girls are often in the same ballet classes with the same teachers—especially before they hit puberty, which is generally when girls start dancing in pointe shoes and boys start focusing more on jumps, turns, and partnering—in those classes they're picking up different unwritten messages about their value and their place in the ballet world.[12]

For one thing, boys tend to start dance classes in general, and ballet class in particular, later than girls do. Stinson argues that starting late gives boys an advantage because, unlike very young girls, "they have developed some sense of individual identity and 'voice.'"[13] Even when they are young, the rules and the opportunities are different for boys, sometimes in very visible ways. Consider, for example, how ballet schools structure their dress codes.

While every dance studio is different, most have a dress code for ballet classes, even for very young students: at each grade level, the girls are assigned a leotard color that denotes their place in the school's ranks. They wear that leotard, sometimes with a matching skirt, over tights and ballet shoes, and sometimes with a thin elastic belt, the color of which also changes as they move up the ranks. Some schools have restrictions on how girls can wear their hair, requiring neat ballet buns from a young age and limiting the kinds of scrunchies, clips, and ribbons girls can put in their hair.

Boys, if they are present, do not wear leotards or color-coded markers of their rank. Instead, at most schools boys wear the same thing, grade after grade, until shortly before puberty: a white T-shirt, black bike shorts, and ballet slippers in black or white. As they approach puberty, they might be asked to replace bike shorts with black tights, though boys often resist this transition. Some dance teachers put it off as long as possible, wary of scaring their few male students out of ballet entirely.

Several male dancers I spoke to remembered that they had resisted wearing tights until their late teens and that their dance schools had not pressed the matter. Sean Aaron Carmon, a Black contemporary ballet dancer who performed with Alvin Ailey American Dance Theater for seven years, took ballet classes as a child in Houston. Carmon vividly remembers the first time he put on tights for ballet class, in his early teens. He was embarrassed about "being looked at, stared at," he says. "For most young boys, the last thing you want anyone staring at is your crotch . . . because you're like, 'Does it look like everybody else's? Are they going to laugh because it's small?'"

After an aunt joked that the tights made his penis look small, Carmon stopped wearing them. It wasn't until he tried out for a college dance program that he relented—and then only because the audition dress code required them.

Eric Trope, a white dancer who performs in the corps de ballet of Miami City Ballet, resisted tights, too. In fact, he resisted taking ballet classes at all *because* of the specter of tights. "I think, in general, I just thought ballet was gonna be boring and not for me," he recalls, "but I also remember the tights just being a huge factor. I didn't want to face that part of it. I didn't want to wear tights. . . . I guess I thought I'd be made fun of. And so, for a good year of ballet class, I took class in basketball shorts."

Trope was embarrassed by the association between form-fitting clothing and femininity. And like Carmon, he was allowed to practice in loose pants until he was fourteen or fifteen years old, when he auditioned for a more rigorous ballet program that required tights.

Because boys are in short supply, teachers loosen the dress code in order to keep them enrolled, while they hold girls to rigid standards that require obedience and conformity. That double standard applies not just to clothing but to behavior, too. Ashley Bouder, a white principal dancer at New York City Ballet, remembers that girls in her ballet school were expected to be "perfect, not only in class but in attitude and decorum," while the boys were "allowed to, in some cases, get away with murder in class, like . . . talking and acting up and doing anything, but it doesn't matter because [the teachers] are just trying to keep them in the class." As Stoner Winslett, the founding artistic director of the Richmond Ballet, puts it, boys in ballet are "treated like baby princes."

British dance scholar Christy Adair explains that the privileged status of boys in ballet is inextricable from the marginalization of ballet—and the arts in general—in the culture at large. "Whilst training," Adair observes, "men are far more likely to receive individual recognition because although they are in the minority, their power status within society is seen to legitimize the art. Therefore, teachers pay more attention to their male students in the hope that more men in dance will ease dance from its marginal position."[14]

Doug Risner, a professor of dance at Wayne State University, has observed the same phenomenon. Boys "are highly prized in this feminized environment," he says, and "it puts them in this weird political situation where faculty know . . . these are the boys they've been able to recruit, and so they get special treatment. . . . If they have conflicts at school, it's much easier for them to be allowed to miss a rehearsal. They're consulted more on their costumes, what they're going to feel comfortable wearing."

Winslett agrees. "If [boys] have to miss rehearsal to go to their soccer game, that's tolerated because there's not another boy to do the part," she explains. "But, say a girl needs to miss rehearsal to go to the soccer game—well, there's somebody else standing in the wings." More likely, there are about a dozen somebody elses.

Boys' dancing gets more attention, too, Risner says. For example, teachers often give boys individualized attention in class, correcting them by name, while the girls are corrected en masse. As in, *Make sure you're bringing that rond de jambe all the way around, Derek, and watch that supporting knee, ladies.* Quite apart from the fact that all students should receive roughly the same amount of attention from their teachers, Risner says, girls "learn a lesson that boys are special. And that ties again back into patriarchy and what's a girl's place."

Adair notes that the double standard for how girls and boys are treated inside ballet schools also finds its way into marketing and other public-facing materials. In one book about the Royal Ballet School, the prestigious feeder school for England's Royal Ballet company, photographs show "the girls, all looking identical, carefully sew[ing] their ballet shoes." The boys? They're "rushing through the woods having a good time."[15]

The major difference, Bouder concludes, is that girls "have to fit in and be quiet and just dance." But the boys "are allowed to be creative, they're allowed to misbehave and try things. . . . That's pretty much how it is in a lot of places—not everywhere, but in a lot of places. They can do whatever as long as they keep showing up."

The gendered differences in ballet's hidden curriculum are one reason for the art form's stark gender gap in leadership as you look up the ranks: the great majority of ballet companies are run by men, and the great majority of choreography that those companies perform, be it old or newly commissioned, is made by men (about this, much more in Chapter 8). When boys in ballet are taught from an early age that they are special and are permitted to exercise more creativity than girls, is it any wonder that they are far more likely to develop the belief that they are entitled to create and lead? Or that, as we'll see later, they might develop the belief that they are entitled to the bodies of the many women around them?

It's true that many boys who take ballet experience disturbingly high rates of bullying outside of their dance schools, sometimes in their own homes (about that, much more later). Inside the ballet studio, however, the hidden curriculum sets out very different rules and expectations, furnishing young boys and girls with very different understandings of their value in the ballet world and their rightful place in it. Girls come to understand that their limited value in a highly competitive environment, where each girl is one of many, lies in conformity and the performance of feminine perfection. Boys absorb the message that they are special and that special people can expect special treatment. And they learn that, as members of a privileged minority, boys who dance ballet will be expected to conform to certain masculine styles of movement—but they will also be permitted to play, transgress, and express their individuality. As we'll see later in this book, the girls and boys who stay in ballet to become women and men carry these lessons with them, sometimes with disastrous consequences.

Of course, these imbalances between what girls and boys learn in addition to ballet technique mirror the differences in the messages they receive from the culture at large. And just like the culture at large, ballet's hidden curriculum furnishes boys with expectations that, as men, they will be entitled to yet more special treatment and allowed to exercise both creativity and control. As Stinson writes, "To a young man, dance training may seem comparable to military training in that the necessary obedience is a rite of passage but not a permanent state. Once he is good enough, he will then have the power to tell others what to do, to reconceptualize what he has learned, to create art and not just reproduce it."[16]

All the same, ballet's gender binary puts extraordinary demands on boys' bodies. The art form demands that boys and men move with the kind of refinement and grace that, outside of the ballet studio, reads as feminine—but its rigid gender binary also requires them to dance with the kind of attack and power for which Katy Pyle was penalized as a student. Some steps are considered too feminine for men to perform, and more than one gay professional dancer told me that teachers and artistic directors had instructed him to "butch up" his dancing, to dance "more solidly," in order to stay within the confines of the binary.

And, Risner says, it's often male teachers who are policing boys and young men this way. "When a boy is not dancing with bravura and strength and masculinity, he's often called out, especially by a male teacher, that he has to dance like a man," Risner says. "'You're dancing like a girl.' And this just gets internalized by everyone, by the girls, by the boys, and it's really challenging." And there are few places where those demands are made more explicit and more visible than in pas de deux class, where students learn two essential components of performing ballet: how to partner and be partnered.

⁓

The pas de deux ("step for two") sits at the heart of most full-length story ballets, the crowd-pleasing classics that ballet companies rely on to fill the theater, like *Swan Lake, Romeo and Juliet, Giselle, Don*

Quixote, and *The Sleeping Beauty*. And it is the pas de deux sections of choreography that are regularly excerpted and performed on their own at competitions and galas: the Black Swan pas de deux, the balcony scene, the *Don Q* pas de deux.

While same-sex pas de deux do exist in contemporary ballet choreography, the default pas de deux, and the most beloved and popular examples of it, are danced by one man and one woman who are depicting a romantic love story. As a general rule, pas de deux is strictly gendered, with a set role for each partner.

In a pas de deux, the woman performs pirouettes and balances assisted by the man, who steadies and spins her in the turns and provides support in the balances. He also lifts her, often onto his shoulders or over his head, and adds his lift to her jumps, throwing her into the air and catching her. Back in the 1830s, when men all but disappeared from ballet schools and ballet stages and the man's role in the pas de deux was performed by women in drag, the pas de deux was considerably less acrobatic. As both male and female dancers have become stronger, pas de deux choreography has become more and more daring and physically demanding for both partners.

Because of the strength required of the male partner, students rarely start learning pas de deux before they hit puberty, and in any case, most local ballet schools have few if any boys to teach pas de deux to. Instead, students usually learn this skill in selective and intensive training programs or at one-off summer intensives that bring together a critical mass of male students.

One such program is at the Joffrey Ballet School (JBS) in New York City, which runs a year-round preprofessional program where students can train full-time from age thirteen onward. At JBS, a ballet trainee's day starts at 8:30 or 8:45 a.m. with a ninety-minute single-sex ballet class, which is followed by a pas de deux class. After a third ballet class, the students take a lunch break, and they spend the afternoon taking classes in other dance disciplines like contemporary and jazz. Trainees head home—to the dorms or to apartments they rent on their own—between 4 and 6 p.m., and those who are still in high school then open their computers and turn to their online classes.

In January 2020, I spent several days at JBS, observing classes and interviewing students and faculty. The first thing I noticed about pas de deux class, where students were between the ages of sixteen and twenty-two, was how chatty and rowdy it was compared to the girls' technique class that had preceded it, in which twenty-four girls had spoken perhaps twenty-four words between them. Now those twenty-four girls, still sweating from their just-ended class, had changed out of their canvas ballet slippers into pointe shoes and been joined by seven boys—two white, two Black, two East Asian, and one Latino—and the mood had become decidedly more social.

On this day, the pas de deux teacher was Marina Bogdanova, who also taught at Joffrey's after-school youth division. In the heavily heated studio, she was one of two middle-aged Russian women with blonde bobs; the other was the accompanist, who sat behind a glossy black baby grand piano with her glasses on top of her head, fanning herself between exercises. Bogdanova instructed the dancers in a mix of heavily accented English and ballet's French terminology, and instructed the accompanist in snippets of Russian.

As the boys stretched and chatted at the back of the studio, Bogdanova marshaled the girls into a long line and split them into groups of three or four. Then she assigned each group to a boy. For the next hour and a half, Bogdanova would demonstrate a series of steps, dancing the girl's part and picking a volunteer boy to demonstrate the boy's part. Then each boy would execute the sequence with each of the girls in his group, one after the next, several times over. When the girls weren't dancing, they stood at the back of the studio, practicing balances, adjusting their pointe shoes, taking a breather. The boys, whose services were needed in the middle of the room at all times, took no breathers. This is a common occurrence when boys are scarce, Risner noted, and it takes a toll on boys' bodies. "They get really injured," he said. "It's too much. How many girls can you lift over your head in one rehearsal?"

One reason pas de deux class is chattier than a regular ballet class is that pas de deux require collaboration and communication between partners. Students are learning to move their own bodies *and* how to work with other people's. And though Bogdanova wielded the kind of top-down, unquestioned authority Stinson describes, there are other forms of learning and teaching happening in a class like this one.

One girl showed her partner the angle at which he'd need to set her down so that her weight would be properly distributed over the box of her pointe shoe. One boy reminded his partner to place her arms properly in a pirouette so that, standing behind her, he had space to place his hands at her waist to spin and stabilize her. Some partners grinned and giggled as they danced, making tiny adjustments and exchanging words as they went. "You're too close"; "It's my fault." When the music ended, before a new girl arrived to take her turn, they debriefed, half in words and half in hand gestures that abbreviated the choreography they'd just practiced. "Better?" "Yeah."

This kind of learning is profoundly intimate given how much the students are required to touch each other and how much trust they have to put in each other. The previous day, in a different pas de deux class, I'd watched as couples practiced a lift in which the girl stood in arabesque on pointe and the boy, standing behind her, placed one hand on her hip and the other on the underside of her raised leg. Bending his knees into a deep plié, he press-lifted her so that her hips were level with his shoulders. When one of the taller boys pressed his partner all the way over his head, her head came perilously close to the ceiling fan.

The teachers touch the students, too. Bogdanova gave verbal corrections, telling students when they had arrived at a position too late or too early, and she demonstrated the way she wanted the steps to look by dancing them herself. But she also gave physical corrections, grabbing girls' thighs to pull them into proper placement and putting her hands on boys' shoulders to correct the angle of their arms. The previous day's teacher, Andrei Jouravlev, a tall and pale-skinned Russian with thick wavy brown hair, had demonstrated the boy's part and picked a volunteer student to dance the girl's steps. On one occasion, he picked a student whose long-sleeved leotard had a large keyhole in the back. When Jouravlev stood behind her and supported her pirouettes, his hands were on bare flesh.

In pas de deux classes, the gendered division of labor in ballet becomes clearer than ever. Combined with the introduction of pointe shoes—which also happens at about eleven years old, as girls are hitting puberty—the advent of pas de deux training marks the moment at which men's and women's paths diverge. At this time, dancers are assigned the deeply gendered roles they'll be expected to play for the rest of their ballet training and, if they become professionals, for the rest of their classical ballet careers. Until this point, there have been small differences in movement—girls curtsy to thank their teachers at the end of class while boys bow—but the pas de deux amplifies those differences and requires dancers to fully take their places in ballet's rigid gender binary.

Men lift and women are lifted. Men stand behind the women, assisting them, hoisting them, steadying them, often half hidden by them. If the man is doing his job well, if he is partnering seamlessly, the audience will at times forget that he's there at all. The woman, meanwhile, entrusts the man with her body—her tool and her livelihood—and allows him to shape and manipulate it, to cart it across the stage, to toss it in the air.

There is a long history of feminist criticism of the classical ballet pas de deux. Some dance theorists maintain that the pas de deux is a prime example of ballet relegating a woman to utter passivity while a man performs his chivalrous duty, carrying her around the stage and displaying her body to the audience.

Of course, as the JBS students were learning, the lived experience of pas de deux is more complicated than that, because being partnered is strenuous work too. Even when a woman is playing a corpse, a deadweight, she is working: as former Miami City Ballet soloist Kathryn Morgan noted, describing the scene in *Romeo and Juliet* in which Romeo finds an apparently dead Juliet in the Capulet family tomb and then dances a grim pas de deux with her limp body, the dancer playing Juliet is still pointing her toes.[17]

But the audience is not supposed to see that work. They're not supposed to notice that, in that arabesque press lift the JBS students were practicing in Jouravlev's class, the woman has her hand braced against the man's hand at her hip and is pressing down with all her might to take some of the strain off him. Similarly, it's not enough for the boys to lift the girls up over their head; they must do it smoothly, gracefully, without grimacing or letting the audience know how complex the lift is and how tired their arms are. In reality, both partners are decorative and both are functional. Everyone was sweating profusely at the end of pas de deux class.

All the same, it's hard to escape the sense that, in pas de deux, ballet's hidden curriculum suddenly stops hiding—that here, the subtext becomes text. In ballet as in life, puberty brings with it a new onslaught of gendered expectations and a new rigidity in gender roles. In pas de deux class, those roles are literal, though pas de deux class does serve as a useful metaphor for the ballet world at large: as hard as the women are working, as beautifully as they are displayed onstage or in the studio, it's the men who are in control.

~

Katy Pyle was pushed out of ballet. After years of being told that their movement style was too "strong," that they danced with too much "attack" and too much power—ballet's code words for "masculinity"— and after years of starving themselves, with the tacit approval of their teachers, in an attempt to stave off the dreaded "athletic" body shape to which they were genetically predisposed, they quit.

Today, Pyle says that they were "very aware" of their sexuality when they were training in ballet. But they didn't come out as lesbian until after they had quit and were in college. "I couldn't come out, like I couldn't make a way for me to see myself in ballet as a lesbian," they say, "and so I had to get away from ballet enough to even recognize myself to myself." They left ballet feeling "incredibly angry," with a sense they had been betrayed by an art form that had required them to conceal themselves from themselves—and then pushed them out anyway. "What was so heartbreaking and painful about leaving ballet was that I gave up so many parts of myself and my identity in order to belong, and sort of denied and repressed myself. And I still didn't belong."

It took some time for Pyle to come back to ballet, but when they did, they brought a radical new vision with them. In 2011, Pyle founded Ballez, a company that is "just what it sounds like: it's lesbians doing ballet. And Ballez is not just lesbians, it's all the queers that ballet has left out."[18] Pyle envisions the company as a haven for people like them who do not fit into ballet's rigid gender binary and have been excluded from ballet training and from the stories that ballet tells onstage.

One way that Pyle's company is building that haven is by staging queer versions of the ballet canon's classics. In Ballez's production of *The Firebird*, the prince is now a lesbian princess, and the female firebird is now "a Tranimal (part bird, part Prince)." In *Giselle of Loneliness*, the cast of queer dancers interacts with the audience as the dancers stage an audition for "the iconic titular role of the frail and tortured ideal of white femininity in ballet." Ballez's take on *Giselle*—a ballet about a woman who dies when the man she loves betrays her and then, in death, forgives and saves him—"reveals our experience as dancers tortured by ballet itself, and asks, 'what parts of ourselves do we have to give up, or kill off, in order to belong? And for how long will audiences participate in that demand?'"[19]

Ballez also runs drop-in classes for adults in New York City and in 2019 posted a series of free tutorials with Pyle to YouTube, so that would-be students can take Ballez classes from anywhere. When the pandemic hit and dance studios all over the country were scrambling to put their classes on camera, Ballez was a step ahead, thanks to their democratizing approach to ballet.

One Saturday in January 2020, I took a Ballez class in Manhattan, in a rented dance studio just a few floors above the classrooms where students at American Ballet Theatre's elite feeder school were taking the kinds of conventional classes Pyle had taken as a child and teenager.

Ballez class began late, something I had never experienced before. And when it did begin, Pyle asked their students—two cisgender men, two nonbinary people, and four cisgender women including me—to arrange the portable barres not in rows, as is often the case, but in a rectangle in the middle of the room. Then Pyle invited us to stand inside the rectangle, and one by one, we shared our preferred gender pronouns and said a few words about our relationship to ballet.

Pyle went first. "One thing I've been thinking about is that ballet has been reserved for the elite, that you had to have a certain race or class or whatever to be let in," they said, gesturing to the space inside the barres. Now, Pyle said, they want "all of us not to just be allowed in [to ballet] but to own it." Pyle was echoing Ballez's mission statement, which demands more than mere inclusion for those who, like Pyle, were allowed into ballet, but only if they suppressed their queerness. "We who have been deemed unworthy of the pride, nobility, and belonging in ballet's centuries long hierarchical history," the mission statement declares, "are coming back into the castle now, to take back the movements, magic, creativity and power that we have always been integral to creating."[20]

Pyle says that some students come to her classes "traumatized," as Pyle was, by their experiences in conventional ballet training. "I'm still working on that [trauma] all the time," Pyle tells me. "There's a tremendous amount of people that have been traumatized by ballet. Hopefully they come to Ballez. . . . It's a lot of pressure for me as well to [provide] one of the only spaces where that can be okay or that can be something that can be acknowledged and worked on."

One of those people is MJ Markovitz, a twenty-one-year-old Ballez company member. As we went around the rectangle in class and introduced ourselves, MJ, who is white, told us they used they/them pronouns and related a story about their ballet training that sounded dispiritingly similar to Pyle's stories from two decades ago. "I've always been told to do less, that I have too much strength and power," MJ said. "I think I probably wouldn't have been told that if I were assigned male."

MJ is a full-time student at the Ailey School, the Alvin Ailey American Dance Theater–affiliated school that trains students to be contemporary dancers and whose curriculum includes a daily ballet class. They identify as nonbinary but are required to take that class in a leotard and pink tights. And, they said, they are also barred from dancing the men's choreography, like doing jumping exercises at a slower tempo to allow for bigger leaps with more hang time.

The first time MJ took a Ballez class, they said, "I cried the entire subway ride home, because I didn't know dance could feel this good." They were coming to terms with their gender identity and hadn't realized the toll that a traditional ballet environment had been taking on them. Like Pyle before them, they "had always been told to make [themselves] smaller and more petite and feminine," and they grew up thinking they could never be a ballet dancer because they lacked the hyperfeminine movement quality their teachers demanded.

MJ said that even though they danced all day during the week, they found the time and energy to come to Ballez's weekend class because without it, they "wouldn't be able to handle" the rigid binary of their traditional ballet training. Being in a dedicated queer ballet space, with a teacher who intimately understood their experience, felt restorative. "Without this," MJ said, "I would feel so shitty and out of my own body."

From its very first moments, a Ballez class is run differently from a conventional ballet class. For one thing, students are permitted to talk—in fact, they are encouraged to talk—during class. And as barre progressed, Pyle urged us to dance in ways that were consistent with our body's limits, even if they were not consistent with ballet technique's desired aesthetic. "Let your back go a lot more than your teachers told you when you were eight," Pyle said as we stood balancing with one leg behind us in attitude. "Save your back." And once we had cleared the barres away and were dancing in the center of the room, all the dancers were asked and allowed to do the kinds of big turning jumps, the tours en l'air, that are usually reserved for men's class—and the only person to put on pointe shoes was a cisgender man.

Pyle, who also teaches ballet at the New School, believes that conventional ballet training traumatizes not only queer dancers but straight women, too. "Women are disempowered from the beginning of training inside of ballet," they tell me, "and that is a value system and a belief system that has become intertwined with the training." Pyle says that some people have told them that the kind of top-down authoritarian pedagogy Stinson criticizes, the rigidity and discipline that is imposed on ballet dancers from such a young age, is "inherent to the training and necessary to the training." But Pyle doesn't think it is necessary or inherent. "I don't think that women need to be in abusive relationships, and I don't think we need to be in those kinds of subservient relationships with art forms as artists."

Pyle says that their company has struggled to find acceptance in the ballet world, and the funding that acceptance would bring. Even amid an industry-wide debate about gender and racial diversity in who gets to dance and who gets to choreograph, Pyle finds that Ballez is often left out of performance programs designed to open ballet's gates a little wider. While the gatekeepers of the ballet world can imagine more dancers of color onstage or more ballets created by cisgender women, they can't seem to see Pyle's larger, more radical vision.

Still, Pyle is optimistic about the queer future of ballet and about the shifts in training and treatment of dancers that it will make possible. Their Gen Z students have them feeling especially hopeful. "There is movement there," Pyle says. "There's this whole generation that is like, 'Why would we continue in this way that things have been?' And I think that the Gen Z kids are gonna make radical change happen as soon as they get the money or some power. . . . Once those people are running things, this whole landscape is going to look really different."

MJ Markovitz, at twenty-one, is just barely older than those Gen Z dancers, and they're hopeful, too. As much as they love ballet, ballet hasn't loved them back, and they want to see Ballez become the art form's new norm in their lifetime. "I don't think ballet should survive a gender-neutral future," MJ tells me. "It's traditionally been very patriarchal and homophobic and racist. Ballet can still exist, but the more we make space for people to exist, the more satisfying it will be to exist."

Pyle knows that their vision of ballet—gender neutral, open to all, a place where girls aren't replaceable automatons and boys aren't, in Stoner Winslett's words, "baby princes"—is radical, and that it might render both ballet training and ballet performance unrecognizable to many people. "But," they said, "that's not unusual in the history of dance. Radical things happen, and the kind of boring, unoriginal shit gets forgotten. The radical things are remembered."

CHAPTER 2

BALLET RUNS ON MOMS

If you are going to have the guts to dream, you
have to have the guts to pay the price.

SUZANNE FARRELL

Anisha Walker is a ballet mom. More specifically, she is a Black ballet mom of a Black ballet student in the suburbs outside of Richmond, Virginia.

Anisha's twelve-year-old daughter, Danya, took her first ballet class at the age of three. She now takes ballet, lyrical, jazz, tap, hip-hop, musical theater, and a beginner pointe class. Danya is on her dance school's competition team, and just before Christmas 2019, she got her first pair of pointe shoes.

"She's so excited," Anisha said in an interview shortly before Danya's trip to the dancewear store to be fitted for pointe shoes. It's a rite of passage that ballet students long for and that many ballet parents document for posterity—and for posting on Facebook and Instagram. The excitement and parental fuss around the day, Anisha says, is "crazy."

As we saw in the previous chapter, ballet's aristocratic origins and its present-day elite associations are embedded in every movement ballet students learn to make. Pas de deux—in which men and women greet each other with genteel bows and curtsies before they begin dancing together and later exit the stage hand in hand, floating away like courtiers leaving an audience with the crown—is a potent reminder of ballet's beginnings in the palaces of French kings. The hidden curriculum conveys coded messages about class, teaching girls to behave with ladylike refinement and teaching students of all genders to carry themselves with the erect and unruffled posture of seventeenth-century royalty. But there are also far more explicit ways of getting that message of exclusivity across.

Take, for example, the practice ensemble, mandated by a school's dress code: a leotard, tights, and ballet slippers. If you shop at a discount dancewear supplier, a quality leotard costs about fifteen dollars. Tights are about eight dollars a pair. Shoes cost between ten and thirty dollars, and dance belts and skirts, which some schools require, are about five and fifteen dollars respectively—a total of about sixty dollars per child.

For some parents, that isn't an onerous price tag, but it's also true that some of the most expensive items, the shoes and the leotard, might not last a fast-growing child more than a few months. It's appallingly easy to put a run or a hole in a pair of ballet tights, and many teachers frown on tights that are grubby or torn. If a student is progressing to a new grade every year, that's at least one new leotard every twelve months, and more if she starts taking additional classes each week, as many schools require for their advancing students. And if, like Danya, she advances to dancing on pointe, which most schools permit starting at about age eleven, prices really start to skyrocket. Canvas ballet slippers are relatively inexpensive and can be bought secondhand. But pointe shoes, which must be bought new, start at $45 and can cost as much as $125.

The cost of gear, though, is nothing compared to the cost of tuition.

Anisha works for the federal government and until recently her husband was a teacher—he has now left the public sector and taken a new job in sales. Danya's dance tuition costs them $5,500 a year.

"Now he works in sales, which makes dance a little bit more affordable, but . . . when we were on government employee and teacher salary it was a bit of a struggle," she says.

Danya is the only African American student in her age group at her dance school, and one of just a few in the entire school. "I can definitely count and name them all, probably six, maybe ten," Anisha says.

The dance school, she says, isn't representative of the town it serves. The Walkers live in a county just outside of Richmond, "so it is majority white, but it's definitely not *that* white." They picked the dance school because, at the time Danya started taking lessons, it was very close to their home. "We became comfortable there, but I can't say that if I were currently looking that I would necessarily feel like this is the place for me, for my child."

Anisha has also noticed that the studio's promotional material doesn't emphasize racial diversity. The image of the school that the director of the studio presents to the world "is white. Essentially . . . I don't know what reason any other Black families would look at her advertising or her community outreach and feel like their Black kid would be able to fit in there."

Anisha is quick to add that "everybody's very nice and supportive" of Danya and that the school does offer scholarships. But, crucially, those scholarships aren't advertised even to current dance parents, let alone prospective ones.

"They have, I guess, options to work with you, but they're not really public, you know. . . . I personally wouldn't feel comfortable going up to [the director of the school] and saying, 'Is there anything you can do for me?' If there were options that were already there that you could apply for, it would be different."

And so, Anisha and her husband made "nine payments or eight payments of $680" in 2019.

It's worth noting that Danya takes dancing very seriously and doesn't do any other extracurricular activities ("It's all dance all the time," Anisha says). For students who are less focused on dancing and who take fewer classes, the costs will be lower. But as students age, as girls approach the age at which they're allowed to go on pointe, and if they are representing the school in competitions, they are generally required to take more classes. In her yearlong study of the school at Alvin Ailey American Dance Theater, Katherine Davis Fishman observed that by age twelve, the most promising students, those on the "A track," were required to take seven classes a week.[1]

Aubrey Lynch is the chief officer of education and creative programs at Harlem School of the Arts Dance (HSA), where most students are Black and many come from low-income or middle-class families. Lynch, who is also Black, says that keeping tuition low is a top priority, but even with his efforts, the school's fees are simply too high for many parents. An eight-year-old ballet student at HSA is expected to take three classes a week, which costs about $2,000 a year. That doesn't include leotards, tights, shoes, competition fees, and costumes for recitals and competitions. Taking five classes a week costs between $2,700 and $3,000, "and then when you're a teenager coming six days a week, that's four thousand dollars, approximately."

"It's expensive. . . . It's a lot as a parent," Lynch says. "And they gotta really believe it's worth it, and they gotta really believe their child can succeed. And some kids don't have the luxury; parents don't have the luxury or time to have that idea." In addition, some families need their kids to help out with childcare or take after-school jobs to contribute to household income. Time spent in ballet class is time that can't be spent watching siblings or waiting tables.

Ty Schalter, a white parent whose son took ballet classes in Lansing, Michigan, until the age of eleven, agrees that the cost of ballet is high, even for recreational students. He worries that the price pushes out students who enjoy it but aren't obsessed with it—who do it for fun but don't have the desire or ability to pursue it more seriously.

"It hits, the cost of ballet, as kids get older," he says. "Even if they're not doing it five days a week, even if it's just twice a week, the cost of it is just, 'Well, if this isn't really what you love, and your public school has organized sports . . . and it's not gonna be what you do for a living, like, tick tock.'"

For Grace Segers, ballet was what she wanted to do for a living: as a teen in the first decade of the 2000s, she took ballet classes or rehearsed for recitals six days a week and spent her summers at intensive programs in New York and Pennsylvania. Segers, who is white, was raised by a single mother in New York City and on Long Island, and she remembers that her mother made considerable sacrifices in order for her to take ballet. "She really was the champion of my ballet education," Segers says.

"Ballet was EXPENSIVE!" Grace's mother, Rebecca, wrote in a text exchange that Grace shared with me. "The more classes you took, the more expensive it got. I think by the end it was around $3000 or $3500 a year."

For a single parent raising a child during the Great Recession and at the beginning of the economic recovery, that was a very significant expense. And while Grace was offered small scholarships from her ballet school, her mom mostly paid off the tuition over time. "I was always scrimping and saving to make it happen," Rebecca wrote, and that often meant going without things she wanted her and needed herself. "Worn out sheets on the bed," she recalled.

Grace's pointe shoes represented a significant burden for her mother, too. "It was a big pull for my mom," Grace says. Because Grace had especially high arches, she needed a special—and more expensive—brand of pointe shoes to ensure that she had proper foot support. Back then, they cost about seventy-five dollars; they now retail for about ninety dollars. "And then because of my high arches I would break through my shoes every six to eight weeks. It was really hard."

When Grace eventually quit, her mother was relieved—not because of the cost but because her daughter seemed burned out and exhausted from juggling ballet and high school. Still, the next step would have been an even more intensive ballet school, perhaps a residential program in another city, where families are responsible not just for tuition and gear but for room and board and travel to and from the program.

At Joffrey Ballet School, full tuition is $21,000 a year for US citizens and permanent residents and $22,000 for international students, of which there are many. If a trainee lives in the dorms, that's another $19,000 a year. It is a four-year program. If trainees pay full freight and live in the dorms, a completed education at JBS will cost them and their families $160,000. That doesn't include annual performance fees ($600), registration fees ($75), access to the affiliated online high school program, or a single pair of pointe shoes.

Even at an all-scholarship training program, like the well-respected HARID Conservatory in Boca Raton, Florida, students and their families have to cover considerable expenses. HARID is tuition-free for all students, but the total cost of room and board, gear, and other fees still tops $17,000 a year for citizens and permanent residents, and international students pay several thousand dollars more (in 2020, because the school moved to virtual instruction in response to the pandemic, fees were temporarily reduced). HARID's is a four-year program.

It wasn't always like this. Ballet lessons weren't always reserved for the wealthy. In fact, there was a time when ballet stages were filled with girls and women from impoverished families, and when ballet moms saw the art form as a potential route to financial security for their daughters—albeit for reasons most parents today would find intolerable.

Ballet began as a royal pursuit, something to be learned, performed, and consumed by kings and their courts. In the seventeenth century, France's King Louis XIV, who was fond of both watching and performing dance, made dancing all but mandatory for his courtiers. He also used the complex etiquette of dance as a form of social and political control.

King Louis had spent some of his childhood in exile after members of the nobility staged an attempted coup, and his early experience instilled in him a belief that "the nobility was a force whose energies needed to be carefully contained," explains journalist Deirdre Kelly in the book *Ballerina: Sex, Scandal, and Suffering Behind the Symbol of Perfection*. "Louis would craft himself as the choreographer, while his courtiers would serve as the performers of an intricately devised court dance in which the king would always play the central role." In implementing this new system of control, Louis "made [dancing] integral to life at court," ballet historian Jennifer Homans writes, "a symbol and requirement of aristocratic identity so deeply ingrained and internalized that the art of ballet would be forever linked to his reign."[2]

Dancing became considered a marker of virtue as well as a way to secure or hold on to the favor of the crown. It was also a way of literally performing one's class and moral character. "Turn-out and a more general openness of posture, had moral and social significances within the aristocracy," explains literature professor Peter Stoneley in *A Queer History of the Ballet*. "It indicated righteousness, style, and power (a slumped, self-concealing posture, on the other hand, was taken to signify deviousness and ignorance)."[3]

Back then, the art form that would become ballet was reserved for men. Stoneley writes that "the noble, dancerly body was also a manly body. The balance of turn-out, and having a fine control of the contour of one's upper body, were essential components of fencing. It was understood that dancing taught one to 'handle matters with seemliness and without disorder,' while also helping one to 'ride horseback and carry arms.' In sum, it 'render[ed] one more skilled at serving one's Prince in battle, and pleasing him in [dancing].'"[4]

After Louis XIV stopped performing in and staging his elaborate court ballets, dance scholar Judith Lynne Hanna explains, ballet moved out of the palace and into the theater, where "courtly social dance developed into a professional theatrical genre." It was still a man's world. "Because well-bred women did not appear on the stage," Hanna writes, "men danced women's roles in travesty"—that is, in drag. "Furthermore, because their dress was not so physically confining, men could be more virtuosic."[5]

Two revolutions, the French and the industrial, would weaken the association between ballet and royalty, and they would remove men from the ballet stage. Before the French Revolution, though ballet had moved out of palaces and into theaters, it still enjoyed royal patronage (and in countries where the royal family was not imprisoned and beheaded by its own people, that patronage still exists, from the Royal Ballet in London to the Danish Royal Ballet in Copenhagen). In France, the Paris Opera Ballet's budget had been provided by the crown. When the revolution came for Louis XVI and his queen, Marie-Antoinette, in 1792, and after the ballet lost its royal license in 1830, the company had to find another way to survive.

Ballet's savior was the bourgeoisie—specifically, the men of the bourgeoisie. In France, the art form survived the cataclysm of the revolution and its bloody republican aftermath by relying on subscribers, or *abonnés*, from the new middle class. "The *ancien régime* had been replaced by a new class of ballet patron eager to emulate the privileges and entitlements that had been the birthrights of their social predecessors," Deirdre Kelly writes.[6] The men of the French bourgeoisie had money to burn, and theaters had budget shortfalls. But there was a problem: the men of the French bourgeoisie didn't particularly want to see other men onstage.

This was in part a result of the Enlightenment and the Industrial Revolution, both of which had reshaped attitudes about what a man should be and how he should spend his time.

"In the Enlightenment era, manliness was increasingly defined in terms of strength and functionality," Stoneley writes, while "gracefulness came to be seen more as a womanly attribute. . . . To the newly confident Enlightenment and post-Enlightenment middle classes, the refinement of aristocratic posture—in the case of men—was seen as frivolous and effeminate." As a result, Stoneley explains, it became unacceptable for men to dance ballet. "There was a sense that the male body could not and should not be graceful; it was too grossly material for aesthetic display."[7]

By the early nineteenth century, the Industrial Revolution had created a middle class and a set of ideas about how the men of that class ought to be spending their time, and it wasn't dancing. "Because the emergent French bourgeoisie attributed the collapse of the monarchy in part to moral laxity," Hanna writes, "they transformed the body from an instrument of pleasure into one of production. In this way the middle class could protect its power." Dancing and other "activities of the body" were seen as "impediments to [the] economic productivity" to which bourgeois men were supposed to aspire. "The work imperative demanded that men bottle up emotion [and] repress sex."[8]

It's no wonder then, that by the 1820s and 1830s, the male dancer was considered undesirable and, as dance historian Lynn Garafola writes, "appealed to a very limited public." Not only did the sight of a regal-looking man on a ballet stage remind audiences of "the aristocratic manner and frippery of the Ancien Regime," but it was now considered unnatural and even immoral for men to learn and perform ballet, or to watch other men doing it.[9]

"In bourgeois culture," Stoneley writes, "the mock-aristocratic male dancer was disturbingly feminine, and he was irrelevant. Who, after all, was supposed to enjoy the display of the male body, and on what grounds? . . . The supposition becomes ever stronger that the presence of the male dancer could only appeal to abnormal men, and to immodest women."[10]

"By the 1830s male dancers were being reviled as disgraceful and effeminate creatures," Jennifer Homans writes, "and by the 1840s they had all but been banned from Parisian stages."[11]

And so boys disappeared from ballet schools and men disappeared from ballet stages, and women took their places. Onstage, *women* now danced *men's* parts in drag. "By the 1830s, the corps had become almost wholly female and leading men the object of sustained and bitter attack," scholar Lynn Garafola explains. "At the school attached to the Paris

Opera, the number of boys plummeted, as it did at La Scala, although the Italian prejudice against male dancers was never as thorough-going as its French counterpart."[12] And, as is so often the case when men leave a profession and women take it over, the prestige of ballet plummeted, too.

Without royal patronage, the Paris Opera Ballet had to become a private enterprise, subject to the forces of market economics. This "led to a new kind of star system," Garafola writes, "one based on drawing power rather than rank, while eliminating, for purposes of economy, the pensions and other benefits traditionally accruing to artists in government employ." And, she explains, it put "the audience—particularly the key group of monied subscribers—in a new and powerful position." Once controlled by the crown, ballet was now controlled by capitalism.[13]

Now that dancing had been devalued, it was done almost exclusively by women; and now that dancers were almost exclusively women, they were paid less and treated worse. And it should come as no surprise that ballet companies soon began using their women dancers to secure the attention of abonnés in ever more exploitative ways.

In 1831, management of the Paris Opera Ballet was handed over to Dr. Louis Véron, the publisher of an arts journal, who envisioned the ballet theater as "the Versailles of the middle class." Véron lowered both ticket prices and dancers' wages, and he made several other big changes to dancers' lives and to the audience's experience. "Under royal patronage," Stoneley explains, "the Intendant of the Royal Theatres had ordered that 'dancers' skirts be lengthened so that carnal thoughts should not occur to the gentlemen who sat close to the stage.' Dr. Véron, on the other hand, shortened the dancers' skirts."[14]

Things looked very different backstage, too. "Véron understood all too well the attraction of beautiful ballerinas," writes Homans, "and to facilitate the 'exchange of goods' between them and their rich admirers, he opened the *foyer de la danse*—the room where dancers warmed up for a performance—to inquiring gentlemen."[15]

Increasingly, Kelly writes, ballet dancers at the Paris Opera "became the pawns of wealthy gentlemen, many of them members of the Jockey

Club de Paris, a gathering of the elite of nineteenth-century France, who, just as they did with horses, traded dancers for sport, swapping them among each other as sexual partners." Jockey Club members had so much power, Kelly explains, that they "saw to it that no opera featured a ballet in the first act, so as to enable them to linger over their dinner and chat up the ballerinas in the wings before their entrances."[16]

The ballet had long been a promising place for an aristocrat on the prowl for a new mistress, but Véron opened the opportunity to hunt there to the men of the blossoming bourgeoisie. By opening up the backstage area to his new wealthy male audience members, Stoneley writes, "Véron inaugurated the age of *prostitution légère*" and the ballet became a "leg show." Under royal patronage, the backstage area had been off-limits to audience members. Now, abonnés were free to roam and prowl for mistresses among the dancers, becoming their "protectors" as the ballet became "the privileged venue of sexual assignation."[17]

"In eliminating the danseur, ballet turned out the remaining in-house obstacle to sexual license," Garafola writes. "Thanks to the travesty dancer, no male now could destroy the peace of [the abonnés'] private harem or their enjoyment of performance and foreplay to possession."[18]

Though the "commerce in dancers' bodies" was not unique to Paris—it happened in London, too—it was most pronounced and most enshrined in policy at the Paris Opera Ballet, where, as Garafola writes, the *foyer de danse* became a kind of luxury brothel, "with madams in the shape of mothers arranging terms."[19]

Dancers and their mothers needed the extra income from these new "protectors" because almost all dancers came from the working class, and with the exception of a few stars, ballet dancers were paid a pittance. Edgar Degas's iconic paintings of ballet dancers in rehearsal and performance at the Paris Opera Ballet are beloved now for their intimate depictions of bygone glamour. But in their time, Degas's works were understood to show the exhaustion, the degradation, and the unseemly sexuality of working-class girls and women who were working very hard for very little money (and if you look carefully at some of them, you will find the tall, dark shadow of a man in a tuxedo or black top hat standing in the wings; he is, most likely, a member of the Jockey Club).

If the financial protection of an abonné was appealing to these dancers, it was because "without outside income, many of them were too destitute to pay for food, fuel, and lodging. . . . So inadequate were the [corps de ballet] dancers' salaries, in fact, that many of them suffered from malnutrition." The many young dancers of the corps were known as "little rats" because they were poor, undernourished, and small (Véron himself called them "gutter sylphs").[20]

In fact, as French writer Camille Laurens has painstakingly documented, the world's most famous *petit rat* appears to have lost her job at the ballet because she attempted to supplement her meager dancing income by modeling for Degas. The body of Marie van Goethem, whom most art lovers know as *Little Dancer Aged Fourteen*, has been memorialized in bronze and with charcoal, though little is known about her life. What seems likely from Laurens's sleuthing, however, is that van Goethem was fired from the Paris Opera Ballet because she missed too many classes and rehearsals in order to model for Degas.[21]

Hanna notes that for some working-class dancers, ballet under Véron's regime did represent a viable route out of poverty and a way to leave the stage for greener and more respectable pastures. Some dancers used ballet's new marketplace to their considerable advantage. "Certainly talented women who achieved acclaim and the attention, dalliance, and commitment of wealthy admirers were envied," she explains. "Respectable wives envied the dancers' freedom from the burden and hazards of childbearing. . . . But respected, in the sense of the dominant culture's view of the proper female role, dancers were not. Ballerinas were branded by the stigma of working-class origins and sexual impropriety."[22]

Nearly two hundred years after the abonnés took over the Paris Opera Ballet, ballet's cultural status has risen considerably, and with it the status of those who learn and perform it. In the United States, the upper classes do not merely consume ballet; they also condone their children's learning it (indeed, as we've seen in this chapter, enrolling a child in ballet is often out of financial reach for middle- and working-class families).

That's partly because, as we'll see in the next chapter, the cultural association between ballet and Europe, and especially France and French femininity, has made it desirable for upper-class Americans and those who emulate them. Ballet became a respectable way for American girls and young women to exercise, a form of physical activity that taught girls grace and good posture and didn't threaten to make them too muscular or masculine.

It's also because, in the twentieth century, boys and men were brought back into ballet, first by the Russian impresario Serge Diaghilev and then by the male-driven ballet boom of the 1960s and 1970s that made glamorous global stars of celebrity Soviet defectors Mikhail Baryshnikov and Rudolf Nureyev.

However, though ballet is no longer solely something done by women and watched by men, it is still overwhelmingly a girls' activity. And because of that, once again, girls and women are at an economic disadvantage.

At the Joffrey Ballet School, as at HARID, students can apply for federal financial aid, and Joffrey does offer merit scholarships. The artistic director of JBS's yearlong trainee program, Era Jouravlev, told me that most students are on scholarships of some kind that contribute anywhere from 10 percent to 100 percent of tuition costs.

Because boys are so outnumbered by girls in ballet, they are, as Wayne State University professor of dance Doug Risner put it, "prized" by ballet schools. They are also, in many cases, cheaper for parents to put through ballet school than their sisters or girl classmates.

Because boys do not dance on pointe, it costs considerably less to outfit them for advanced ballet training than it costs to outfit girls. Girls who are training at Grace Segers's level can expect to "kill" at least one pair of pointe shoes every month, more when they are preparing for competitions or performances. At JBS or HARID, where girls dance all day, every day, they can expect to go through multiple pairs of pointe shoes each month. Boys' shoes, which are simple canvas slippers, are much harder to kill.

Another reason why it may cost less for boys to train is the widespread practice of offering boys scholarships simply because they are boys.

"There's a lot of different things, incentives, to get them to continue through, because you have to get them there, but then you have to keep them there," says Lauren Fadeley Veyette, a white soloist at Miami City Ballet whose husband is a former principal dancer at Pennsylvania Ballet and whose brother-in-law is a principal dancer at New York City Ballet. Sometimes boys are lured into taking ballet with scholarship money for other classes, contingent on their showing up for ballet. Eric Trope, the Miami City Ballet dancer who was so reluctant to put on tights, remembers that his dance school covered his tuition for theater classes and jazz classes with a scholarship that required him to take ballet. Sending him to ballet class became a rational choice for Trope's parents.

"And I kind of protested it a little bit," he says, "but the only way I was gonna be able to get my scholarship was if I took ballet. So my mom, of course, was like, 'I don't want to pay for it when you can get it for free.' So I took the ballet class begrudgingly."

Francis Veyette, Lauren's husband, had a similar experience as a boy: after watching *Singin' in the Rain*, he wanted to be Gene Kelly, and when his parents went to sign him up for tap lessons, they were told that if he took ballet, both his ballet and tap classes would be free.

Megan Fairchild, a longtime principal dancer with New York City Ballet, attended that company's feeder school, the School of American Ballet, a few years ahead of her brother Robbie, who also went on to become a principal at City Ballet. The two grew up taking classes at the same dance school in Salt Lake City, with one big difference: the cost.

"Almost every boy that does ballet is doing it for free, anywhere that they are," Fairchild tells me. "From the basic level, like at the strip mall that we all started at, guys dance for free. They are just trying to get guys interested. So my brother always danced for free." Whereas Robbie received a full scholarship for his early training, the Fairchilds' parents paid full freight for the demonstrably equally promising Megan.

Full scholarships are rare at JBS, according to Era Jouravlev, who says she awards scholarships on merit and doesn't take gender into consideration. "Yes, boys, it's always difficult to get them in the school," she concedes, "but I have this belief that I can also do ballet without boys." Still, in the 2019–2020 academic year there were only three trainees in the whole school who were awarded full rides: one girl and two boys.

Adrienne Kisner is a white mother in Boston whose nine-year-old son has been taking ballet classes since he was four. A student at the feeder school for Boston Ballet, he's on a yearlong scholarship, which she suspects has less to do with his talent and more to do with the school's desire to keep him from quitting ballet.

"In my heart of hearts, I feel it's because he's a boy," she says, "but I don't know if that's accurate. That he got it because there are some beautiful little girl dancers who did not get it, and he did." Her son, she says, is "diligent but not a prodigy."

Alec Shyman, a nineteen-year-old student in the BFA program that Alvin Ailey's dance school runs with Fordham University, is a little more blunt about what he calls his "privileged experience" as a boy taking ballet. He remembers being one of just four boys at a different Boston dance school and says that at some point in their time there, every one of those boys received a merit scholarship, regardless of their talent.

"We called it the 'dancer with a dick award,'" says Shyman, who remembers feeling self-conscious as he walked past a line of twenty girl classmates to collect his award. "And [the girls] were all good and worked hard . . . but there's no equivalent for them."

As Megan Fairchild put it, as a boy, "basically you just have to be willing to put on the tights, and you'll get a scholarship anywhere, if you're, like, a breathing dancer." And, as we've seen, sometimes the tights are optional.

Amy Brandt, who was a professional ballet dancer before becoming editor in chief of *Pointe* magazine, argues that giving boys scholarships solely based on gender reinforces their privileged minority status and can result in a culture of sexist entitlement in dance schools and, later on, professional companies. "Guys feel very entitled because they've been given scholarships all their lives or have always been in the minority," she says.

On the other hand, Aubrey Lynch at Harlem School of the Arts notes, the perks for being a boy who does ballet can make it easier to overcome parental objections, especially among the low-income families of color who send their children to his school. "It begins with education and showing [parents] the end goal," he says. With dance, "you can make ten shows a week on Broadway; you can be in movies and television. You can travel the world. The dance education can pay for scholarships because all universities are looking for male dancers. So if you're good, you might pay for college and go to college as a dance minor and major in business."

There's one route to ballet scholarships that dancers of both genders can take: competing for them. On the growing ballet competition circuit, students can compete for subsidized admission to elite full-time training programs in the US and abroad. At competitions, dancers can perform in large groups, small groups, or in pas de deux couples. But it's in the solo competitions that they compete for the attention of schools that might grant them admission and scholarships.

But there's a high financial barrier to entry to the competition scene itself. The list of expenses is long: costumes, travel, and accommodations (for the dancer as well as for a teacher or parent, since many competitors are too young to travel alone); fees for the choreographers who create custom solos; fees for the coaches who train dancers for competition; and the cost of renting studio space in which to rehearse.

Regina Montgomery is a demi-soloist at Tulsa Ballet. At age nine, she started competing in the international Youth America Grand Prix (YAGP), which holds regional competitions that culminate in a final round in New York City. She continued to compete in YAGP every year until she got her first job in a ballet company at eighteen. "We were pretty well off," says Montgomery, who was born in China, adopted by white parents as an infant, and grew up in Los Angeles. Still, on top of her regular tuition and gear, competing was an expensive proposition.

"I probably had four [private lessons] at least a week for an hour, and we had to cover studio space as well," she says. "And then even for competitions, my parents would pay for one of my teachers to come to New York with us for finals to coach me whenever we were traveling."

It's easy to see how training and competing, at both this advanced level and at the less expensive recreational level, become financially prohibitive for many American families, especially families of color, who are disadvantaged by both a wage gap and a wealth gap. It's important to note that middle-class and upwardly mobile Black families have been sending their daughters to ballet class for well over a century: as dance historian Melissa Klapper explains in her social history of ballet in America, it was "seen as a path towards respectability" for parents who had fled the South in the Great Migration and were raising their children in the North. "I gave my daughters ballet so they could know how to walk and create the picture I wanted," said one such father, quoted in Klapper's book *Ballet Class*. "I wanted them to have an excellent education. I didn't want them to suffer the pangs of racism."[23]

Still, in the United States white men outearn men in all other racial groups except Asian women and men, and white women outearn women in all other racial groups. The average Black family has about one-tenth the wealth of the average white family. And there's a clear correlation between parental income and childhood exposure to formal and private arts education: a study of American arts attendance and education between 2002 and 2012, released in 2015, found that "the more educated the parents or the higher the family's income, the more likely children were to have taken arts or music classes in or out of school." While about 31 percent of white parents said their child had received formal arts or music education outside of school in the last year, 19 percent of Black parents and 10 percent of Hispanic parents said the same. For parents earning over $100,000 a year, the number was 39 percent, while for parents earning less than $50,000, it was 14.5 percent.[24]

It's little wonder that, among both the parents of color and the white parents I interviewed, none described their child's dance school as racially or economically diverse. Without serious efforts to decrease the cost of all ballet training—or to subsidize it for dancers from middle-class and low-income homes—ballet training, and thus the chance to join the ranks of a professional ballet company, will remain largely reserved for white and wealthy children.

~

There's another price to be paid for ballet training, and that is time—more specifically, a parent's time, and most specifically, a mother's time. For students who are living at home rather than at a residential program, ballet training involves an enormous amount of parental time and a not-insignificant amount of parental labor—and that most often falls on mothers.

The lobbies, observation areas, and parking lots of American ballet schools are full of moms. Moms waiting, moms keeping one eye on their dancing child and the other on their wandering toddler, moms taking mental notes about when spring recital auditions will be held and which shoes their daughter will need to take to them.

Dads are there, too, dipping in and out to execute drop-offs and pickups or backstage in November building sets for the annual production of *The Nutcracker*. One father in Charlottesville, Virginia, reported that because he works from home and his wife travels often for work, he does about 60 percent of ballet drop-offs and pickups, and they both volunteer backstage come *Nutcracker* time. He's made friends with other fathers he's met during his time at the dance studio, and they've formed a pub trivia team; they call themselves the Dance Dads.

Stories like this one are charming, but they're also unusual. For the most part, the division of parental labor in the ballet world can be best summarized by a T-shirt in the store at my local ballet school that says "Dance Dad . . . I don't dance, I finance." Dance dads exist, but ballet runs on moms.

In addition to scrimping and sacrificing her own comfort to afford ballet classes and pointe shoes, Grace Segers's mother, Rebecca, spent a great deal of time ferrying her back and forth to the ballet school, which was a half hour's drive from home. "By the end I was taking ballet six days a week, so that was at least a one-hour or two-hour round trip for her, because I couldn't drive," Grace remembers. "And she did it every day, while working full-time."

Adrienne Kisner, whose young son is on a scholarship at Boston Ballet School and takes classes three afternoons a week, describes the time commitment of ferrying kids to ballet as "like having a part-time job." In fact, Kisner has a full-time job, one that requires her to be available or on call during her son's ballet classes. Her family doesn't own a car, and her son is too young to take public transportation on his own. Still, she says, he had perfect attendance in 2019. "It would be much easier if he liked something like his sister does," she concedes. "Like clay on Saturdays."

Even mothers who don't spend hours taking their children to ballet put in a lot of time and work, and that labor is gendered, too. The wife of the Charlottesville dance dad agrees that her husband does "a lot of the physical running back and forth" to get her daughter to and from the dance school, but, she says, "the planning, making sure she's got what she needs, teaching her to do her hair, all those kinds of things have definitely been on my end." She's also been responsible for doing her daughter's hair and makeup for recitals and making sure they pass ballet's meticulous muster. At twelve, her daughter "can almost do a performance-quality bun at this point. She does almost all of her own stage makeup, to a point where I'm comfortable with her going onstage—she doesn't look like a clown."

The first time I interviewed Anisha Walker, she was in the car, driving a child to or from an extracurricular activity. Her experience as a ballet parent has been both gendered and raced. For example, for that year's production of *The Nutcracker*, her daughter Danya was cast as a flower in "Waltz of the Flowers," and the school's director "decided that all the flowers have to have the ballet-pink tights."

But Anisha was informed that "apparently the tights that Danya had on at a rehearsal weren't the right pink," she recalled. "They need to be more peachy. I'm just like, 'No matter how peachy . . . when they go on her brown legs, they're not going to look quite as peachy.' I did have to kind of explain that."

Anisha went out and bought another pair of pink tights all the same. "And we put them on and they looked the same as the pair we'd worn to practice because I think we always get ballet pink."

For another recital, Danya was asked to wear "nude" gear that actually matched her skin. "We had to put makeup on the straps [of her costume] because they were like a light beige-y color and [the school] wanted them to blend in with the skin. So we put makeup on them," Anisha told me. Who in the family found the makeup that matched Danya's skin and used it to color the straps? I asked Anisha. "Yep," she said, "that was me."

The work of supporting young ballet dancers can fall especially heavily on mothers of boys who dance, because those boys often find that their fathers are unsupportive of or hostile toward their dance training. In Doug Risner's research, boys reported that they got the most support from their dance teachers and their mothers, and the least support from their fathers.

The answers to Risner's survey question "What important person gives you the least support for your dancing?" are heartbreaking, because they tell stories about dismissive or outright neglectful fathers. "The person that gives me the least support as a dancer would have to be my father," one boy said. "The males in my family show little or no support," said another. "My father [has] never seen me dance."[25] But these answers are also infuriating, because they raise the question of which adult in the family *is* putting in the time, effort, and emotional labor to support these boys.

And then there are the parents who must choose between making enough money for their child to take ballet classes and having enough time to spend with that child. Sean Aaron Carmon, the former Alvin Ailey dancer, says he saw very little of his father growing up, mostly because he worked so much to pay for Carmon's dance training. Carmon characterizes his dad's mentality as, "No one is going to remember that I wasn't there at the beginning of Thanksgiving . . . but they will remember that they were able to do what they needed to do because I could get time and a half working." Carmon's mother taught him how to write letters to local businesses requesting sponsorships to cover competition fees, travel, and accommodation. Meanwhile, his father worked all the time to afford the tuition, room, and board at the summer intensives that Carmon auditioned for.

"I'm going to work," Carmon says, describing his dad's attitude, "because my son needs six thousand dollars [for a summer intensive]. He's not going to see me all the time, but he will be able to do what he needs to do this summer."

Twelve-year-old Danya Walker has been dancing since she was three years old, and with every passing year, she has spent more time at the dance studio. She now dances three week nights a week plus Saturday, and "Sunday depending if there's a production coming up," Anisha says. That's a lot of tuition, a lot of shoes, and a lot of time carved out by two parents who work full-time. At the end of 2019, when Danya progressed to learning to dance on pointe—a rite of passage she was "crazy" excited about—she only added more classes to her schedule and her shoes only got more expensive. By August 2020, she was in her second pair of ninety-dollar pointe shoes, and each pair required a twelve-dollar tube of "pointe paint" in order to match her skin.

Anisha says she and her husband have talked to Danya about the cost of ballet and made sure she knows that she can stop any time she wants.

"I don't want to put the burden of the cost on her," Anisha says, "but I do definitely, every year, make sure that she understands that it's not a requirement. Like, as long as she loves it, we'll continue to do it. But I want to make sure that she's all in before I commit to the amount of money."

It's a sentiment I heard from several parents who balked at the cost of ballet training: *As long as they love it, it's worth it.* But that love cuts both ways. As Anisha told me, "It's definitely very expensive. I feel like I'm stuck at this point because my daughter loves it."

CHAPTER 3

A TOLERANCE FOR PAIN

To some extent it requires its practitioners to give up on having a normal body, and the pain involved in this transformation is part of ballet's mythology.

PETER STONELEY

Mark, twenty-eight, is a dancer in a small contemporary ballet company in a major US city. One night during a performance in early 2019, Mark—who agreed to let me write about his experiences if I used a pseudonym—felt "something in my back kind of pop. It was my back and side, and I was like, 'What is that?'"

"When it first happened, it felt like my back was out, like I had lost an inch on the left side—it was just unhinged. It went all the way from my lower pelvis to my knee." He hobbled off the stage and was soon diagnosed with a muscle tear in his groin.

The damage wasn't severe enough for surgery, Mark says, and the only prescription in the short term was to rest, ideally for between four and six months. "Boy, did it hurt," Mark remembers. It hurt to walk, to stand up, to perform basic daily functions—let alone to dance. But Mark didn't stop dancing, because he couldn't, not really. His small company had no understudies to take his place onstage, and, more importantly, if he stopped performing, he'd stop getting paid.

"I can't believe I'm saying it, but I was dancing still, almost throughout the whole injury," he remembers. "I just kept going, and I was taken out of a lot of shows, but I performed still, doing some partnering here and there."

During a performance season, Mark doesn't get paid if he's not onstage. Knowing he couldn't afford to take time off to heal, he "took the personal decision to stay on my feet, at the very least, even if it's in the back of the row."

"I was dancing through pain," he remembers. "I was walking through pain. Sitting down, for weeks, it was painful. To even bend over."

Mark's employer doesn't provide health insurance, and whatever thin coverage he has, he buys out of his own pocket. The company will pay for medical care if an injury is sustained during a rehearsal or a performance, but not through a formal insurance policy: instead, dancers go for treatment, pay their full bills out of pocket, and are reimbursed from a company cash fund. Mark, whose company salary is about $40,000 a year, doesn't go to the doctor or the physical therapist if he doesn't know he can cover the expense himself, at least in the short term.

So, he says, he felt he had no real choice but to stay on the stage. "I would not have any way of getting treatment without being able to pay these bills," he says. He kept performing, sticking to roles that required as little movement as possible. His grandmother flew in from out of state to see him perform during that season, but given his limited mobility, she barely saw him dance.

Injuries are a fact of life for dancers, especially high-level students and professional dancers, who dance for many hours a day. As with any highly physical line of work, the dancer's body is at risk for sudden acute injuries like Mark's groin tear and for repetitive stress injuries accumulated over hours and years of class and rehearsals. Although they are common, injuries represent an existential threat to a dancer: her body is her tool and her livelihood, and her ability to remain employed depends on its functioning at its highest possible level. Ballet is a fiercely competitive field, and careers are short (in part because of the toll it takes on the body). When your career only lasts until your early or mid thirties—if you're lucky—a few months lost to injury can feel like a year.

Mark's story is an unusual one for a ballet dancer who is employed full-time by a company: although Mark's company doesn't provide health insurance, many ballet companies do provide their dancers with adequate coverage, and many provide on-site physical therapy and other specialized care for their dancers. (It is unusual in other ways, too; Mark is Black, and he dances for a respected and racially diverse company.)

But even dancers who have the security of a full-time company job and proper health insurance are in a precarious position, one that makes injuries especially distressing. With rare exceptions, they're employed on one-year contracts. If they're just starting out, if they're on the bottom rung of a company, or if they're afraid of getting a reputation for being injured often, they might understandably decide that they can't afford to take time away to let their injuries heal properly. In a highly competitive industry, dancing through an injury can feel all but mandatory.

It wasn't just Mark's primary job on the line. He, like many dancers with full-time company jobs, uses his unpaid vacation time ("layoffs," in dance terms) to take other performance opportunities that supplement his income. Once his regular performance season with the company finished, Mark had a contract to dance a series of these gigs overseas, and he was counting on that money. A year of good gigs—playing the *Nutcracker* prince in ballet school productions, teaching master classes—can add up to $10,000 to his annual income. "I never stopped, to be honest . . . because I just needed to make money at the time, and I wasn't really prepared for an out injury like that."

Mark's injury *was* an "out injury"—one that should have taken him out of daily classes, rehearsals, and performances for a significant stretch of time. He should not have gone back onstage mere days after he had hobbled off. But he did, like so many dancers who get hurt but don't have the chance to stop and heal, who rehearse and perform through extreme pain, and who often reinjure or do permanent damage to their body as a result.

⌒

Dancers often say that they feel most like themselves when they're dancing, that onstage is where they can express themselves most freely, most honestly, most naturally. It's the truth, no doubt, but so is this: there is nothing natural about ballet.

Humans did not evolve to turn out from the hip at 180 degrees or bend backward at the spine until the body is almost folded in half. They certainly did not evolve to dance on pointe. As dance journalist Joseph Mazo once wrote, "If God had wanted us to stand with our toes pointing in opposite directions, he would have bought a load of ball bearings and installed them, instead of using hip joints."[1]

The demands that ballet places on the human body and its hip joints—along with its feet, ankles, knees, spine, and shoulders—have increased over time as ballet has become more athletic and acrobatic. For both men and women, ballet demands more flexibility, more strength, more control, and more endurance than it did a generation ago, and more than would have been imaginable for dancers even in the mid-twentieth century. And even though dance medicine has improved, it cannot prevent or fully repair the extraordinary strain that ballet puts on dancers' bodies. "It is this exquisite, intimate tyranny to which one accedes in becoming a dancer," writes the dance historian and choreographer Brenda Dixon Gottschild. "It is a battle with the body to make it something other than what it is."[2]

Whether or not ballet is a sport—a debate that sporadically roils the dance world—is largely beside the point here: whether or not you think a ballerina is an athlete, she gets injured like one. In fact, sometimes she's more likely to get injured than a traditional athlete is. In one 2013 study, ballet dancers were more likely to sustain knee and lower back injuries than gymnasts and volleyball players. Professional ballet dancers have a lifetime injury rate of 90 percent, and, according to one study, "nearly all professional dancers employed for more than 1 year will have an injury," most likely in the foot or ankle. An earlier study found that dancers had a 61 percent chance of being injured in an eight-month period and got injured with the same frequency and severity as athletes playing contact sports like football and wrestling.[3]

Even those lucky few who don't get injured will dance through pain. Injuries, and pain in general, are inextricable from dance, and the toll that ballet takes on the body is, as Peter Stoneley notes in the quote that heads this chapter, part of its mythology. Ballet is beautiful, and beauty, after all, is pain. The mystique of ballet relies on the dancer's suffering, on the dissonance between the serene and immaculate ballerina on the stage and the gruesome, grueling reality of her body underneath her beautiful costume. There's a reason why no ballet movie is complete without a shot of a dancer wincing as she examines her blistered and bloodied toes, and why ballet Instagram is full of images of mangled feet posed beside pristine satin pointe shoes. Ballerinas, in exchange for their extraordinary beauty, are expected to endure extraordinary pain.

For professional ballet dancers, New York City Ballet dancer Abi Stafford wrote in *Dance Magazine*, "pain is simply a fact of life," and it comes in a variety of forms, "from niggling bruised toenails to crippling torn ligaments. There is temporary pain from pulled muscles and chronic pain from tendonitis. Nerves make stomachs hurt. Performances make lungs burn, leg muscles cramp and arms tingle. And at the end of the day, exhaustion can bring on all-encompassing suffering." Little wonder, then, that those who are drawn to dance and those who succeed as dancers have been found to have higher pain thresholds (i.e., the amount of pain they experience before noticing it) and higher pain tolerances (i.e., the ability to dance through pain) than other people.[4]

Nowhere is the movement demanded of dancers less natural, less in line with how human bodies evolved to move, than in the feet. The lower extremities (toes, feet, and ankles) are the most common injury sites for ballet dancers of both genders, accounting for between 34 percent and 62 percent of ballet injuries. Far more common than acute injuries, like bone breaks or ruptured ACLs, are stress injuries caused by "repetitive micro-traumas" to the tendons, muscles, and the five bones of the foot known as metatarsals—although acute injuries are made more likely by underlying chronic-stress injuries.[5]

Some injuries to the lower extremities are so closely associated with dance that sports medicine doctors have named them after dance, a dubious honor. A dancer's fracture is a foot injury that occurs most often when a dancer on demi-pointe (on tiptoes, in nondancer parlance) pushes her weight too far over the outside edge of her foot and rolls it. The result is an oblique spiral shaft fracture, a diagonal break in the metatarsal that connects to the pinky toe.

Dancer's tendinosis (also known as dancer's tendinitis), which manifests as pain under the big toe, at the back of the ankle, or on the underside of the foot, is a degeneration of the tendon that runs from under the calf down under the foot to the knuckle of the big toe, the flexor hallucis longus tendon. This tendon is put to work when a dancer jumps or rises up to demi-pointe and comes down again. When those motions are repeated, as they are over and over again in ballet, "the tendon becomes frayed, which causes swelling and microtears. This in turn causes more aggravation . . . and a vicious cycle ensues."[6]

But the most common cause of lower-extremity injuries in ballet dancers is, unsurprisingly, dancing on pointe. That's because pointe work forces the human body to do things it was never intended to do.

The toe end of a pointe shoe is known as the box. The hollow box, along with the stiffened sole of the shoe, which is called the shank, is made of a layered mix of fabric, paper, and glue. With the support of the hardened box and the shank, and by pointing her toes and feet and pressing down through the shoe, the dancer is able to lift up until her foot is perpendicular to the ground and the ends of her toes are pressing into the floor. Thanks to the stiffened shoe, she can stay there for long stretches of time—as long as her balance and tolerance for discomfort will permit.

When pointe shoes were first introduced in the early nineteenth century, they were a revelation. For some time, choreographers had been experimenting with ways to make dancers float and fly; some had used wires to literally lift their dancers off the ground. When dancers started darning the ends of their soft slippers to create more support in the toes and using that support to pull themselves up higher than the standard demi-pointe, the illusion of floating and fluttering was created without the need for harnesses or pulleys. Suddenly the ballerinas were not merely dancing women; they were flying birds or flitting fairies. It's no coincidence that one of the first ballet roles to be performed on pointe, in 1832, wasn't an earthbound human woman but a floating, otherworldly sylph. Pointe allows dancers to circumvent the rules of normal human movement.

Breaking those rules comes at a considerable cost. Pointe shoe technology has evolved since the days of shoe darning, but not nearly as much as one might expect. The fabric-glue-paper combination has barely changed in a century, and while some pointe shoe brands have developed a proprietary plastic blend that makes for a more supportive and durable shank, and others have inserted shock-absorbing foam into the shank, most have stuck to the old ways.[7] As basketball sneakers and running shoes have been engineered almost beyond recognition, pointe shoes have remained largely unchanged for generations of dancers, even though the technology exists to make them more durable and safer.

Yet even in those more supportive and more durable shoes, there's no truly pain-free or safe way to dance on pointe. When a dancer is on pointe, the toes are held tightly in the shoe's box, pressed together from the sides so that the five toes act together like a single rigid digit. The human foot isn't designed for that lateral compression, and it's certainly not designed for the longitudinal compression that happens when the weight of the entire body presses down into the box, where most of it is borne by the big toe.

Nick Cutri, a Los Angeles–based physical therapist who treats a lot of dancers, explains that, in a nondancing body, the big-toe joint performs one major function: it helps you walk. The articulation of the toe joint allows a person's weight, as they take a step, to move through their back foot and onto their front foot. "As that body is transitioning forward in gait, most of the weight is falling forward, outside of our center of gravity, as we transition forward," Cutri says. It's a fairly low-impact movement that doesn't put a great deal of pressure on the toe joint. When you're walking, the big-toe joint only bears about 30 percent of the body's weight. "It's just kind of the end of that push-off. So there's relatively very little body weight going through it," Cutri says.

But in dance, and especially on pointe, a joint that doesn't usually carry much body weight is instead required to take all of it—and in a completely different position from the one it evolved to bear weight in. Pointe is only possible because the toe joint is made rigid by the shoe, and in that rigid position, it is asked to carry the weight of the entire body.

Some joints are designed to do that, Cutri explains. The knee, for example, is a large hinge joint with a surface area capable of bearing the weight of the body above it. The largest joint in the foot, the subtalar joint—where the heel bone meets the bottom of the ankle—is built for that, too. The joints in the toes, on the other hand, are not. "They're really relatively very small," Cutri says. "They're not designed to take a ton of impact force. They're designed for just push-off as the body is transitioning forward in gait."

But dancing on pointe puts knee-level demands on a toe-size surface area. "The big, big issue," Cutri says, "is that they're now taking that very small joint that's meant to roll and really transition very little of the body weight forward, and they're compressing all their body weight down into that joint, just like the knee, but it's a hundredth of the size of the knee."

"The knee has a lot of big muscle groups that wrap around it to protect the motion that is needed from that structure," explains Cutri's practice partner Traci Ferguson, who specializes in treating dancers who do pointe work and is a former ballet dancer herself. "You have your calf, you have your quad, your hamstring—you have those big hitters. The big toe doesn't have that system. . . . There's no big muscle that will reinforce that joint."

Unsurprisingly, Cutri says, he and Ferguson treat a lot of dancers with bone stress injuries (sometimes referred to as stress fractures), which occur when the impact on a bone outpaces the bone's capacity to repair itself. He also sees a lot of arthritic toes, inflamed big-toe joints, dancer's tendinosis, and sesamoiditis, which is the inflammation of tiny bones distributed in another tendon and manifests as pain under the ball of the foot. Those tiny bones are designed to bear up to half a person's body weight, but when dancers push through the front of the foot to rise onto demi-pointe or to jump, the bones can experience up to three times the body's weight, six times what they're meant to bear.[8]

A big-toe injury might sound like a small problem. But the big toe is essential to a ballet dancer, regardless of whether she's dancing in pointe shoes. And if left untreated or danced on without rest, these small injuries can lead a dancer to overcompensate with other parts of the foot or ankle, passing the injury further up what sports medicine physicians call "the kinetic chain."

Just up the kinetic chain from the toes and metatarsals is the ankle. One of the most common problems Cutri sees in younger dancers is os trigonum, a congenital condition that tends to flare up in dancers because it's exacerbated by spending a great deal of time in plantar flexion, the position that the ankle is in when the foot is pointed. Os trigonum occurs when a bony growth develops between the ankle and the Achilles tendon, leaving the dancer a smaller and smaller amount of space at the back of the ankle. "It will cause pinching, it can cause some soft tissue damage back there," Cutri says, "and it's just quite painful, because basically there's something hard there that shouldn't be there." The growth can be fixed with physical therapy, but often it requires surgical removal.

Without rehab or surgery, os trigonum decreases a dancer's range of movement, which makes it harder to dance and makes it more likely that she will compensate by using other body parts. Those body parts, in turn, are at risk of overuse and acute injuries. Risk flows up the kinetic chain, from the toes all the way to the hips and spine. When dancers aren't using their feet correctly, whether it's due to os trigonum, a bone stress injury in the second metatarsal (the most common bone stress injury site for dancers), or an inflamed big-toe joint, they increase the already sky-high risk of hurting their ankles.

Ankle sprains are the single most common dance injury, accounting for between 67 percent and 95 percent of injuries among professional dancers (in other sports, they account for about 25 percent). Ballet dancers are significantly more likely to sprain their ankles than modern dancers or musical theater dancers are, and women ballet dancers are far more likely than men ballet dancers to sprain an ankle.[9] The reason? Pointe shoes. The height and precarity introduced by pointe shoes, added to the plantar flexion, make it astonishingly easy to roll an ankle and damage the ligaments and tendons that support the joint.

I nearly witnessed one of these bread-and-butter ballet injuries during the time I spent observing classes at the Joffrey Ballet School in New York City in early 2020. Full-time students in this four-year program take multiple ballet classes every morning, including boys-only classes that focus on high-octane jumps and turns, and girls-only classes that focus on pointe technique. Then they reconvene for a pas de deux class in which they learn to partner and be partnered.

During one pas de deux class, students were practicing a common element of partnering, the assisted pirouette: the man stands behind the woman and, with his hands at her waist, helps her to spin around. With his help, she is more stable and can complete many more rotations than she can working alone. Toward the end of class, a couple who were dancing near the front of the room were completing a series of pirouettes when, suddenly, the woman's weight shifted and her ankle buckled. Every dancer watching—and I—gasped as she put her other foot down to right herself. In the back of the studio, one of her classmates exhaled in relief and shook her head. Every one of us knew we had just witnessed a very near miss.

The student, a sixteen-year-old I'll call Carmen,[10] told me after class that her pointe shoes were nearly "dead" and needed to be replaced. Dead pointe shoes—that is, shoes that have been so softened by sweat and repetitive motion that they are no longer supportive enough to hold a dancer up—are dangerous to dance in, as Carmen's experience makes clear. It's one thing to entrust your ligaments and joints to a shoe made of burlap and glue when it's brand-new; it's quite another to entrust them to a shoe that's tired or close to dead.

Injuries happen when pointe shoes are tired, and they happen when bodies are tired. A reliable predictor of whether or not a dancer will get injured is whether they dance more than five hours per day, which full-time students and professionals certainly do. "When dancers' muscles are fatigued, their technical mechanics break down and they lose the protective capacity to prevent injury," one study explains. For example, they might not jump high enough to provide themselves with enough time to land correctly, resulting in damage to the foot, ankle, Achilles tendon, or knee. Another study found that professional ballet dancers were more likely to sustain an injury at the end of the day and at the end of the performance season, when their fatigue has accumulated. By the same token, bone stress injuries in the lower body can cause fatigue: a stress fracture in the fibula, the slimmer of the two bones in the lower leg, is "frequently the cause of poor balance and fatigue when initiating a turn." Dancing on tired legs or tired shoes can be disastrous.[11]

The technology exists to make hardier pointe shoes, ones that offer more support than the traditional model and that wear out far more slowly. About twenty years ago, an American brand, Gaynor Minden, released a pointe shoe with a box and shank made of malleable plastic, which resists deterioration from sweat and motion (a few other brands, including Capezio, followed suit while continuing to sell shoes made the traditional way). Gaynors last longer than a traditional pointe shoe, and they cost more—about $140 compared to about $70—but their cost is not the reason that large parts of the ballet world have met them with disdain and rejection. It's because of what they do to a dancer's line.

In ballet, the line is sacred. It is a cardinal rule that the dancer's body should make a long and smooth line; depending on the position, the body becomes a sleek parabola or a perfectly straight dash, uninterrupted by breasts or buttocks or bulging quadriceps or unpointed feet.

The line has been used as a pretext for barring Black dancers, and fat dancers, and dancers who are in possession of breasts or hips that interrupt their lines. Melissa Verdecia, a white Cuban American dancer who performs with Ballet Hispánico in New York City, remembers the day in her teens when a teacher told her that she didn't have the lines to become a professional ballet dancer.

"I was always skinny, so to speak—I was always petite—but I had a butt," Verdecia explains. "I had a butt and muscular legs . . . and I had a teacher who was like, 'Stick in your butt.' And I was like, 'I can't, that's just my butt.'" Her teacher's response? "Well, you're never gonna dance ballet like that." That teacher was wrong, kind of: Verdecia has had a career in which she's danced contemporary ballet. But she also remembers looking around at her class at American Ballet Theatre's summer intensive as a teen, noting that she was one of the only Latina girls and also one of the only curvaceous ones, and realizing that there probably wasn't a place for her in that company.

Even when more curvaceous dancers are admitted into ballet, the pursuit of the line can come at a considerable expense to their physical health. Harper Watters, a soloist at Houston Ballet, is Black and has spent a lifetime trying to flatten the curve in his lower back to lessen the appearance of what he calls his "big ole curvy booty"; the result is a compressed disc and an imbalance between how much he uses his gluteal muscles and how much he uses his core muscles. The compressed disc, he says, is "so painful."

And, in the name of the line, dancers like Carmen are still pirouetting in shoes that have barely changed since the 1920s.

Detractors of Gaynor Minden shoes argue that they're "cheater" shoes, that the plastic shank makes it too easy for dancers to get up on pointe and stay there without developing the kind of strength that's required of dancers in traditional shoes. And they worry that the new material makes it hard to rise up and come down slowly, gracefully, and elegantly—instead of "popping" up. While Gaynors now have a solid share of the market and have gained more widespread acceptance among elite students and professional dancers, some teachers (including the former head of the ballet program at my local dance school in Iowa) bar their students from learning the basics of pointe in these shoes.

"Cheating" and "popping" aside, some of the resistance to the new shoes comes down to this: traditionalists think they're ugly. They're too clunky, too square at the end, too bulky. They ruin the line. One former New York City Ballet principal dancer who went on to become an influential teacher called them "space-age shoes." Another called them "appalling" and said that even on a good foot, "it looks like she's got a skate on. It's not a foot anymore. It's a shoe!"[12]

Gaynors are, according to the company's founder, "the first and . . . the only pointe shoe that was ever designed with dancers' health and safety in mind." (But she's quick to note that her shoes won't make dancing on pointe painless or even comfortable. "You'll still suffer," she says.) One proponent of Gaynor Mindens, a dancer in the Royal Ballet's corps de ballet, described them as feeling "just like trainers." But traditionalists aren't interested. "Ballet isn't about health," said the aforementioned celebrity teacher. "It's an art form."[13] It's not about your ligaments; it's about your lines.

"It's not the look everyone is going for," Traci Ferguson, the dance PT, says, "because so much of ballet is rooted in tradition. I think that's a big part of it." It is true that an expert ballet audience member with a very expensive seat could see and understand the difference between a traditional pointe shoe and a "clunky" one. But those audience members make up an extremely small percentage of ballet-goers, and, after all, they're not the ones incurring the long-term orthopedic damage.

Pointe shoes could be made even more functional, and even safer, than Gaynor Mindens are. A more "foot-forward" shoe, Ferguson says, wouldn't be tapered at the tip, so that the box would be the same width at the top, where the toe knuckles are, as is it as the bottom, where the shoe hits the floor in the pointe position. That would make some steps more difficult, Ferguson concedes, because the widened box would make for a bigger structure. And "a foot-forward shape would take away a lot of the aesthetic of the pointe shoe."

So, I asked Ferguson, a safer shoe might change the movement, and it might change the line, but it also might not result in serious musculo-skeletal damage? "Exactly."

This resistance to safety in the name of beauty has a long, gruesome history in ballet. In the mid-1800s, theaters in Europe and Britain introduced gaslights, an innovation that meant that theaters could light the stage and the house separately, which "brought radiant drama and otherworldly atmosphere" to ballets like *Giselle* and *La Sylphide*. There was just one problem: dancers kept coming into contact with the gaslights' open flames. Their costumes would catch fire, and the dancers would be horribly burned or even killed. This was an American problem, too: Deirdre Kelly notes that in Philadelphia in 1861, "seven young ballerinas at once caught on fire, all subsequently dying."[14]

When a solution was invented—dipping costumes and props in a flame retardant—and mandated by the French government, some dancers refused. Why? Because "the chemical yellowed their muslin skirts, making them look dark and dingy," and "stiffened them, compromising the illusion of lightness and buoyancy ballerinas of this era worked so hard to achieve." In the words of one Paris Opera Ballet dancer who opted for beauty even if it meant burning to death, "We'll burn but once, but have to suffer those ugly skirts every night."[15]

⁓

The purpose of a pointe shoe is to enable the kinds of abnormal movements demanded by ballet without concealing the strength and flexibility of the dancer's foot. But it's jarring to realize that the very characteristics that make for "good" feet are the ones that can predispose them to injury. A "good" foot for ballet is one that can point into a deep curve; colloquially, some dancers call them "cashews." A genetic predisposition to high arches—the medical term is "cavus foot"—makes it more likely that a dancer can acquire that kind of shape in plantar flexion. Combined with strong foot muscles, a cavus foot gives a ballet dancer a smooth, curved finish at the end of the leg line. And though a good foot is valuable for dancers of both genders, it's especially important for women, who dance on pointe and whose feet must be strong and arched enough to manipulate a pair of pointe shoes. Without properly pointed feet, her line is ruined.

Cavus foot is seen as an built-in advantage for dancers, who obsess over their own feet and envy others'. But cavus foot, the marker of naturally good feet, doesn't distribute weight as well as a normal or flat foot does. That increases the load on a dancer's first metatarsal, the one that connects to the big toe, and raises the risk for bone stress injuries in the fifth metatarsal, the one on the outside edge of the foot. It also increases the stress on the ankle, a joint that is already under considerable pressure in ballet.[16]

Another congenital advantage that some dancers enjoy is genu recurvatum, or hyperextended legs, which make the backs of the knees appear to curve slightly upward when the leg is fully straightened. Genu recurvatum improves the dancer's line, making her legs look longer and straighter and accentuating the curve of her foot. It also likely contributes to lumbar lordosis, or swayback, which can cause pain in the lower spine as the muscles spasm and seize.[17]

Similarly, the practice of "winging" the foot—flexing the ankle slightly when the leg is extended so that, when viewed from the side, the line ends a slight upward flick—is widely considered to improve a dancer's line. It can also cause inflammation of the ankle joint lining, which results in bunions. These bony growths are painful and disfiguring, and they make it difficult to fit properly into a pointe shoe, and as the deformation progresses, the dancer's weight is transferred sideways onto bones that cannot bear it. "Pain from overload of the lesser metatarsal heads," one paper explains, "can be more debilitating" than the bunion itself.[18]

While it used to be acceptable for girls to start dancing on pointe before adolescence, in the United States it is now standard for teachers to hold them back until they are at least eleven. Some schools require an assessment by a physical therapist to ensure that each dancer has the strength, as well as the ballet technique, to begin learning pointe work.

Some dance schools go further than that. Abbe MacBeth, whose twelve-year-old daughter takes ballet classes in Charlottesville, Virginia, says that after her daughter passed the medical assessment, she was required to have X-rays taken. "They take X-rays of the ankles and feet, and they look for where their growth plates [are] and if they're seeing anything strange now, so that as you're going on pointe you're really aware of how your bones are and how your body's going to react," Abbe tells me.

And after all that, Abbe says, the girls in her daughter's class, along with their parents, were invited to an informational session hosted by the school, where a local podiatrist began her remarks by saying, "I'm here to talk you out of going on pointe."

"I actually appreciated that the studio owners did that session," Abbe tells me. "You could tell from the girls' faces, they were like, 'What?' And she looked at them and said, 'I'm not going to convince you not to go on pointe, but I want you to think about what this is going to do to your body.'"

The podiatrist, whose own two daughters had been ballet students at the school, proceeded to explain to the perplexed girls what kind of a toll pointe takes on the body. "She talked to them about the pressure you're putting on your toes and your ankles," Abbe remembers, "and how in addition to the calluses and things like that, this can cause your foot shape to change." Most of all, she warned the students against spending more time on pointe than their teachers had sanctioned or attempting steps they weren't yet approved to execute. "You may not be ready to do turns yet; you're not ready to jump leap across the floor. . . . You increase your skill, and then you plateau for a while."

This is the best way for young people to learn pointe work: in the best available shoes, with close supervision from well-trained teachers and medical attention throughout the process. But even then, Cutri says, it's not really that safe. He's heartened that the standard age for beginning pointe work has risen to eleven or twelve, but if he had his way, it would be much higher. At age eleven, the female skeleton is still years from maturity—typically, growth plates close two years after menstruation begins—and the risk of doing permanent damage is considerable.

When I asked him what he'd do if he could snap his fingers and set the minimum age, he said he'd "probably" make a policy that girls shouldn't be allowed on pointe before they turn fifteen.

"Hopefully one day we'll be like, 'You can't do it until you're fully skeletally mature,' so they haven't had all the stress by the time they get to their teenage years on these bones that are soft and pliable."

⌒

One factor that makes it difficult to treat bone injuries acquired doing pointe work, and one that makes them more likely to occur, is the "dancer's triad," or, as one sports medicine journal article referred to it, "the dreaded dancer's triad."[19]

The triad's components are (1) malnutrition, which leads to (2) hormonal disruptions, including delayed menarche or halted periods, which can (3) diminish bone density and make it more likely that bone fractures or breaks will occur, as well as making it harder for them to heal. (It is sometimes called the "female athlete triad" and tends to show up in other "aesthetic-athletic" or "physique-conscious" activities, like figure skating and gymnastics.)

Dr. Jessalynn Adam, a sports medicine and rehabilitation physician who specializes in treating young athletes, notes that the contemporary term for the triad is "relative energy deficiency in sport," or RED-S, in part because malnutrition has serious consequences for male athletes, too, including decreased cardiovascular capacity and a weakened immune system (and, she notes, the acronym formed by "female athlete triad" is hardly helpful for those who are diagnosed with it).

The inadequate nutrition that forms the first leg of RED-S is sometimes caused by an eating disorder (about which more later), but even dancers who do not have diagnosable eating disorders might be taking in too little food, to the point that they kick-start the other two legs of the triad. Osteopenia, in which the bones weaken in a precursor to osteoporosis, is of particular concern. This is not only because it can make it easier for women to get injured during their dance careers, but also because it swallows up the valuable and limited time that women have to develop bone density, a window that closes around age thirty.

In the sports and dance medicine literature, doctors urge each other to assess dancers for RED-S and to refer them to the appropriate specialists (nutritionists, endocrinologists, psychologists) if they think it's present. This, the literature stresses, is essential to creating an effective treatment plan for the physical injuries that physical therapists and orthopedists are trying to repair: if the dancer's bones are weakened by malnutrition and hormonal dysfunction, they're not going to heal properly—and even if they do, they're just going to break again.

Ferguson, who treats a lot of dancers in their teens and early twenties who are enrolled in intensive preprofessional training, says she checks for signs of RED-S in every dancer—as a matter of habit and principle, she refers to them as athletes—that she treats. She says she starts by asking the athletes about their daily eating habits, presenting it "as a math equation: What's their energy expenditure? How many calories are going in, and how many calories are going out? . . . If they're not eating to the demands of an eight-hour rehearsal day where you're dancing the whole day, which requires a lot of energy, they're still burning more calories than are coming in. So that's their daily check-in."

Then she asks them to zoom out for a monthly check-in, as in: Are they menstruating regularly? Late periods and skipped periods, or periods that haven't started at all for athletes in their midteens, can be a sign that malnutrition is causing hormonal changes. That's when Ferguson starts to worry about estrogen levels and whether or not the athlete's hormones are affecting her ability to build and maintain bone density.

"When women enter menopause, that's when we start to lose density," she explains. "So when the athlete is within that [RED-S] system and they're not menstruating at a normal rate, they can cause their body to think that they are entering menopause. It mimics the same bone density loss as menopause."

In other words, because ballet is so physically taxing, and because dancers are under pressure to remain thin, they can consume too little food to fuel their bodies to perform basic functions. Because they are encouraged to maintain a sleek and lean line, uninterrupted by breasts, thighs, or hips—all markers of the hormonal changes that accompany the transition to physical adulthood—dancers can look like they have yet to reach puberty. The bone-deep reality is that they have simply skipped it and proceeded straight to menopause, about three decades early.

—

While women ballet dancers are much more prone to ankle problems than men, hip problems don't discriminate. That's because ballet demands extreme turnout of both men and women.

In one five-month study of the Norwegian National Ballet, among the 75 percent of dancers who were injured, hip and back injuries were the second-most common complaint, though, unlike lower-extremity injuries, they did not result in dancers missing class, rehearsal, or performances. In a later study, this one of a larger sample of American pre-professional ballet students, hip injuries were more common than knee and ankle injuries and did cause dancers to miss some or all of a class, rehearsal, or performance.[20]

Just as pas de deux has become more demanding as dancers have become stronger, the ideal turnout has evolved considerably over time. In the court of Louis XIV, the perfect turnout for a courtier was a forty-five-degree angle. In the 1820s, French ballet students "took to strapping their feet and legs to [the barre] in order to stretch their limbs and force their insteps."[21] Today, the ideal turnout is 180 degrees: in first position, the feet should form a perfect straight line, and that turnout should be maintained as much as possible when the dancer moves through other positions. It is profoundly unnatural, or, as sports medicine physicians term it, nonphysiologic.

Anyone who has ever taken a ballet class has been told to turn out from the hip, using the muscles of the inner and outer upper thighs and the gluteal muscles to fan the feet out. In reality, the hips can only achieve a turnout of about sixty degrees, and the rest of the work is done by the foot and the knee.[22] This results in yet more damage to the foot and knee, and dancers might also arch their lower backs to increase the appearance of their turnout, which puts strain on the spine.

But even when these other body parts aren't pitching in to achieve a perfect line, turnout and the range of movement demanded by ballet wreak utter havoc on the hips. Nick Cutri, who estimates that hip injuries are, along with ankle injuries, the most common dance problems he treats, explains that because dancers begin their training at such an early age, the time they spend in the turned-out position can twist the soft and malleable young thigh bone, reshaping it permanently.

Cutri stresses that research into this phenomenon is relatively limited. But he believes that "when you take somebody that's skeletally immature and you're excessively rotating their hips in really one direction only, you're torsioning the actual long bone, the femur," he says. "So you actually create a torsion in the femur and in the tibia where you're twisting the bone."

Cutri draws a comparison between the thigh bones of dancers and the upper arm bones of youth baseball pitchers, which have been studied in more depth. "We see it in young pitchers, and they've actually been able to establish a link between too many pitches in young prepubescent males and actual twisting of the humerus bone."

Before the dancer reaches musculoskeletal maturity, he explains, "the bone isn't complete from end to end. . . . It's a soft cartilaginous growth plate at either end, and so you're taking that growth plate and because it's soft, it can be twisted. And so it will grow bone in the manner in which you're stressing it. . . . It will put support where it feels like it needs support."

The body adapts to ballet, and that adaptation is permanent. "If that stress is in a rotational fashion," Cutri extrapolates, "it will lay down bone in a rotational fashion."

In young dancers, Cutri says, the thigh bone may grow so twisted that walking or standing with the feet in parallel, the way a nondancer would, puts the kind of strain on the knee that a nondancer would experience when attempting to walk or stand turned out.

As is the case with cavus feet and genu recurvatum, the very congenital hip traits that make for a good ballet line—the ones that mark a person as a promising dancer early in life—could also be the ones that, when danced on, worsen into serious conditions. One example is femoral retroversion, in which the angle of the top of the femur to the ball of the hip joint makes it feel more natural for a person to stand in a slight turnout position. Another is hip dysplasia, a congenital condition that results in shallow hip sockets. Shallow sockets make for better turnout, and just as ballet teachers may note a young student's cavus feet, they may note his promising turnout and encourage him to keep training and to deepen that turnout.

"Anybody that's got any kind of dysplasia," Cutri says, "they already don't have a really deep hip socket. You're taking them and you're going, 'Ooh, that's really pretty. Let's keep going with that.'"

Cutri worries that, in young people with shallow hip sockets, spending a lot of time turned out from the hips can make the hip deformity worse—and permanent. "The theory is that you're creating a very shallow socket [and] you're not allowing that bone to form completely around the ball."

Marc Philippon is one of the country's most respected hip surgeons. The father of two daughters and a son who all took ballet, Philippon, who practices in Vail, Colorado, has operated on numerous elite ballet dancers as well as dozens of Olympic and professional athletes.

Philippon notes that even dancers with "normal, boring anatomy"—that is, dancers without dysplasia, femoral retroversion, or hip impingements—put their hips under tremendous strain from a very young age.

Ballet requires both an extreme range of movement from the hips (picture a développé in second, in which the working leg is both extremely turned out and lifted as high as possible) and a great deal of repetition (picture all those hours, all those tendus and battements at the barre). "Just the repetition and the demand on the body can lead to overload of the joint, can cause damage to the body and damage to the structures," Philippon says. "The dancer has to do a range of motion that is sometimes extreme. For example, the développé, where they have to rapidly rotate and flex their hip . . . puts a lot of stress on the joints."

Philippon specializes in repairing the labrum, the cartilage cushion in the hip socket, which enables the ball of the joint to move smoothly and prevents the two bones from scraping against each other. Labrum tears, which are very painful and can seriously inhibit the movement of the leg—an obvious problem for a dancer who is required to do high battements or big split jumps—can be acute injuries or repetitive stress injuries. Philippon also estimates that as much as 15 percent of the cases he sees began further down the kinetic chain, as foot injuries, ankle instability, or tendinitis in the knee.

Philippon stresses that very few people are genetically predisposed to good turnout, and he worries about teachers pressuring students to achieve the 180-degree line that has become the ideal. Like many dancers and parents I interviewed, Philippon worries about "old-school" teachers who encourage students to force their hips—with the help of their knees, ankles, and feet—into a position for which their body simply is not built.

"I think it's very important for [teachers] to understand that not everybody is the same," he says. "For some people it's very easy to do a turnout because their thigh bone or femur is retroverted. For them it's super easy. But you have dancers who have what we call 'anteverted' [leg bones]. For these people it's very hard to do turnout. So if you have a teacher telling students, 'Hey, your turnout is bad, you need to force it,' and they don't understand it is a mechanical issue and not lack of trying, some of these injuries probably could be avoided."

Once those injuries have occurred, it can be very difficult to repair them well enough to restore a dancer's full range of movement with surgery—sometimes impossible, if the injury is too advanced. "They need to meet criteria," Philippon explains, "meaning . . . the structures are reparable, in good condition, and they have good function at the time of injury, very good function." Dancers who meet that criteria, he estimates, have a 95 percent chance of regaining function "at the same level or better." Still, the surgery is invasive, recovery time is significant, and, as we've already seen in Mark's case, some dancers simply cannot afford the cost—in time, in money, in guaranteed employment—that surgery and recovery require.

Philippon says that at the highest echelons of the ballet world, in large and prestigious companies, there has been "a lot of progress," in the last decade toward helping teachers understand that unsatisfactory turnout isn't a question of effort but a matter of mechanics. "Instead of sometimes pushing through," he says, now "they actually will stop, assess the dancer, and then take them to a professional to evaluate them, instead of going the old way, where you basically have to push through the pain."

But Cutri, who has done postsurgical rehab on many of Philippon's patients, is less optimistic. He says that teachers forcing students into positions their bodies can't handle isn't only an "old-school" problem but one he sees taking a toll on his young patients today.

Cutri worries about young dancers overrehearsing and overstretching to achieve the huge ranges of motion that have become de rigueur in ballet. Without proper strength training, without teachers who can teach young dancers how to control their very flexible muscles, there's a real risk for long-term damage to the hips.

"Taking a stretch and then making them hold the splits for an hour or twenty minutes or thirty minutes . . . Congratulations, you just overstretched an eight-year-old," Cutri says sarcastically. "But to teach that eight-year-old then how to control that split is really difficult because they don't have the motor control for that yet."

Ferguson, too, is concerned about the "borderline contortion-like movements" that have become standard in ballet. "For a very long time ballet was so controlled and purposeful that it wasn't that big of an issue, but it's definitely pushing more," she says. She's especially concerned about the influence of the youth competition circuit, which has long rewarded displays of acrobatic flexibility in jazz and other disciplines. While ballet competitions are not new, the emphasis on acrobatics and hypermobile "tricks" is.

She sees patients who are increasing their flexibility by stretching in "oversplit"—that is, pushing their legs beyond 180 degrees by placing one or both feet on a box or a chair, with the hope of achieving leaps and kicks that go beyond a straight line. She also sees dancers who are trying to mimic the congenital conditions that make for a better line, like genu recurvatum. "They are pushing for more hyperextensions because they like that line in the knee that almost bends backwards, and it has that bend in the tibia that counteracts the toe. And they'll strap themselves into things and [try] all sorts of crazy ways of going about it."

(The demand for extreme flexibility, which was once reserved for girls, is now directed at boys, too, the dancer Mark observes. "More and more boys, at a younger and younger age, are becoming extremely flexible, like a rhythmic gymnast," he says, and are "trying to have a thin frame [for] a better line.")

Cutri explains that it takes a great deal of flexibility but very little strength to, for example, "whack" the leg up into a high battement in second position, so that the knee is next to the ear. It takes both flexibility and control to lift the leg slowly into position, hold it there, and lower it slowly down again. When dancers are trained to whack but not to control the motion, the muscles stop working and the surrounding structures take over.

"They don't know how to activate their muscles at these end ranges," he says. "Then they tend to hit those static structures, the ligaments, the bones. . . . So what tends to happen is they create this joint that is really, really loose and, in ballet terms, very pretty. But they have zero control over it. So when they get to these end ranges, there's nothing stopping it. It just goes. And then you end up hitting those two bones together, or you end up pinching that labrum and that labrum ends up tearing."

Ferguson worries that as ballet moves towards hyperflexibility, "we'll start to see a higher rate of these injuries, either while the dancer is active or as the dancer ages." The danger doesn't end when your dancing career does, Ferguson explains, because "your ligaments don't tighten. They stay at the same level they were stretched to. If you're no longer at the same strength level you were at when you were doing it initially, you won't have the same support." Jessalynn Adam warns that "extra-stretchy" athletes, the ones with overextending elbows and knees, should be screened for connective tissue disorders that can cause hyper-mobility, like Ehlers-Danlos syndrome.

Cutri says that preventing the kind of long-term damage Ferguson describes would require a fundamental shift in ballet training: not just holding off on pointe until age fifteen but also not asking dancers to de-velop extreme flexibility until well into their teens. "I would just say un-til we know that that body is skeletally mature and their growth plates are closed, I wouldn't let them start doing extended splits and things like that."

Cutri knows this would "absolutely" change ballet training and the shape of a field where currently many dancers become professionals at seventeen or eighteen. But, he says, the old-school ways of training are demonstrably bad for young bodies and have permanent consequences for older bodies. "It's just a different era. We know so much more. Are we doing this because we want them to love this sport, and do some-thing that's good for themselves, and it's going to help their self-esteem, their self-confidence? Are we asking them to do something that's fun-damentally really bad for the longevity of their skeleton?"

⌒

Most American girls who take ballet will stop taking regular formal dance classes by the time they graduate from high school; a small group will continue to dance in college, and an even tinier sliver will become professional dancers. But the lessons they learn in early dance train-ing can live in their muscles for decades. Take, for example, the appar-ent overlap of two populations: people who had ballet training in their youth, and people who experience pelvic floor dysfunction that makes penetrative vaginal sex painful or even impossible.

Studies have found high rates of pelvic floor dysfunction in elite female athletes: one 2018 meta-analysis found that the athletes most likely to experience urinary incontinence are gymnasts, and an earlier study found that 43 percent of elite ballet dancers experience urinary leakage.[23]

The pelvic floor works hard in ballet, helping to provide the body with the kind of stability that makes it possible to balance on one leg, go up on pointe, and land big jumps. Along with the rest of the core—which includes the abdominal muscles, the lower back muscles, and the diaphragm, among others—that stability allows a dancer to create the illusion of "isolation," that the leg doing a battement is the only part of the body moving while the rest stays solid and still (or, as one of my teachers used to call it, "quiet"). Isolation is a central principle in ballet: the arm lifts without shrugging the shoulder, the leg lifts without hoisting the hip, the knees plié while the lower back stays straight and long.

But if those other core muscles are weak or aren't firing appropriately, the pelvic floor might be called into additional service, says Kathryn Maykish, a physical therapist who specializes in treating pelvic dysfunction and treats a lot of dancers and former dancers (and who is herself a former dancer).

One example Maykish gives is the case of turnout: as Marc Philippon says, many dancers do not have the bony anatomy, the underlying body structure, that will permit the 180-degree turnout currently considered ideal for ballet dancers.

"There are natural differences in our bony joints, how much external rotation we can actually get" even when the muscles that contribute to turnout are strong, Maykish says. "If a dancer was born with less external hip rotation, in order to get that picture, that ideal shape we want from ballet, she might start to force or grip or compensate elsewhere so she can get what *looks like* that hundred-and-eighty-degree turnout her teacher is asking for."

One such place is the pelvic floor, where the dancer might "hold" or "grip," Maykish says, "instead of isolating that movement to just her deep hip external rotators." As a result, the pelvic floor muscles, overworked and weakened by lack of rest, can stay tense and unable to release or relax. When female athletes experience urinary incontinence, one study explains, it can be because their "pelvic floor muscles are overloaded, stretched, and weak because of increased intra-abdominal pressure."[24]

Which brings us to painful sex. The first time I attempted vaginal penetrative sex, when I was sixteen and taking three or four dance classes a week—ballet, jazz, and theater jazz—it was simply impossible. My vaginal muscles felt, in the words of one former dancer who has pelvic floor dysfunction similar to mine, "like a brick wall." Nothing was getting inside me, no matter how much I wanted it to. When I forced it, the stinging and burning pain that resulted was excruciating; another former dancer who experiences this pain described it best when she told me it feels "like rug burn." This was how penetration continued to feel for me for a decade, and not just during sex but also during pelvic exams, IUD insertions, and even when I tried to use tampons.

A string of mystified ob-gyns misdiagnosed me with urinary tract infections, offered me topical analgesics for my vulva, suggested I might be allergic to condoms or lubricants, told me to simply drink an extra glass of wine to relax and "loosen up" before sex, and wondered aloud if I had been raped (thankfully, I had not). The problem didn't go away, and in the meantime, my inability to have the kind of sex I wanted— the kind of sex my straight male partners most wanted—without consistent, excruciating pain took a toll on my relationships and my self-esteem. Sex, even consensual sex, became a traumatic self-fulfilling prophecy, a source of conflict rather than closeness with my partners.

It wasn't until I was referred to a pelvic floor physical therapy clinic that I found the understanding, diagnosis, and treatment that I needed. Pelvic floor dysfunction can result in all kinds of chronic pain conditions, including vulvodynia and vaginismus, as well as urinary incontinence and constipation. My pelvic floor physical therapist, like Maykish, treated a lot of former dancers.

"There are some biomechanical reasons that we could point to for a higher prevalence of pelvic pain in women who train in ballet," Maykish says, although she's careful to note that it's not clear if the ballet-trained population is at higher risk than the rest of the population. And, she says, the psychological and social aspects of dance training are "an even greater driver when we're thinking about pelvic pain and especially pain with penetration."

For example, ballet's demand for thinness (about which much more in Chapter 4) puts pressure on dancers to hold their bodies in a particular way. And "if we're always holding our tummy tight, then we're also always holding our pelvic floor tight," Maykish explains. "They go along with each other. So that habitual pulling up, or trying to pull the belly up and in, even when we're not dancing, can cause 'cross talk' over to the pelvic floor and encourage it to hold tight."

Then there's the matter of whether a dancer feels safe in the place where they're dancing or is bracing for hurtful critique of their body or sexual harassment (about which much more in Chapter 7). That, too, can show up in the body and stay there for years. "We know that trauma doesn't just have to be something that happens one time," Maykish says. "Trauma is also systemic, and trauma can be chronic. And our pelvic floor muscles are one of the groups of muscles in our bodies that most readily respond to stress and trauma."

In fact, the pelvic floor is even more responsive to stress and fear than the muscles we usually associate with those feelings, the upper shoulders. "Before your upper shoulders are feeling tension in them, your pelvic floor is already contracting and trying to defend you or protect you," Maykish explains. "That hypervigilance, that fear and anxiety, can start to be somaticized—we take it and we put it into our bodies because we don't have a chance to express it elsewhere."

One result of a pelvic floor that's been taught to hold on tight—whether by movement, or pressure to look skinny, or fear and trauma—can be painful sex. I'll never know if my dance training (or my gymnastics training) played a role in my own years of suffering, though I have my suspicions. What I do know is that my experience of stumped ob-gyns and the relief I felt at finding specialist care are both common.

One former dancer I interviewed had been diagnosed with over a dozen UTIs and had taken antibiotics each time, only to have the pain return the next time she tried to have penis-in-vagina sex. Another was told the problem was all in her head, and then that the only solution was surgery. Yet another has simply built her life around avoiding PIV sex and physical intimacy in general. In a culture that neglects research into the female body, cares little for women's pain, and places a low value on women's sexual pleasure, this is all quite predictable.[25]

Maykish has found that the most effective treatment is a team approach, meaning a combination of pelvic floor physical therapy, rehabilitation medicine, and mental health therapy. She was unsurprised to hear about my experiences with ob-gyns or the similar ones I'd heard about in my reporting; she hears those kinds of stories every day. "Our ob-gyns are really trained to look at a very small part of our bodies," she says, and they're not taught to assess the pelvic floor muscles for strength or tonicity. "So they just don't know." But, she says, "if a young woman is thinking that perhaps her pelvic floor is leading to dysfunction, particularly with pain with vaginal penetration, there are professionals who can help."

Mark started taking dance classes when he was seven years old and took his first ballet class in sixth grade. In addition to his snap groin injury onstage, he has a slew of standard repetitive stress injuries amassed over two decades of dancing, including something like os trigonum, the floating bone in the ankle that Cutri sees so often in his practice.

Like many dancers, Mark has a lot of repetitive stress injuries in his lower extremities. Mark says that "almost everyone"—that is, almost every one of his ballet teachers and artistic directors—has given him "the foot talk." One long-standing stereotype about Black dancers is that they are genetically unlikely to achieve the "cashew" foot that ballet prizes, that their feet are naturally flat and therefore less suited to the deep curve that is required to complete the leg line.

"There is . . . a weird stereotype that white people have good feet [and] Black people have bad feet, but I know some Black guys with some incredible arches, like I've never seen," Mark says. "There's all these other dancers that are out there, that are Black, with amazing feet. . . . And I've seen white people with bad feet." Nardia Boodoo, who is a member of the corps de ballet at the Washington Ballet and who is Black, says that the bad-feet stereotype was enforced in one of her ballet schools. "I remember one teacher having a talk with just the Black girls in class about our feet and how, technically, Black people's feet have low arches," she says. "And I remember being like, 'That's so not true,' because I actually have really high arches."

Mark's barrier to good feet has little to do with his race and more to do with the shape of his thigh bone and shin bone. "I have bowed femurs and bowed tibias, so I'm bowlegged, like, doubly," he explains. "It makes my line look extremely weird," and it also means that in order for his foot to continue a straight line at the end of his leg, he needs to wing "as far out as possible, just to achieve a straight line."

Winging causes inflammation in the ankle, and that, combined with the beating his feet take in class, rehearsal, and performances, has meant Mark's career has been marred by repeated foot and ankle issues: ankle sprains, dancer's tendinosis, and a severe case of floating bone that will probably require surgical correction.

Like Harper Watters, the Black Houston Ballet soloist who has focused on straightening his lower back to minimize the disruption of his line, Mark has felt extra pressure to have good feet that do not confirm a racial stereotype.

"I've tried to break my feet. And I think a lot of Black dancers do. . . . There's always this self-conscious thing in my head, like, 'What are your feet doing, what are your feet doing, what are your feet doing?'" Because of his particular bone curvature, he says, the need to coax his body into a different shape is exaggerated. "You know, it can't feel good. If it feels good, it's probably wrong."

Just a few months after his groin tear, Mark was almost back at full strength. The company was on tour in Europe, and he had resumed dancing most of his regular roles. But then he got injured onstage again. His floating bone, which sits at the front of his ankle, got caught on a tendon or a muscle as he landed a big jump. It was a bad sprain, one he thinks was made more likely by his repetitive stress injuries. Whatever caused it, it was excruciating.

Again, he kept dancing. This time, the company made a physical therapist available to the dancers while they were on tour. But Mark didn't have the option of skipping performances—in part because other dancers' calling out meant that he had to step into their roles, so in fact, he was dancing more than he would on a usual tour. The tour lasted four weeks, and Mark was dancing through pain through the very last show.

Both Philippon and Cutri say that rushing back to training and performance like this is common in both students and professionals. Philippon describes dancers as "very much motivated" and says they have a tendency to "push the envelope" on returning to training or work after an injury. "They're overachievers, so they want to get back early," he says. In sports medicine literature, doctors warn each other about this envelope-pushing tendency; in numerous articles about ankle and foot injuries, for example, doctors warn against putting dancers in removable controlled ankle motion boots ("cam boots") because dancers will simply take them off and dance on their injury.

"Because noncompliance is high in the dancing profession due to internal and external pressure to return to training and performance, casting is preferred," one article warns.[26] In other words, the only way to stop a dancer from dancing—the only way to counteract the pressure she feels to return to work—is to make dancing literally impossible. Immobilize her.

Mark certainly feels the external pressure. His company is small, about eighteen full-time dancers, and the choreography they're known for is extremely demanding. A small company means more opportunities to perform but less time to rest during rehearsals and between shows, and, as Mark experienced on tour, there are few people or even no one to take your place in a performance if you get hurt. While many dance companies are unionized under the American Guild of Musical Artists, his is not, which means he isn't guaranteed a set amount of rest time during rehearsal days. There are no in-house physical therapists or trainers.

"You're going to get injured [in the company] because the caliber and the level of intensity of the work is so brutal, and [the artistic director] will say it himself, that you are going to get injured. You're putting a lot on the line every time you go onstage. So there are injuries all the time. . . . That's just what it is, and it's common knowledge."

Most of those injuries—about 80 percent, he estimates—are repetitive stress injuries. "The work is repetitive and intense. We don't really have time where we're not working together; we're always working together as a group. . . . In a [big] company you might have the principals have rehearsal at ten, and then the corps, and then these couples. It's not like that—it's all day, all day."

Many dancers told stories of rushing back to dancing before they were fully healed and before their pain had abated. "I was just needed," Nardia Boodoo says. She had just started at a new ballet company when her injury happened—a second bad sprain in her left ankle, which did serious damage to her tendons—and she felt like she couldn't afford not to be dancing. After her first sprain, doctors had told her to rest, and she'd taken a few months off. "And it all healed well, but then I jumped into dancing a little too soon, and then I ended up reinjuring my ankle again."

"I had to," she says of returning to work. "I couldn't spend a year injured. Directors don't really like injuries. . . . They just don't know what to do with you, and [it's] like, 'We need you for this, we need you to do this, we need you.' And so you feel like you have to, regardless of whatever's going on."

At twenty-eight, after three years in the company, Mark is thinking about what comes next. After his year of back-to-back injuries, he fell into an "awful" monthlong depression and started wondering if he was done with dancing. "It was a tough time," he says. "I had this on my mind a lot."

He loves to perform—needs to perform—but he also needs a job that's easier on his joints, and that might not be in a ballet company. He's thought about dancing on Broadway, where some of his skills will transfer and he won't be under quite so much physical pressure.

"I do think I need to do less, and I'm definitely looking for my next step out," he told me in late 2019. He still had some time to decide if he'd sign another one-year contract with the company, and he was hopeful another option would materialize so that he had a real choice in the matter. In the meantime, he said, "I'm just taking it step by step and taking care of my body."

CHAPTER 4

TURNOUT AND BURNOUT

[Balanchine] would speak of the "suffering faces" of dancers . . .
spiritual suffering. To George dancers were saints because they worked
harder and longer, were obedient, never talked back, were always
paid the least, and then went onstage and danced like angels.

Vera Zorina

In 2001, at the age of sixteen, Lauren Fadeley Veyette achieved the dream of so many American ballet students: she became a member of New York City Ballet. Fadeley Veyette, who is white, started taking dance classes at age four in Orlando, Florida, and was accepted to the School of American Ballet (SAB), City Ballet's feeder school, when she was fifteen. She moved to New York and into the SAB dorms, assuming that she would spend three years in the school and then join the company. But after just one year she was made an apprentice, the lowest rung of the company, and thrown into rehearsals for that year's marathon season of *The Nutcracker*.

"I was in high school," she says. "I was still going to school and that was something that was very important to me. . . . All of a sudden they're like, 'Okay, you start with the company.'" It was the middle of the school year, Fadeley Veyette remembers, when she was informed that she'd get a chance to do what so many young ballet students dream of doing: dance George Balanchine's iconic Christmas ballet on the Lincoln Center stage at what was then called the New York State Theater. She had been planning to go home to Florida for Thanksgiving break, but that was no longer an option, because the six-week, forty-seven-show *Nutcracker* season usually begins the day after Thanksgiving.

"I didn't realize that this was a full-time job yet," she says. "I was not mentally prepared to be a part of that, at that age, at a company of that size. I mean, they have a hundred dancers and it's really just a machine."

Fadeley Veyette remembers the pressure she felt to accept the opportunity she knew thousands of other students would kill for, even though she had serious reservations.

"You don't say no to that, seriously. You can't say, 'Hey, I don't think I'm mentally or physically ready to join the company, can you wait a few years?'" Fadeley Veyette had been handed the opportunity she'd been working for her entire childhood—her entire life. Declining or deferring it was unthinkable.

By the time she was eighteen—the minimum age at which the company now promotes people to the apprentice rank—Fadeley Veyette was finished. Burned out and depressed, she "hated ballet and wanted to quit dance forever."

"I would wake up in the morning and think, 'I can't go in there anymore. . . . I'm done. I don't wanna dance.'"

When she told her parents, they could barely believe it. "You've changed your whole life for this; you've achieved your dream. Why is it now you're giving up?" she remembers them asking. "I was like, 'I just can't.'"

The intervening two years had been enormously hard on Fadeley Veyette's body and spirit. At SAB, while she was still going through puberty, her teachers had told her she needed to lose weight.

"I had never encountered that before," she says. "I didn't even know about dieting or anything. I was always a normal kid. . . . I didn't have crazy ballet parents or anything." And though her teachers at SAB had told her to start losing weight, they never told her to stop. "They never told me when I looked good again," she says, "so I kind of went too far." She developed what she calls "major body issues," but she also found that her extreme weight loss was rewarded. "I think that's potentially what got me into the company," she says.

She also believes it's what contributed to a serious injury, a "dancer's fracture" she sustained onstage while performing "Waltz of the Flowers" in *The Nutcracker* two seasons after she was made an apprentice. She had been told to lose weight "many times," and her weight had yo-yoed as a result of crash dieting; at the time of the injury, she remembers, she was "too thin for myself"—that is, unnaturally thin for her frame. She rolled her ankle, as so many pointe dancers do, "and it just broke my whole first metatarsal. . . . Somehow I finished the piece. I don't know how I finished dancing on a broken foot."

She spent the next several months on crutches and in physical therapy, with her foot in a cam boot. During that time—unable to walk, let alone dance—she naturally gained weight. The company let her know in no uncertain terms that it was unacceptable. "I was literally in a boot and crutches," she remembers, "and they were like, 'We can't put you onstage like that.' And I said, 'I know, I can't walk,' and they were like, 'No, the way your body looks.'"

"They didn't care that I was injured. It was how I looked physically."

Her foot healed nicely, but she still felt broken. "It was really during that injury where I was like, 'I'm so happy to not have to go to work right now.'" She knew that wasn't a normal response, that it wasn't what a happy person thinks about their dream job. "This is what I've dreamed of, and now that I'm *not* doing it, I'm happier than when I was?"

"I was just like, 'What am I doing? I can't keep doing this.'"

When Fadeley Veyette left New York City Ballet, she was depressed and exhausted. "This sucks, my life is over," she remembers thinking. "I achieved my dreams, and I hated it and I'm never dancing again."

But at her parents' urging, she did something she had never planned to do: she went to college. Most dancers aspiring to a career in ballet skip college because the four years between eighteen and twenty-two are crucial dancing years, time that should be spent in a preprofessional program like the one at Joffrey Ballet School (which also accepts high school–age dancers), dancing in a second company. Second companies, like American Ballet Theatre's Studio Company or Alvin Ailey American Dance Theater's Ailey II, are small professional outfits where young dancers can become familiar with the rhythms and demands of company life, and they act as talent pools for the first companies at their institutions.

Also at her parents' suggestion, Fadeley Veyette enrolled at Indiana University as a ballet major. They wanted her to keep the door open to professional dancing and knew that if she took four years off entirely, that wouldn't be possible. She was quite sure she was done and started a minor in kinesiology. The physical therapist who had treated her when she broke her foot had been a dancer, and Fadeley Veyette had loved working with someone who understood exactly what was required of a ballerina's body. "My first two and a half, almost three years in college, I was not going back to dancing professionally. I was very much like, 'No, I'm gonna be a physical therapist.'"

But at the end of her junior year, she finally heard what her teachers at Indiana had been telling her: "You know you still have it in you. You're not done—you still love to be dancing." She had to concede that they were right.

After graduating, she auditioned for several companies, and in 2007 she secured a place in the corps de ballet at Pennsylvania Ballet in Philadelphia. A few years later, she was promoted to soloist, and then she was promoted again to principal dancer. After nine years, then in her early thirties, she joined Miami City Ballet, one of the top five ballet companies in the country. Miami is considered a "Balanchine company"; its founding artistic director was Edward Villella, a former New York City Ballet star who danced under Balanchine, and a significant proportion of its repertory is Balanchine choreography. Fadeley

Veyette's SAB training made her a good fit for the company, and she joined as a principal soloist, the company's second-highest rank.

Now thirty-five, she's glad she went to college, she says, "because I realized you can't dance forever and it's good to have a backup plan. But . . . you can't dance forever, so you'd better dance while you can."

⁓

The happy ending to Fadeley Veyette's story—a fifteen-year professional dance career, a happy marriage to a fellow ballet dancer, a college degree to fall back on as she approaches retirement age—is as unusual as it is heartwarming. For advanced students and professional dancers, ballet's physical rigors and injury rate, its fierce competition, and its precarious employment all take an enormous emotional and mental toll. And while one form of mental illness, the eating disorder, has become emblematic of the art form, the reality is that depression, anxiety, and burnout also run rampant in the ballet world.

"There are increasing levels of anxiety and mental health issues in the profession," says Griff Braun, director of organizing and outreach at the American Guild of Musical Artists (AGMA), the union that represents dancers at the many unionized ballet companies in the United States (including New York City Ballet and Pennsylvania Ballet, but not Miami City Ballet).

Braun says that some of those anxieties are "inherent" and inevitable in a highly competitive field in which careers are short and dancers "feel an incredible amount of pressure to maximize their time." But, he says, the stinginess of arts funding in the US also puts companies under pressure to squeeze as much work as they can out of their dancers, "requiring this breakneck pace of churning out art and consequently churning through dancers."

Fadeley Veyette's experience of being channeled at a young age into a demanding full-time job is a common one. And it demonstrates the pressure that dancers are under when they give their lives over to the control of adults who are unwilling or improperly equipped to attend to their mental health.

Dr. Linda Hamilton, who trained at SAB and is now a psychiatrist who treats dancers, says that the most common reason a ballet dancer comes to her is occupational stress. While many dance companies have physical therapists on staff or on call and are equipped to take care of their dancers' physical well-being, they are unlikely to dedicate significant resources to their dancers' mental health. At the end of 2019, the editors of *Dance Magazine* put "access to a full medical dance team" on their wish list for the next decade in dance: a psychologist in the studios, as well as a dietitian, and complementary care from chiropractors and acupuncturists ("Basically, all the resources that major sports teams take for granted").[1]

"Dance institutions are failing their dancers with a lack of support for mental health," writes Kathleen McGuire, a *Dance Magazine* writer and former ballet dancer who quit because of untreated depression. "When I call up so many of the great training institutions in this country to ask for an interview with the psychologist they refer their dancers to, they can't produce one." While physical health care is easy to justify as necessary for dancers to keep dancing, mental health care, McGuire says, is too often dismissed as an unaffordable luxury, not something worth making room for in a company or school budget: "We don't have time or money for that."[2]

Little wonder, then, that in a 2017 survey conducted by the magazine, 81 percent of respondents said that the dance world wasn't doing enough to keep students and professionals mentally healthy. By the time dancers make it to a mental health provider, they're often at a crisis point that might have been prevented with earlier intervention. "We typically see dancers when the wheels have already fallen off the wagon," says Dr. Brian Goonan, a sports psychologist who consulted with the Houston Ballet company for almost a decade.

Mental health professionals who care for dancers say that the youth of their patients presents a particular challenge. To be ready for a career by eighteen, dancers have to commit to ballet so young: the intensity of the training requires them to act like adults when they are still children. Many miss out on the experiences that their peers have at the same age, including full-time school. "They have to decide how seriously they want to pursue it much younger than other artists," says Dr. Nadine J. Kaslow, a clinical psychologist and consultant for Atlanta Ballet. "The developmental pressures are different for things like socializing and dating. There's much more homeschooling."[3]

One result of the youth imperative is that dancers have limited chances to develop an identity outside of dance: dance is their identity. One popular sweatshirt design for dance students, available in any font you can imagine, says, "Sorry, I can't. I have dance." It's meant as a joke, a nod to the answer that so many young dancers have to give when they turn down opportunities to live a "normal" adolescent life: "I can't." They can't socialize with their classmates, can't be in the school orchestra, can't go to church camp. They have dance.

Until, of course, they don't have dance. Because they commit to ballet so early, and to the exclusion of most other pastimes, dancers have limited chances to discover other activities they love, other routes to artistic and emotional fulfillment, other appealing career options. If they get injured or for some other reason aren't able to continue dancing, they're left stranded not just without a plan but without a full sense of self.

As was the case for Mark, the injured dancer we met in Chapter 3, physical injury is often accompanied by, or is the cause of, severe emotional distress and depression. This is hardly surprising given all that is at stake when a dancer is injured: their health, their livelihood, and, as was the case for Fadeley Veyette, their sense of identity.

"Many dancers get depressed when they are injured," Hamilton says. "They need support and they may retreat from physical therapy, or they may find that they are rushing back too soon. They basically need guidance."

Hamilton argues that, as ballet companies diversify their repertory and add more contemporary choreography to their performance programs, dancers' bodies—and then their minds—feel the strain. "Choreography has become more demanding," she says. "They're not just doing ballet anymore; they're doing many different techniques. . . . And there's research that supports [the idea that] the more techniques you do, the more you stress different body parts, the more injuries you have."

The push to diversify is a survival tactic for companies, who are trying to hold the interest of patrons, and for individual dancers, who are trying to maximize their chances for employment. To an outsider, there might be few visible differences between the neoclassical Balanchine-heavy repertory that Fadeley Veyette performs at Miami City Ballet and the high-octane contemporary ballet Mark performs with his small company. But each style makes different demands on the dancer's body, and switching between them can result in injuries from fatigued and underprepared muscles. But few companies, and few dancers, can afford to specialize in just one style of movement, and many ballet students, while they are encouraged to perfect their ballet training, are also encouraged to carve out time and energy to become proficient in other styles.

Hamilton believes that this shift towards versatility is contributing to an uptick in injuries and burnout, and pushing dancers out earlier. "We're seeing injuries in young people that we used to see in older teenagers and certainly in professionals," she says. "There are more injuries now than there ever were, and much shorter careers." Meanwhile, as we saw in the previous chapter, the demand for hypermobile legs, spines, and feet continues unabated.

Griff Braun has a different but related explanation: ballet companies are trying to do more with less.

"My instinct is that it may have more to do with the volume of work than the diversity of styles," Braun says. "The amount of work that's being crammed into short rehearsal periods . . . It seems like in every company that we're working with, the dancers are pretty heavily taxed. The companies are trying to do more with less."

Again, Braun says, diversifying is an economic imperative for companies—but it's the dancers who bear the burden of that extra work. "They have to do more repertoire to entice audiences to come in and see them, but they are trying to cram that into as little rehearsal time as possible, because more [time spent rehearsing] is more money to spend."

Regardless of the causes of injury and burnout, it is a mistake for companies and schools to choose to treat physical and mental health as separate, because dancers—given the intimate relationships they cultivate with their own bodies—do not experience injuries as solely physical events. Dancers are shaken by injuries, which, even when they don't end careers, yank ballet dancers off the narrow path to success and cost them precious time in an already-short career. "In addition to dealing with the pain itself (and all the doctor visits, medications and exercises), other feelings crept in," *Dance Magazine* writer and former dancer Abigail Rasminsky wrote about a hip injury that required several months off.

"I felt lonely, depressed and angry—I had never been alone in my apartment for so many hours. I felt aimless, like a failure lounging on my couch. And I was terrified of my future. What would I do if this didn't get better? Who would I be without dancing?"[4]

The very things that make dancers well-suited to ballet can be their undoing. Physically, it's inborn advantages like high arches, shallow hip sockets, and hyperextended knees; mentally, dancers can be undone by the very psychological traits that make it possible for them to succeed in ballet. Chief among these is perfectionism, an entirely necessary trait in a hypercompetitive field that demands near-impossible feats of the human body.

It is impossible to talk about ballet's mental illness problem without talking about perfectionism, about the inevitable mental and emotional toll of an art form that requires its practitioners to spend hours in front of mirrors, comparing their fallible bodies to an unattainable ideal, and to each other.

In 2003, researchers at Duke University surveyed students about the campus culture, particularly as it was experienced by young women. What they found was that Duke women felt enormous pressure to be socially active—party, drink, date, and hook up—while also getting high grades, participating in extracurriculars, and being beautiful. They were supposed to do all of this without seeming to try at all, without showing the strain, without breaking a sweat. Failure was unacceptable, but so was the appearance of trying to succeed. The researchers dubbed this set of absurd and gendered expectations "effortless perfection."[5] (Stanford University has its own version, "Stanford duck syndrome," in which the goal is the appearance of smooth, effortless gliding that's only made possible by frantic, unseen paddling.[6])

In the mid-2000s, I was a student at a similarly elite university, no longer working toward a career as a dancer but still rehearsing several days a week with a campus dance company. When I heard the term "effortless perfection," I recognized the concept instantly. *This*, I remember thinking, *is just ballet*. This is what we were taught in dance: to be athlete-strong but artist-unruffled. To work just as hard at concealing the work as we did at the work itself. The goal, as Edward Villella wrote about Gelsey Kirkland, a dancer whose mental illness eclipsed her dancing, was "steel-like legs that are doing the most fantastical feats while the upper body is soft and lovely as though nothing was going on underneath."[7]

We have already seen how attempts to achieve the perfect ballet line can damage the body as dancers try to make their hips and spines and feet and toes do things they were never designed to do. The ideal dancer, in addition to having impossible flexibility and strength, is impossible in other ways, too, and the unending effort to achieve that which cannot be attained damages the mind and spirit.

The relationship between a dancer and her body is a deeply intimate one. Many dancers began taking classes out of a childhood need to improve their coordination, balance, and strength, and those who stick with it are rewarded with all three of those things, along with a deep knowledge of and connection to how their body works. They enjoy exceptional proprioception, awareness of the body's position and its place in space.[8] By the time she's dancing professionally, a dancer knows every muscle and has control over each tendon's tiniest movements. Many of the dancers I interviewed rattled off explanations of their injuries in the highly technical terms you'd expect from someone who's spent a great deal of time in a physical therapist's office learning why a part of their body isn't working the way they need it to.

Dancers also monitor their appearance in minute detail from day to day or even hour to hour, noticing tiny changes that might be invisible to outside observers but are obvious to someone who spends hours every day moving in front of a mirror. And when you're lined up in the studio or on the stage with two dozen fellow girls or women, all of you in the same practice leotard or costume, it's hard to avoid comparing your body to everyone else's.

Ballet teaches you a way of looking that is hard to shake even after you stop dancing, a way of spotting minute details—minute flaws—and fixating on them until they're fixed. Years after I stopped dancing, this is still how I watch ballet, noticing the mistakes first and reflexively imagining the correction a ballet teacher would ask for. Long after I stopped moving around in front of wall-to-wall studio mirrors, it is still how I look at myself in the bathroom mirror, noticing the flaws first, incapable of unseeing them, and struggling to see the whole as beautiful until they're corrected. It's a kind of all-or-nothing thinking in which the tiniest mistake dwarfs and cancels out everything else.

There is a thrill in the perfectionist discipline that ballet cultivates, a satisfaction to be found in relentlessly asking more of yourself, in practicing until your muscles don't just remember the right way to do the steps—they can't forget it. "I think [ballet] attracts perfectionists," Hamilton says, "because if you were not a perfectionist, I don't think you would be doing the same tendus over and over again."

"I do think that being a perfectionist is actually a very valuable trait," Hamilton says, but in ballet, the gap between the ideal and the dancer's reality can be—or feel—so wide that it becomes too much for the dancer to tolerate. But "the perfectionists that I know who've left ballet because it was so painful ended up being the same perfectionists when they went on to a different career," Hamilton says. "It doesn't go away. You have to learn to work with it."

Marc Philippon, the hip surgeon who treats dancers and athletes, says that the perfectionism that pervades the ballet world can be channeled into productive uses. Dancers tend to be eager to return to dancing as quickly as possible, which can result in their dancing on still-mending injuries—but it can also make them highly motivated and methodical participants in their own recovery. In other words, if you tell a dancer to do her PT exercises twice a day, every day, for a certain number of days, she will follow your instructions to the letter.

This can work in a dance teacher's favor, too. For example, when Philippon observes that dancer is being trained in a way that is damaging her hips, he takes the opportunity to explain to her, or her teachers, what's causing her injuries. "Most professionals in that field . . . are perfectionists and they are eager to learn, so I feel that if you go up to them and explain to them the basic principles that can lead to injuries, usually they will be very responsive. That has been my experience."

There is an illusion of control to be found in systematically correcting mistakes, fixing one thing at a time until the whole is polished and beautiful. But there is a difference between discipline and destructive perfectionism. The former is admirable and necessary for success in any fiercely competitive field. And there are forms of perfectionism—"adaptive perfectionism," for example—that can serve dancers well. "An adaptive perfectionist," McGuire writes, "has a lot of positive striving toward high standards but is not rigid in their goals."[9] If something's not working, they stop trying to force it and come back to it later, or they accept that, for reasons beyond their control, it's never going to work.

But destructive perfectionism, in which dancers focus on their failures and see their successes as worthless because of those failures, can make dancing unbearable and push dancers to quit. It's perfection or nothing. An adaptive perfectionist recognizes that the depth of her hip sockets places anatomical limits on her turnout and works to achieve the best turnout she can without forcing it from the knees, feet, lower back, or pelvic floor. Destructive perfectionism says nothing but 180 degrees will do, however you get there.

But in ballet, the lines between discipline, adaptive perfectionism, and destructive perfectionism are often blurred. Just as dancers feel enormous pressure to dance through pain and injury—to hold on to a role, or a contract, or the good graces of the few people with the power to make casting and hiring decisions—they're also made to feel, as students and as professionals, that any sacrifice is worth making if it will bring them closer to the ballet ideal.

But perfection, as McGuire notes, is a "horizon that vanishes as you approach it."[10] And ballet's perfectionism epidemic leaves dancers vulnerable to eating disorders, anxiety, and depression, and threatens to rob them of both the creativity necessary for making art and the joy that they experience performing it.

Fadeley Veyette's case is instructive here. She has never had, she says, the kind of "stick figure" body that ballet gatekeepers insist creates perfect lines. She is "a broad muscular person," and her build is a genetic trait she cannot alter. "That's something I've had to deal with my entire career. I still deal with it." When her teachers and company gatekeepers told her to lose weight, she attempted through dieting—and then starvation—to turn her body into something that it could never be. The exercise achieved nothing but to reinforce a destructive perfectionism that resulted in depression, burnout, and what might have been very early retirement.

And in an ironic twist, the widespread attitude that mental illness is a sign of weakness adds unimpeachable mental health to the list of attributes a dancer must possess in order to be perfect, in order to "make it."

"The ballerina or the student with an eating disorder—it's true, but it's also a cliché, and in a professional company, those dancers unfortunately just don't last. Or fortunately," says Sascha Radetsky, a former American Ballet Theatre soloist who is now the artistic director of ABT's Studio Company. "But they just can't handle the physical stress if they're not getting proper nutrition. So they kind of winnow away and you're left with dancers, largely, with really healthy habits."

McGuire notes that the ballet world is ruled by a ruthless logic best encapsulated by a common response to her own writing about why she quit: "Dance isn't for everyone." Some people can't hack it, and they don't survive. "This may as well be a mantra in the dance world. We have become entrenched in the Darwinian notion that the emotionally weak will be weeded out. There is no room for them anyway."[11] If ballet breaks your spirit, this logic says, it's not because there's something wrong with ballet—there's something wrong with you. You weren't resilient enough, hardworking enough, competitive enough, focused enough. You didn't want it enough. You weren't willing to do what it takes to achieve perfection.

⁓

Perfectionism can be found at the root of many of the mental illnesses that plague dancers, but none so much as body dysmorphia—the inability to see your body as the size and shape that it truly is—and, of course, eating disorders.

Eating disorders are not simply a matter of yearning to look a particular way. They're about asserting control—the one thing dancers decidedly lack. So much of their lives are out of their hands: their schedules, their employment status, whether or not they're performing well in the eyes of artistic management. As Balanchine saw it, the best dancers were the ones who "worked harder and longer, were obedient, never talked back, were always paid the least, and then went onstage and danced like angels."[12] They had no control at all.

And while men's bodies are on display in ballet and are considered fair game for scrutiny and critique, the glut of girls and women makes competition for the few spots—at elite schools, in companies, and in any given performance—fiercer for women than for men. "We spend more time than men focusing on everything that's wrong with us," white New York City Ballet principal dancer Lauren Lovette says. "You're constantly being criticized for your weight, being too skinny or too fat. Or, 'Your technique is good but not perfect.' Or, 'Oh, your feet don't bend in exactly the right way.'" Is it any wonder that the perfectionists who inhabit this world turn to unhealthy behaviors to exert control and feel successful?

In the early and mid-1990s, ballet's pressure-cooker, eating disorder-friendly culture came in for some unwelcome attention, as American media spread the word about the eating disorder crisis unfolding among teenage girls.[13] Ballet, like gymnastics and figure skating, was under scrutiny (and the focus on eating disorders in these activities contributed to the inaccurate public perception that eating disorders are a problem that only afflict thin, well-off white women). Harrowing tales of dancers being instructed to starve themselves, of smoking or snorting their appetites away, made for bad ballet PR as the rest of the nation moved towards a new, tenuous, and conditional "body positive" culture in which emaciation was no longer considered the height of feminine beauty.

That body positivity is now best expressed in the popular slogan "Strong is the new skinny" as fitness culture creeps out of the gym and slowly takes over the rest of women's lives, from sweatproof makeup to yoga pants you can wear to the office. But "Strong is the new skinny" only goes so far. Now women are permitted, or rather expected, to be muscular—but never bulky, just lean and toned. They are expected to be the *right kind* of skinny, in the right places; they have to look like athletes, but not like water polo players or shot put throwers. Strong is the new skinny, as long as you're also still skinny.

As the ballet world has become more sensitive to eating disorders, and as the emphasis in the culture at large has shifted from mere slenderness to visible but still acceptably feminine athleticism, ballet teachers and company directors have learned that they can no longer simply instruct their dancers to lose weight.

In her infamous memoir *Dancing on My Grave*, Gelsey Kirkland told a story about George Balanchine that was corroborated by fellow New York City Ballet dancers who told comparable anecdotes in their own memoirs.

Balanchine stopped a class one day in the late 1960s to examine Kirkland's body and "rapped his knuckles" down her sternum. "Must see bones," he told her. "He did not merely say, 'eat less,'" Kirkland remembered. "He repeatedly said, 'eat nothing.'" Kirkland weighed less than a hundred pounds. By then, Balanchine's preferred female body type—swan-necked, slim-hipped, long-legged, impossibly thin, and capable of terrifically difficult footwork—was on its way to becoming the global standard for ballet companies and schools. "Mr. B did not consider beauty a quality that must develop from within the artist," wrote Kirkland, who remembered that she and her fellow dancers used infant emetics to purge even after eating fruit. "Rather he was concerned with outward signs such as body weight."[14]

In those days, it was "lose the weight, we don't care [how]," says Atlanta nutritionist Emily Harrison, a former ballerina who was the in-house nutritionist at Atlanta Ballet for six years and now consults with the company, "and lose it by *Nutcracker*—and by the way it's November 15—and [do it] without getting injured and without passing out." Katy Pyle, the founder of Ballez, remembers a teacher at their elite North Carolina ballet school who, in the mid-1990s, "definitely encouraged us to have eating disorders. . . . She would look at our stomachs and . . . be like, 'Did you have pancakes for breakfast?'"

The days of American ballet teachers and company directors telling their dancers to eat nothing, or telling them exactly how many pounds they should lose, are largely over. The focus now is on optimum performance, on strength, on food as fuel—or at least, it appears to be. Now company directors say they want dancers who are "fit," provided that they also *look* fit. That is, in addition to having the strength and stamina to dance a full ballet, they must adhere to the conventional understanding of what a fit person looks like: it's not enough to lift your pas de deux partner over your head; you also need to have a six-pack while you're doing it.

Company directors can still fire or refuse to hire dancers for not being this kind of "fit." Marcello Angelini, the artistic director of Tulsa Ballet, concedes that "it has happened a couple of times" in his years running the company. Angelini points to the company's two nutritionists and its partnership with a local gym, which gives dancers discounted membership and access to personal trainers. "I'm proud to give our dancers all the tools necessary to succeed," he says. But, he argues, how much a ballerina weighs is a concern for her partner.

"If I see that [there is a] lack of will to overcome this challenge, then I don't have much of a choice, and I'll tell you why. It's not a question of discriminating, but being a former dancer, my back remembers every dancer that I danced with," Angelini says. "And so sometimes the hard choice that I have to make is, do I look after the wellness of that male dancer twenty-five years from now, or do I say 'It's okay' to the lady?'"

In Angelini's view, maintaining an appropriately low weight is a question of teamwork for women. "Somebody is behind you that has to lift you up and down and up and down, and eventually you might damage his back. . . . And if I am a girl, understanding that if I am as fit as I possibly can be I am going to make the life of that person that is going to make me look beautiful and light and ephemeral easier, well, then, the equation works." This apparent concern for the long-term spinal health of men dancers is admirable, but surely the short-term mental health and job prospects of their women colleagues merits equal consideration.

Defending the practice of hiring and firing dancers based on their size and shape, teachers and directors will point to the sacredness of the line, which must not be interrupted by the inconvenience of breasts, hips, or buttocks. But because of the new cultural injunction against outright telling dancers to lose weight, gatekeepers have developed a suite of euphemisms that all amount to the same message: slim down.

"I have had two people in the last year who were younger dancers in their midteens and were told they needed to lengthen; they were told they needed to elongate more," Harrison says. "Which was code for, 'You need to lose ten pounds.'" One student's mother emailed Harrison recounting what her daughter's dance teacher had said, insisting that the girl had done her best to comply. "The poor child has spent the past year working on her technique and trying to pull up in class and she's pulling up everything; she's practically lifting up her eyebrows in class." It was on Harrison to translate the truth: "lengthen" doesn't mean get longer; it means get thinner.

"There's more awareness of eating disorders and, perhaps, more early intervention," Hamilton says, but "thinness is admired." Now, she says, teachers and directors communicate in code words. "Like 'tone.' You need to be more 'toned.' . . . Every dancer knows that means they have to lose five pounds." This collective exercise in euphemism calls to mind the scene in the movie *Knocked Up* in which a television producer insists that he doesn't want an anchor to lose weight (because he cannot legally ask her to do that). "We didn't say, 'Lose weight,'" he clarifies. "I might say, 'Tighten.'" His colleague adds, "We don't want you to lose weight. We just want you to be healthy, you know, by eating less."[15]

The language of health and fitness has thoroughly replaced the blunter language of weight loss and thinness, and though it's possible that ballet's gatekeepers understand these two regimes to be different, ultimately, the demands they place on dancers are not meaningfully distinct. And while it is easy to imagine that having a woman in charge would result in a shift in policy, especially if that woman herself was subjected to the old-school way of talking about weight, that's not necessarily the case.

"Our company's not full of skinny people," Stoner Winslett, the founding artistic director of Richmond Ballet tells me. "Our company is full of fit people," she says. "They look really, really fit, and they want to look that way. And they pretty much do look that way, and I'm pretty lucky that it doesn't take much maintenance."

Still, Winslett says she's very explicit about what happens to dancers who gain weight—or rather, who don't "look really, really fit": they're denied professional opportunities. "Every now and then somebody gets a little bit off track and [you] just, you know, tell 'em that could be that. 'Maybe you're not gonna be cast in the things you want to get cast in until [you] get this back under control.' And then they usually do."

That's not a conversation she has to have often, she says, because the dancers take their positions as role models for students in the company's school seriously. "Dedication, discipline, work ethic, fitness," she says, not-so-subtly linking weight gain to a lack of discipline and work ethic. "They take it very seriously, and it's a beautiful thing."

Christine Cox, the cofounder and artistic director of BalletX, a small contemporary ballet company in Philadelphia, says that she herself "didn't come with a natural balletic body" and felt pressure from artistic management to stay thin. She "battled it"—"it" being her natural body shape and size—by adding extra gym workouts on top of her class and rehearsal schedule.

Now, as an artistic director herself, she says she's "very direct" with her dancers. "In fact, I had one [of these conversations] yesterday," she tells me.

> You know, some of them are just not as fit as they need to be . . . and I just say, "You know you guys have to be fit, you have to have a six-pack." . . . I'm not talking about thinness. I'm talking about fitness. To be the most strong athlete you can be. Preparing ourselves like we're Olympians, that's what I talk about. I'm like, "You guys, you gotta come in early [and] get your body ready for class. You gotta leave here, eat a nice meal, and then go work out. Three times a week. Don't take the whole weekend off."

The purported turn towards dancers' health is "a double-edged sword that is making it healthy for the individual but so much harder because there's not enough hours in the day," says Sean Aaron Carmon, the former Alvin Ailey American Dance Theater dancer. Before the ostensible shift toward health and fitness, "it was, 'We don't care how you lose the weight, just lose the weight. We don't care if it's unhealthy, we don't care if you're unhealthy. . . . Do what you got to do. Put your feet under a couch [to make your arches better]—we just want the line. Go do some coke—we just want the waistline. We want the bones, honey.'"

Now, faced with a culture that purports to care about health but still glorifies thin bodies, companies are protective of their reputations, Carmon says. "So now no one wants the bones. Granted, they want you to be thin, [but] that media coverage of, 'Oh, such-and-such starved themselves' . . . Well, that's almost as bad as having fat dancers."

The eye on that needle, Carmon says, "is so, so small . . . because their stance has switched to 'We want you to take care of yourself . . . but it's not working right now and it's a little thick.'"

"In my day, they didn't care how you lost it, you just had to lose it," agrees Rita Corridon, a white Cuban American dancer who performed with the Joffrey Ballet in the 1980s. But in 2019, when her daughter Isabella was preparing to graduate from American Ballet Theatre's full-time training program and start looking for company jobs, she got a different message—or rather, the same message, phrased differently—conveyed to her by Radetsky, the director of ABT's Studio Company.

"What they told Isabella is that they needed her . . . to lengthen more when she's dancing. . . . 'Lengthen' is the 2019 word for 'lose weight.' Okay? Or 'get into shape' is what they're saying when you need to lose weight. They won't say, 'You need to lose weight.'"

"Nowadays . . . everything has to be so politically correct on how everything's done weight-wise with dance. And I would always tell [her], 'Isabella, it's a dirty little secret.' They don't tell you now, really, to lose weight." At least, not in those words.

Isabella did lose some weight—she says she got her five-foot-six teenage frame down to "about 111 pounds"—and along with a lot of praise from her classmates and approval from her teachers, she did get a company job. "They want you to be healthy, and they want you to do that," Rita says, "but it's really the skinny girls getting the part."

"Message received," says Carmon of casting decisions like this. "I understand what you are saying to me. I am a disappointment; I need to figure out how I can be better for you. Because the way I look now, I'm not valuable to [the company]. . . . It not only sends them right back to unhealthy habits but it preys [on them] emotionally. . . . But publicly, the companies are doing the right thing. They are saying what they are supposed to say to make sure their image is protected."

One former dancer who worked under Angelini remembers that it was at Tulsa Ballet that his weight came up for the first time. "In my midyear review," he tells me, "it [said] that 'artist is not in good physical shape,' and I didn't even get what that meant. . . . 'Like I'm too small? Like I need to be less short?' And one of my friends was like, 'No, you need to lose weight.'"

"The way it was written in those vague terms," the dancer remembers, "no one talked to me about it. . . . It was just so cold, and then I realized maybe this is why I'm not doing so well here, [and] this is something I can control." He went on a "very intense" diet and dropped about twelve pounds in six weeks. Predictably, he "started getting all this attention, like, 'You look great, you look great.'" His peers and his company staff told him, of course, that he looked "longer."

For all the talk about fitness and optimal performance, dancers who are strong and fit are still asked to slim down if they don't have what New York City Ballet soloist Georgina Pazcoguin calls "the impossibly thin ectomorph body type that [is] asked to be even thinner." And for all the talk about health, the belief that it's unhealthy or unsafe for dancers to be larger or heavier than the current ideal demands is just that—a belief, and an inaccurate one.

"There's simply no scientific evidence that you have to be skinny to do ballet. These are issues of tradition, not biomechanics," Julia Iafrate, a doctor of osteopathic medicine and the founder of the Columbia Dance Medicine clinic told *Dance Magazine* in early 2020.[16]

"The reality is, it's an aesthetic art form," Harrison says. "Dancers have to look a certain way. They still have to wear tights, and the choreographic demands just get more and more intense. The lifts get crazier and bigger and harder, and everything is faster. It's just really hard now. Even in the last ten years, the choreographic demands have come so far." All this, even though the ideal ballet body has barely strayed from the Balanchine ideal: long-limbed, bones exposed, all superfluous flesh eliminated.

Kathryn Morgan knows about the ballet world's doublespeak about health and thinness better than most. In 2010, her promising career at New York City Ballet, where she had been rapidly promoted to soloist after dancing one of the title roles in *Romeo and Juliet* at just seventeen, was derailed by an autoimmune condition that left her too exhausted to dance. Her muscles would give out under her every time she tried to go on pointe. Her hair fell out. And she put on forty-five pounds in six weeks.[17]

Morgan quit ballet and left New York City to seek treatment for what—after many misdiagnoses from dismissive doctors—was finally identified as Hashimoto's thyroiditis. Though her health improved, she assumed she'd never dance again: she hadn't trained in years and, crucially, she no longer looked like a ballet dancer. But in 2017 and 2018, she started to train again, and she lost almost all the weight she had gained. In April 2019, she auditioned for Miami City Ballet and was offered a position in the company as a soloist. At thirty, having taken more time away from professional ballet than some of her peers will spend in it, she finally had her happy ending.

Except, she didn't. As her first season with Miami City Ballet drew closer, Morgan was asked to learn several parts she could perform, including the title role in *The Firebird*. She was fitted for costumes, and audience members who wanted to be part of her unlikely comeback were eager to know which performances they should come to.

"Basically I was rehearsing [*Firebird*] for the entire season," Morgan told me in early 2020, "and then the day before the casting went up I was told that I would not be doing it because of my body."

Morgan had "never been the smallest in the room," she says, even when she was healthy and at her ballet weight. But now she was healthy—that is, her autoimmune condition was under control, and she was fit and strong—but Miami City Ballet artistic director Lourdes Lopez said she could not appear in *The Firebird* because she was not "presentable."

"I was told that I would not show the company in its best light," Morgan says. "In one of the meetings she said to me, 'I know you're supposedly this inspiration to all these young kids through your [YouTube] videos and blah blah blah and what you've done . . . but I don't think you can fully be an inspiration until you look like a ballerina again.'" Morgan left Miami City Ballet after one season, during which she barely appeared onstage. In late 2020, she recounted her experience at Miami City Ballet in a YouTube video, and she was soon joined by several other former MCB dancers who said they, too, had been fired, kept offstage, or threatened with reduced performance opportunities because they were not thin enough.[18]

For Morgan, the message was clear: despite being a size 2 or 0, despite having regained her technique and her strength, and despite her selling power with audiences who were invested in her triumph over adversity, "everything I'd done was not enough unless I was skinny."

Despite the purported emphasis on health and optimum athletic performance, the line trumps all. Strong isn't the new skinny; strong has simply been added to the list of things that skinny dancers are now required to appear to be. The perfect ballet body is still thin by definition. Only now, with crash diets and eating disorders ostensibly frowned upon, dancers must accomplish that perfection the "right" way, achieving an unhealthy appearance through healthy means. As if such a thing were even possible.

The rise of social media as a ubiquitous part of young adult life and a significant tool for dancers' self-promotion has deepened ballet's perfectionism problem. Now dancers don't only compare themselves to the girl next to them at the barre or dancing with them onstage but also to an endless scroll of competitors, delivered via algorithm straight to their pocket. Ballet Instagram is no different from the rest of the app: like most users, dancers post their best photos and videos, their most flattering angles, the most curated and perfected versions of themselves.

The result is that it is upsettingly easy to spend hours on Instagram staring at photos of dancers who are thinner than you, who have better feet than you, whose développés go higher than yours. Who seem to have perfected or been born without (or photoshopped away) every physical flaw you can catalog so intimately in yourself. "For dancers—most of whom already have a laser focus on their appearance—the images they see on Instagram can seem to exacerbate ever-present issues," notes *Dance Magazine* writer Rachel Rizzuto.[19]

Dr. Linda Hamilton, the psychiatrist who treats dancers, says that many of her clients talk to her about what Instagram does to their self-esteem, "about how bad they feel. . . . It's not very good." Carmen, the sixteen-year-old Joffrey Ballet School student who nearly sprained her ankle in pas de deux class, says that when she first started using Instagram, she "was comparing everything," always noting when a dancer's photos showed better lines than hers or videos showed better execution of turns and jumps.

"I feel like everyone goes through that stage," says Cecilia, a white twenty-year-old Joffrey student from Iceland who's one grade level above Carmen. "But with age you realize you can't be them, and [you understand] what your strengths are." Now Carmen is trying to use Instagram productively, to find nutrition tips and exercises she can do before and after class to improve her feet and her turnout. But, she admits, the version of her life that she posts on the platform is still the best version she can curate.

"I think Instagram in general is bad for body image," says Cecilia's classmate Jennifer, a white twenty-two-year-old from New Jersey, because "they only show the good stuff." Jennifer says she rarely posts any photos or videos of herself "because I don't feel confident enough," and because she can't help but compare her own photos to those of the professional dancers she follows. "It just makes me feel bad."

Perhaps aware of both the dangers of a highly curated, best-angles-only feed and the premium the social media economy places on authenticity—or at least on the appearance of authenticity—some dancers post footage of rehearsals gone wrong or reflections about less-than-perfect performances. Cecilia likes following American Ballet Theatre corps de ballet dancer Scout Forsythe because "she's honest. She posts stuff that's not perfect."

New York City Ballet principal dancer Lauren Lovette posts often about the inevitability of failure, both in the studio and onstage. "I stumbled. I flew. I wobbled. I grew," Lovette posted the day after a

2020 performance of *Swan Lake* in which she didn't pull off the famous thirty-two fouetté turns in the Black Swan second act solo. "I felt fearful. I felt brave. I missed my fouettés. I cried on stage. I felt every moment, and the moments were clear. . . . p.s. The crying on stage is a good thing!"[20]

Two years earlier, Misty Copeland had had a similarly difficult time with those turns, and a video of her imperfect performance was posted on YouTube, prompting a wave of negative responses, some of which alleged that Copeland had been cast in the iconic role not because of her skill but because of her race.

Copeland responded with an Instagram post of her own, a long reflection on her place in the ballet world and the balance between technique and artistry. "I will forever be a work in progress and will never stop learning," she wrote, but "people come to see ballet for the escape. For the experience of being moved through our movement and artistry, not to score us on the technicality of what we do. This is why ballet is not a sport. A ballerina's career is not, nor should be defined by how many fouettés she executes."[21]

Still other dancers use the platform solely to talk about the inevitability of failure. White American dancer Shelby Williams, who performs with the Royal Ballet of Flanders, uses Instagram to post on behalf of her alter ego, a self-serious dancer named Biscuit Ballerina who posts fake-deep musings about artistry beneath cringe-inducing videos of Williams dancing with sickled feet, bent knees, and gawky arms ("biscuits" is ballet slang for unpointed, floppy feet). Williams uses humor to undercut her own deep and demanding perfectionism and to cope with the anxiety that, as a ballet student, made her hate ballet as much as she loved it.

"Ballerinas are supposed to be perfect, and we're not supposed to show when things are hard. That carries into our personal lives as well," Williams told *Pointe* magazine.[22] In addition to footage of "Biscuit" failing farcically, Williams also posts user-submitted supercuts of dancers falling or otherwise messing up in the studio and onstage—America's funniest ballet home videos. The aim is to destigmatize mental illness and to poke fun at the culture of perfectionism in which it germinates. "The dance world has come so far in terms of nutrition and injury prevention, things that were cutting dancers' careers short," Williams told *Pointe*. "But the mental side of things can cut your career short just as quickly, and it's rarely addressed."

Some dancers opt out of Instagram altogether, not only because it introduces yet more competition for best feet and best fouetté but also because it introduces another form of competition entirely: for most followers. Now it's about not only your appearance but the appearance of popularity and approval. "I have gone through many Instagram holes where I see likes going up and how many turns someone can do," says Stephanie Rae Williams, a member of Dance Theatre of Harlem. Williams says that she's largely stopped using Instagram because she doesn't think it properly represents dancers' ability to perform onstage—their movement and artistry, as Copeland put it—and because it does too much harm to her mental health.

At the same time, a significant Instagram following can make it easier for a dancer to get a job or allow them to supplement their income with sponsorships. The dancers who don't want to play that game, Hamilton says, who want "to concentrate on class and do it the old-fashioned way," know they're taking a professional risk. They "are constantly questioning whether they're doing harm to their career."

Like physical injuries, the enormous mental and emotional demands that ballet places on dancers have become part of its mystique, part of its glamour and mythology. Though they train like athletes and get injured like athletes, dancers are not—or are not only—athletes. Dancers are artists, and artists are meant to suffer. In fact, the mystique says, art isn't possible without suffering. Ideally, artists should be a little bit mad; madness, we've been taught to believe, is where the genius lies. This isn't limited to dance artists—Mozart, van Gogh, and Pollock are all popularly depicted as mad artists—but from *The Red Shoes* to *Black*

Swan, the connection between ballerinas and madness is long-standing and deeply entrenched.

But as aesthetic athletes—a term sports medicine physicians also use to describe gymnasts and figure skaters—dancers are expected to execute as reliably and flawlessly as professional athletes (without, as the editors of *Dance Magazine* have noted, the kind of support and salaries that many professional athletes enjoy).[23] In this regard, the humanity that is central to their artistry is wiped out by their status as athletes. Dancers at the elite level are held to exceptionally high standards not just by their teachers and company directors but by audiences, who arrive at the ballet—a live performance conducted by human beings—expecting a flawless show.

"People just see you as a commodity or robot," Copeland told ESPN in 2019. "They look at athletes, dancers and artists like they're not real. Like we don't have the same experiences and doubts as everyone else. It's like, 'I'm spending money to see you. So you have to be what I want you to be.' . . . With all of that pressure, it's hard to perform at such a level."[24]

The eating disorder is the archetypal ballerina affliction. But anxiety and depression are also predictable consequences of ballet's culture, the pressure it puts on dancers, and the perfection it demands of them.

Grace Segers, the ballet student who quit late in high school after years of elite-track training, developed an eating disorder while she was dancing—but that wasn't the mental illness that ended her dancing life.

As a student, Segers says, she felt pressure to lose weight because she "didn't necessarily have the body type [that] you think of when you [think of] a ballerina." "I was too tall [and] my hips were kind of big," says Segers. "And looking back I was a perfectly fine and healthy weight, but . . . I just always felt like I was physically bigger."

She was never told directly to lose weight, as Fadeley Veyette was, "but I think indirectly I was given that impression, because the girls who got the best parts always had a certain kind of body type. They were a lot skinnier, just naturally very skinny and generally shorter."

Segers was "always very much a perfectionist," she says, "so I would really push myself to do better, in ways that were sometimes not the healthiest." She was so burned out by taking ballet class six days a week while also taking high-level academic classes in high school that she "basically gave [herself] a psychosomatic illness." She had "all the symptoms of mono without actually having mono" and was eventually diagnosed with chronic fatigue syndrome.

"I couldn't make it out of bed. I was running low fevers; I couldn't make it to school during that time," and she certainly couldn't dance. Knowing that a job at a top company was not in her future, she decided to quit dancing altogether and focus on school. "With a lot of hard work and therapy I was able to go back to my normal self," she says.

As Hamilton noted, the perfectionism that ballet requires, cultivates, and rewards doesn't go away once a dancer hangs up her pointe shoes. It's a way of seeing, a way of being, and unless it's moderated by adaptation, it finds other outlets. In college, Segers developed an eating disorder that lasted into her early twenties. She's currently in remission from bulimia.

My own eating disorder took longer to develop—I had been out of college for a year and a half—but when it did, my ballet training, the way of seeing I had learned in the dance studio, kicked in. I could only see my failures, and they rendered my successes meaningless. I was either perfect or worthless, under my own ruthless control or revoltingly untethered. There was no gray area.

In her 2007 book about young women and perfectionism, *Perfect Girls, Starving Daughters: The Frightening New Normalcy of Hating Your Body*, feminist author Courtney Martin discussed the fine line between disciplined dedication and mental illness. "The competition inherent in athletics can teach girls to set a goal, practice in order to achieve it, and be resilient if it doesn't pan out," Martin wrote in a passage about high school sports that could have been written about ballet. "But it may also teach them to drive forward like crazy, tolerate real pain, compare themselves constantly."[25]

And when the game is over or the dancing stops, "they often channel their drive into other things. . . . They are the most obsessive about their jobs, staying into the wee hours of the morning even when everyone else goes home. They often continue to see their bodies as projects, as opposed to parts of them, and aim to sculpt their bodies, deprive them, harness their wild urges."[26] It is "hellishly hard," Martin wrote, to be a serious youth athlete and then lose the structure, identity, and support system that your sport once provided. And for people who have stopped dancing, it is horribly easy to rebuild some of those structures for yourself using the most powerful imperative of all: be perfect, whatever it takes.

CHAPTER 5

THE UNBEARABLE
WHITENESS OF BALLET

*Surely, no dancing body—black, brown, or white—is inherently unfit for
any kind of dance. . . . Instead, cultural preferences by the established pundits
of taste set and shape the exclusive criteria that distinguish one culture's
values from another, one dance form from another. It's really more about
what we like to see than about what the dancing body can be taught to do.*

BRENDA DIXON GOTTSCHILD

Wilmara Manuel and her eleven-year-old daughter, Sasha, were
at the world finals of a ballet competition, the Youth America
Grand Prix, in 2015 when it happened. Shortly before the competition
began, the young dancers were on the performance stage with their
parents, warming up and preparing to dance the solos they'd been rehearsing for months.

As Wilmara, who is Black and originally from Haiti, and Sasha,
who is biracial, stood there, a young white dancer looked around the
stage, checking out the competition. "And her eyes land on Sasha,"

Wilmara remembers, "and I saw her look [Sasha] up and down, and then look at her mom.

"And her mom said, 'Don't worry. They're never really good anyway.'"

Wilmara did her best to contain her shock. Sasha didn't hear what the white mom had said, and Wilmara wasn't about to tell her, because "that's not the thing I want to discuss ten minutes before she takes the stage." But Sasha could sense that something was amiss. "Just the look on my face, she was like, 'What? What happened? What did she say?'" Wilmara brushed her daughter off.

Don't worry. They're never really good anyway. An entire worldview of white resentment of Black progress and excellence passed quietly from mother to child in just seven words.

That white mother could not fathom that Sasha, a biracial child with a Black mother, might be *really good*—as in very good, or truly good—at a traditionally white art form at which her child was presumably also quite proficient. She could not imagine that Sasha might deserve to be at that competition, might have qualified on her merit— her talent and skill and persistence—rather than because of what she might consider a misguided or even unjust attempt to diversify ballet by lowering standards. They're *not really good, but* they *are allowed to be here. In this space that is rightfully yours, in this art form that is rightfully yours.* They're *never* as good as the white girls, a sweeping generalization that grants no individuality, no humanity, to any nonwhite dancer. *They're all the same, and they never deserve to be here. But don't worry.* Your *excellence is a given. You belong here, while their presence is conditional or even ill-gotten.*

A few minutes later, Sasha took the stage and performed her solo. She ended up placing ahead of that white dancer.

From then on, Wilmara traveled with Sasha to every competition, paying the additional travel costs to make sure that, if something like that ever happened again, she'd be there to support her daughter.

"That has stuck with me," she says. "And it's one of the reasons I make the sacrifice and I go with her everywhere. Even if there are others going, I feel like I need to be around should comments like that pop up. I just don't feel like I can take that chance, you know? And what cracks me up is that . . . she doesn't even look as dark as I do, which makes me feel like, 'Oh my God, if you were darker, like, what else?'"

Sasha grew up in a suburb of Indianapolis and is now sixteen. She trains at the Royal Ballet School in London, an exclusive training ground that serves as a feeder school for the Royal Ballet. It's widely acknowledged to be one of the best ballet schools in the world.

Wilmara says that people often express their surprise at the quality of Sasha's training and technique. "Oh wow, you're really good," Wilmara says by way of example. "Where do you train? Have you been dancing for a long time?" She says that while she tries to give these white people the benefit of the doubt, she knows what they usually mean, and she'd prefer they just come out and say it: "I'm surprised you're that good. You're Black and you're dancing and you're good."

Now that Sasha is a little older, Wilmara talks to her about the racist assumptions embedded in those surprised comments. "You know she's asking because she doesn't think a person of your color can do this," she's told Sasha, who now "gets it when she hears that tone of voice."

And, she says, she's been frank with her daughter about the kind of resistance she should expect from the overwhelmingly white ballet establishment if she keeps excelling—which she shows every sign of doing.

It's moms who do the bulk of the work of ballet parenting: the sewing of costumes, the schedule keeping for rehearsals and recitals. And when you're a ballet mom to a dancer of color, there's an even higher price to pay.

"Not everybody's gonna be thrilled," Wilmara says, paraphrasing her conversations with Sasha. "Even if you're not a dancer of color, it's cutthroat. And on top of that, you *are* a dancer of color, and so that poses another threat in some ways. So you have to be mindful of your things and what you are doing, and know what things are okay, and [pay attention to] when you are uncomfortable." This emotional labor, the work of helping young dancers understand what "that tone of voice" means and why it's being used—or the work of deciding whether to tell your child about the racist remark you just overheard or absorb it yourself and shield them from it—is a part of parenting not demanded of mothers of white dancers.

Then there's the payment in time and money required of Wilmara to make sure that Sasha's ballet experience is as fair and worry-free as possible.

Once, at a competition, Wilmara forgot to color in the "nude" pale-pink straps on one of Sasha's competition costumes. Wilmara scrambled to find brown foundation because none of the vendors at the competition had a leotard in Sasha's skin color.

"Come on, people, you are here," Wilmara remembers thinking. "There may not be that many [dancers of color], but they are all here and you should be able to bring various shades of nude leos."

Succeeding in ballet, or even just surviving, requires extra talent, extra work, extra resilience, and extra sacrifices from dancers of color, especially Black and brown dancers, and their parents. White ballet moms might have to talk to their white daughters about how cutthroat ballet is. But they don't need to issue additional warnings about how a white girl's success will be received by that cutthroat culture, because almost all the successful girls and women in ballet are white.

"They've had to grow up a lot faster," Wilmara says of Black and brown ballet dancers. "I think the ballet world makes you grow up a lot faster, but on top of that," there are the "extra hurdles that other dancers don't have to think about." There are the overtly racist comments backstage before a performance and the subtly racist "compliments" after. There is time spent frantically searching for the right leotard or adapting the default pink leotard. There is the knowledge, internalized first by parents and then by their kids, that if you make it over all those hurdles your success will be viewed with suspicion and resentment. That ballet does not have a "diversity" problem; it has a white supremacy problem.

"Our kids," Wilmara says, "are thinking about this and thinking about it early on."

⌒

The organizing principle of ballet—of training, of performance, of making a ballet body—is control. Control of your rigid torso while your foot shoots upward from the hip in a battement. Control of a silent and compliant class of otherwise giggly nine-year-old girls.

"The traditional and classical Europeanist aesthetic for the dancing body is dominated and ruled by the erect spine," wrote dance scholar Brenda Dixon Gottschild in her landmark book *The Black Dancing Body*. "Verticality is a prime value, with the torso held erect, knees straight, body in vertical alignment. . . . The torso is held still."[1] It all demands control.

Control of your smiling face as your feet scream in your pointe shoes at the end of a long pas de deux. Control of your weight, of your turn-out, of your stretched and strengthened feet that now arch into a shape no ordinary foot can make. "The ballet audience, attuned and habituated to view control as a prime value, applaud its display and are embarrassed when it isn't fulfilled," Gottschild wrote.[2] Discipline, order, adherence to strict and unquestioned rules. That's what ballet is.

When Gottschild asked Seán Curran, a white dancer and choreographer who performed with the Bill T. Jones/Arnie Zane Company, what he pictured when he thought of white dance or white dancing bodies, he said, "Upright. . . . For some reason, 'proper' stuck in the head a bit, something that is built and made and constructed rather than is free or flows."[3] A body that is rigid, obedient, and disciplined, remade from something natural and unruly into something refined and well behaved. Proper. "Whiteness," Curran said, "values precision and unison."

Curran's assessment identifies a central underlying prejudice of white supremacy: the belief that people of color, and their bodies, are wild. Uncivilized, animalistic, subhuman. That white people—who, by contrast, are assumed to be organized and civilized—have both a right and a responsibility to tame that which is untamed and impose order, precision, and unison on it. To suppress and control that which is savage; to press it into something that approaches whiteness but will never be truly white, and thus never truly equal.

This is the logic that underpinned white colonization and American slavery. It is also the logic that makes racial segregation possible: that which is pure and organized must be kept separate from that which is profane and undisciplined. And central to this worldview is the idea that the work of white supremacy is unending, not because white supremacy is flawed, but because the very people it seeks to suppress are inherently inferior, naturally incapable of complying. Because of some inborn lack—of will, of understanding, of discipline—people of color will never fully obey, never properly assimilate, never be redeemed by whiteness. In this way, white supremacy perpetuates itself, justifying both its worldview and the permanent need for its existence.

It's little wonder, then, that ballet—with its fixation on control, discipline, and uprightness—wraps itself so neatly around whiteness. It makes sense that white Americans, reared on the belief that whiteness is synonymous with order and refinement, also believe that people of color have no place, or a limited place, or a conditional place, in classical ballet.

Furthermore, it is easy to see how the ideal ballet body—so controlled, so upright—is everything that white supremacy imagines a Black body is not. And because of deeply ingrained American cultural associations with musculature, loose movement, brute force, and untamed sexuality, the Black body is believed to be everything a ballet body is not permitted to be.

"When we talk about the ballerina," says Theresa Ruth Howard, a former dancer and a teacher, diversity strategist, and the founder and curator of the digital ballet history archive Memoirs of Blacks in Ballet (MoBBallet), "we're talking about the ideal, our stereotype of the desirable woman, and that is reserved for white women."

Howard has made a career of helping the people who run ballet companies and schools to examine their ideas about what makes for a "good" ballet body, asking them to question their biases about the inherent fitness of white bodies and unfitness of other bodies, especially Black bodies.

She says that long-standing racist tropes about Black women's bodies make Blackness and ballerinas seem antithetical. "You have the trope of either the jezebel, the mammy, or the workhorse of the black woman," which are incompatible with desirability, fragility, and sexual purity, the ideal of white womanhood at the heart of the ballerina's appeal.

"She's desired. It's the epitome of beauty, of grace, of elegance, and these are not adjectives that are assigned to Black women," Howard says. "Especially not darker-skinned Black women. This is why the closer you look to the white European aesthetic as a Black woman, the better chance you have at occupying that role. Especially at a higher level [of ballet]."

George Balanchine famously said that "ballet is woman," but that's not the whole truth. Ballet is *white* woman, or, perhaps more precisely, white womanhood. Ballet is a stronghold of white womanhood, a place where whiteness is the default and white femininity reigns supreme. Despite the long tradition of Latin American dancers carving out successful professional careers in the US and the enormous success of Misty Copeland—a light-skinned Black dancer whose ascent to the pinnacle of American ballet was a watershed moment for Black dancers and audiences alike—the archetypal ballerina is still a pale-skinned white woman with slender limbs, negligible breasts and hips, and long, sleek hair. In the American cultural imagination, the ballerina is still white.

That's partly because to be a ballerina requires the very characteristics that white women are presumed to have (with rare exceptions) and that Black and Latina women are presumed to lack (with rare exceptions). The ballerina is graceful, elegant, and refined. She is imagined to be wealthy yet restrained. She is asexual and innocent, yet desirable and aspirational. She is barely earth-bound; she floats, ethereal. And though women ballet dancers are not weak or delicate, they are required to appear as though they are. According to the racist stereotypes that shape the white American imagination, none of these characteristics are inherent to darker-skinned women, especially Black women—though they are sometimes granted, equally stereotypically, to East Asian women.

It's important to be explicit about the racist stereotypes that make it so easy for many Americans to imagine a white ballerina and so difficult for them to imagine a Black one, or only willing to make space in their imagination for light-skinned Black and Latina ballerinas, not darker-skinned ones. The deep-seated association between Blackness and brute force, a natural athleticism and strength that lacks refinement or skill, means that the kind of delicate and refined femininity that ballet demands of women is considered impossible for Black women to achieve and—and this part is just as important—a given for white girls and women. Howard has made a career of excavating these biases and holding them up to the light—and holding ballet gatekeepers accountable for making choices that further entrench ballet's racial inequities.

Ballet is imagined to be synonymous with whiteness and thus antithetical to Blackness. It is not simply that many nonwhite dancers are up against racist barriers if they want to become ballet dancers; it is that white dancers benefit from those barriers. They benefit from the fact that the word "ballerina" evokes the image of a white woman, a mental shortcut that exists because white women are imagined to be graceful, pure, and desirable until proven otherwise. The cultural default that disadvantages so many dancers of color smooths the way for their white classmates.

Ballet, in other words, is white woman. That's not to say that dancers of color have not made centuries' worth of essential contributions to the art form in America, because they most certainly have. Dancers of color were present at the birth of ballet in the United States: as Howard notes in her digital timeline of Black ballet dancers, the nineteenth century's "only male American ballet star" was George Washington Smith, a Philadelphia man who was "said to have been a mulatto" and who performed with international ballet star Fanny Elssler when she toured from Europe to the US.[4] The first star of New York City Ballet, Maria

Tallchief, was Native American, and the first American dancer to join the famed Ballet Russe de Monte Carlo was Japanese American Sono Osato.

Dancers of color have continued to shape American ballet despite concerted efforts by gatekeepers to keep ballet companies white or mostly white. The history of ballet in America is a history of reluctant, sporadic, and conditional inclusion of nonwhite dancers, especially those who are not exceptionally slim or fair-skinned.

To understand the extent to which ballet is synonymous with whiteness and a very particular kind of white femininity, consider how the image and the idea of the ballerina is used outside of the ballet world to market luxury lifestyle products.

While most consumers who take ballet as girls stop dancing before they finish high school, the ultrafeminine mystique of the ballerina is used to market to them for the rest of their lives. Ballerinas are everywhere in consumer culture, their images deployed to sell us perfume, watches, couture, and designer footwear. (Some of these "ballerinas" are not in fact ballerinas at all but models who have been strapped into unbroken-in pointe shoes and asked to make it fashion. The Instagram account @modelsdoingballet curates the most egregious examples of this attempt to use the idea of the ballerina to convey luxury, desirability, and femininity. The account's slogan is "Just stop. Hire dancers.")

Ballet dancers have been closely associated with couture and luxury goods for decades, and ballerinas have been a regular fixture in luxury fashion magazines like *Vogue* since the 1950s. But ballet's transformation from exotic (and unseemly) European entertainment to an aspirational and acceptably chaste American art form began decades earlier.

Between 1915 and 1925, Russian ballet star Anna Pavlova made regular tours of the United States, performing her famous "Dying Swan" solo night after night in bustling cities and tiny towns. "On one tour," dance historian Melissa Klapper writes, "she performed in Battle Creek, Michigan, in the afternoon, Kalamazoo, Michigan, in the evening, and then boarded the train to Muncie, Indiana, that night in preparation for the next day's shows."[5] European (and faux European) ballet troupes had toured the United States before, but Pavlova's influence was unrivaled.

"She became a fashion icon and a fitness guru," Klapper explains, "gently scolding American women for not taking care of themselves . . . and parlayed all the attention into a lucrative side career endorsing an array of products, from face creams to hats. Beginning with Pavlova, ballerinas became icons of femininity for Americans."[6]

The "balletomania" that seized the US and UK in the 1930s made ballet not just respectable but fashionable and glamorous. Since then, ballet-inspired styles from tutu-esque gowns to leg warmers and pink crossover sweaters have continued to cycle in and out of style.[7] But as streetwear trends moved toward more casual styles—as the fashion behemoth that is athleisure rose to dominate huge swathes of the industry and of women's wardrobes, especially during a pandemic that saw so many people working from home—ballet dancers have become more effective fashion emissaries than ever.

Look closely at athleisure marketing and you'll find dancers everywhere. Between 2015 and 2020, as the athleisure subsector of the fashion industry ballooned to be worth tens of millions of dollars, dancers modeled for athleisure lines made by Nike, GapFit, Zarely, and Cole Haan. Misty Copeland developed her own line with Under Armour, and across the Atlantic, Royal Ballet principal dancer Francesca Hayward developed a limited-edition line with Lululemon that included products like the Principal Dancer Funnel Neck Sweater.[8] New York City Ballet partnered with Puma, which provided the women of the company with athleisure wear; the company's dancers modeled for the brand and taught Puma-branded workout classes in the US and abroad. The dancer is the ideal model for athleisure: visibly muscular without being bulky, as slender as a fashion model but a real-life athlete. The ballerina is strong without sacrificing femininity—in fact, she is about as feminine as it can get.

And then, of course, there is the activity for which the athleisure is supposedly designed: working out. Perhaps the most successful recent use of ballet to move products is in the rise of barre classes, the workout trend that burst onto the already-crowded fitness market in 2015 and saw rapid growth into massive popularity in 2016.[9] Barre, which borrows from basic ballet classes as well as Pilates, yoga, and aerobics, has become the go-to workout for women looking to acquire toned, lean muscles without bulking up. In addition to bestowing a dancer's posture and a perked-up posterior, barre promises to "lengthen" and "elongate" its practitioners' muscles. Barre devotees will be strong but not too muscular. You'll look athletic but not masculine. Heaven forbid.

This kind of marketing relies on the popular image of the ballerina: she's extremely slender and has exquisite upright posture, and while she's very strong, she is graceful and hyperfeminine. There is no such thing, in the popular imagination, as a bulky ballerina. To achieve this look, barre class participants do tiny Pilates-inspired squats and work with very light weights and resistance bands. Sometimes they are tethered to the barre while performing these exercises. (In her 2019 book *Trick Mirror*, *New Yorker* journalist Jia Tolentino described barre as "a manic and ritualized activity, often set to deafening music and lighting changes," and wrote that its movements "resemble what a ballerina might do if you concussed her and then made her snort caffeine pills—a fanatical, repetitive routine of arm gestures, leg lifts and pelvic tilts."[10])

Whether or not barre classes resemble the first half of an actual ballet class is largely beside the point (though they don't). In borrowing an iconic piece of ballet equipment and the ideal of the ballerina body, barre is also borrowing our cultural understanding of ballet and using that understanding to sell twenty-five-dollar fitness classes.

The ballerinas who are employed to help brands market their luxury goods and athleisure lines are sometimes women of color. Copeland, as noted, has her own Under Armour range and appeared in an ad campaign for Stuart Weitzman, as well as a campaign for Breitling watches; American Ballet Theatre corps de ballet dancer Courtney Lavine, also a light-skinned Black woman, has appeared in commercials for Avon perfume and L'Oreal foundation; and Nardia Boodoo, a darker-skinned member of the Washington Ballet's corps, has modeled in pointe shoes for Banana Republic and Lunya, the Instagram-friendly silk sleepwear brand. But the vast majority of dancers (and fashion models posing as dancers) who are helping to market goods and services to women using the idea of the ballerina are white, marketing a white-coded body and lifestyle to an implied white audience.

That's in part because of the stereotypes activated by the body shape barre classes promise—long, lean, graceful!—and in part because it is one of the few exercise trends that emphasizes what fitness historian Natalia Mehlman Petrzela calls "extremely traditional ideas of femininity."

"This is not to say that barre does not cultivate strength," Petrzela notes. "However, when I see most barre studios advertising a long, lean dancer's body, I see the movements [they are] mimicking are very much about restraint and discipline." Unlike other fitness trends, like CrossFit and other explosive full-body workouts that have become increasingly popular with women in recent years, the movements in a barre class are small and contained (just like white women are supposed to be). There are no full-out sprints or big-momentum lifts here. The movements in barre are, for the most part, pulses and shallow pliés. These are minute and unruffled motions that are executed with—and promise to deliver—*control*.

It's not only the how of barre class that screams "strong, but in an appropriately feminine way!"—it's the where. Some barre fitness studios are decorated to mimic dance studios, the feminized space in which many participants, it's assumed, spent their girlhoods, Petrzela says. "They tend sometimes to almost mimic domestic spaces. Some have carpets on the floor. To me, that whole vibe of barre, from the marketing to the decor to the movement, promotes a pretty traditional notion of what attractive femininity looks like." Just as CrossFit depends on a particular kind of rugged and military-adjacent masculinity to market itself to men (and some women), barre depends on the hyperfemininity of ballet to market itself to women. In barre, you'll work extremely hard for an hour, but the labor will be barely visible and you'll never break a sweat—and what's more feminine than that?

It is impossible to separate barre's restraint and control, or its associations with domesticity and childhood, from the whiteness of ballet. As we've already seen, restraint and self-control are core to the American conception of whiteness: where people of color are imagined to be wild, white people are civilized—and white women, those queens of domesticity, are the most civilized of all.

Barre, a prestige lifestyle product (undiscounted classes cost between twenty-five and thirty dollars each in major cities and between fifteen and twenty dollars in smaller metro areas), depends on the mystique of the ballerina, and the promise of "the ballet body" for its appeal. In this sense, sociologist Jessie Daniels says, what barre classes are selling is not so much white womanhood as white *lady*hood. Barre depends on the implied whiteness of ballet, and its overwhelming femininity, to market those luxury fitness classes and all the gear one is supposed to wear while doing them (and while traveling to and from them, and while brunching afterward). Without the implied whiteness of ballet, without its heavy association with a very particular kind of femininity, barre's prestige would fall away.

Inside the ballet world, the art form's overwhelming whiteness has real professional and psychological consequences for dancers of color. As we saw in Chapter 4, it's no longer widely acceptable for ballet teachers and company directors to explicitly tell a dancer to lose weight; that kind of critique of a dancer's body has been replaced by euphemisms about "health," "fitness," "elongating," and, of course, "the line."

A similar doublespeak has developed for white teachers and directors attempting to justify their biases against Black dancers, especially the darker-skinned ones who are the furthest away from the white "European" aesthetic.

"African Americans," Gottschild wrote, "have also been stereotyped as genetically best suited for *certain* types of dance that exhibit what is supposedly our innate sense of rhythm, but innately ill-equipped for other 'white' dance forms." And there is no dance form whiter than ballet.[11]

Because it is still acceptable for ballet teachers and company directors to dismiss any dancer on the basis of their line, there is little to stop white ballet gatekeepers from dismissing Black dancers, especially women, based on the belief that they simply are not capable of the kinds of lines they believe are inherent to that white European aesthetic.

And, just as a tech start-up might decline to hire a Black engineer on the grounds of "culture fit," a ballet company can offer the vague justification that, in hiring only white dancers, or all white dancers and one light-skinned Black or Latina dancer, it is preserving the company's "standard" or "aesthetic."

Because ballet is an art form without objective measures of success beyond box office takings—because it is not a sport in which success can be measured on a scoreboard—it is easy for directors to hide their biases against Black bodies behind this "aesthetic" defense. It is still acceptable, even in an age of dutiful lip service to racial and ethnic diversity, to argue that because ballet is defined by unison, conformity, and order, and because a company's corps de ballet must move as one, a director has every right to assemble a company that is mostly white and in which all the dancers have similar physiques. This, the argument goes, is what best serves the company and the director's artistic vision. It's not bias; it's just that ballet is an aesthetic art form.

Except, of course, that it is bias. As Howard reminds the institutions she works with, it is a deep-seated, often-unconscious bias built on the notions that ballet is synonymous with whiteness and bodies that are not white are inherently unsuited to the upright, aristocratic discipline ballet demands. "Ballet is so subjective," Howard says, "it's basically who's looking at that body, whether it's a teacher or an artistic director, and how they perceive that body."

In the US, that bias, informed by resilient racist tropes, makes it especially hard for white teachers, directors, and audience members to see Black ballerinas, especially darker-skinned ballerinas, as acceptable, let alone aspirational.

It is somewhat easier, apparently, for those same white gatekeepers and audience members to accept men dancers who do not fit the "European" aesthetic.

The ballet world is awash in girls and always in need of boys. "There are never enough boy dancers," Katherine Davis Fishman wrote in her book about the Ailey School. "Anywhere."[12] And as we've seen, the low supply and high demand makes life in the ballet studio somewhat easier—or at least, very different—for boys than for girls. There's less competition, more leeway, and a better chance of winning scholarships, competitions, and jobs.

The experience of boys in ballet training and men in professional ballet is one of relative privilege compared to the experience of girls and women. "With women," Howard says, "the standard, the criteria, is greater, it's more intense. There's more of them, [and] they're seen as more replaceable than men."

One result of the boy shortage is that the ballet world is a little more welcoming of Black boys and men than it is of Black girls and women. This has been true for decades: New York City Ballet hired its first Black male principal dancer in 1962. It has never had a Black woman principal, ever.

"The function of the classical corps de ballet explains why Black men do not fall prey to the color barrier," Howard wrote in 2017. "Men never stand in lines as swans, wilis or sylphs, so the depth of their brownness is never an issue in regards to the aesthetic of 'classicism.'"[13]

"Usually if a company has a Black dancer or a dancer of color," says Joan Myers Brown, a former dancer and founder of the long-running and predominantly African American contemporary ballet company Philadanco, "it's a male. . . . Because they pick somebody up, throw them around, so they don't care what color they are."

But that's in part because the rigid gender norms of ballet—its deep investment in the image of strong men partnering fragile women—lend themselves to racist stereotypes about Black men as hypermasculine. In ballet, men of all races and ethnicities are expected to be extremely muscular, with very little body fat, and for Black men this adheres to the stereotype of the athletic and virile Black man, a trope rooted in race-based enslavement.

Overlaying ballet's gender norms on top of stereotypes about Black masculinity makes for a curious cocktail. "Another reason why the black male body is more acceptable is rooted in the very function of the male ballet dancer itself," Howard explained in her 2017 article. "His role has always been in service to his ballerina. Since the white eye is accustomed to seeing the black male body in that station, it fits the stereotype of the black subservient laborer."[14]

At the same time, the trope of the Black man as a laborer makes it harder for white ballet audiences and gatekeepers to see Black dancers as romantic leads. In ballet, these roles are traditionally danced by the men who fit the description of a danseur noble, a regal leading man who looks like the white ballet establishment's idea of a prince. Black dancers are relegated to comic sidekick roles, the Mercutio to the white man's Romeo.

In predominantly and traditionally white companies, this can mean that some iconic roles stay de facto off-limits to Black men. At New York City Ballet, for example, it took decades to cast a Black dancer in the role of Apollo in the 1928 Balanchine classic of the same name. And even when soloist Craig Hall danced the role, in 2011, it was in a single "dancers' choice" performance for which his fellow dancers, not management, did the casting. Until then, the role of the young Greek god had been danced almost exclusively by danseur noble types, blond and bronzed men whom the audience and artistic directors had no difficulty imagining as divine. And it wasn't until 2020 that American Ballet Theatre, City Ballet's main US rival, cast Black dancers in the roles of Romeo and Juliet in a single production, though its premiere was postponed because of the coronavirus pandemic.[15]

The experience of being one of the few or the only dancer of color in an otherwise white ballet company comes, as it so often does in mostly white workplaces, with extra labor. For Black dancers, that might mean the work of pointing out to a white creative team that their aesthetic is designed around the bodies of white women.

For Chyrstyn Fentroy, a twenty-eight-year-old soloist at Boston Ballet who identifies as mixed—her mother is white and her father is Black—this work started at an early age. When she was a girl, all the dancers playing guests in the party scene of *The Nutcracker* were given fake ringlet curls to pin into their hair. "And they'd have their hair down, and those just don't work for my hair," she says. "Even those fake ponytail curls, they just don't look the same on me. It looks fake. So my mom made fake hair for me to have my hair down. My mom was crafty like that."

And that work has continued at Boston Ballet, a predominantly white institution where Fentroy was the first Black woman to join the company in over a decade. "Boston Ballet did [the Balanchine ballet] *Chaconne*, and the whole ballet starts with all of the women with their hair down," she says. "And it was a whole conversation that I had to have."

For other dancers, there is the literal cost to be paid and a psychological one. Nardia Boodoo, a twenty-six-year-old member of the corps at the Washington Ballet, identifies as mixed—her mother is Black and her father is Indian—and is one of two Black women in her forty-person company. Recently, the director of the company, former ABT principal dancer Julie Kent, who is white, initiated a conversation with Boodoo about performing in shoes and tights that matched her skin tone. "She was like, 'If you feel comfortable or more empowered wearing flesh-colored tights and shoes, then you can do that,'" Boodoo remembers.

But when Boodoo opened up her costume packet, she found that her company-provided allowance of shoes and tights were pink. If she wants to perform in skin-tone shoes and tights, she has to pay for them out of her own pocket. "They are providing me only pink tights and pink shoes. . . . It's kind of like [Kent] said that just to say it."

Luckily, Boodoo is sponsored by a dancewear retailer; she models for the retailer in exchange for tights and posts the resulting "brand ambassador" photos to her Instagram account. It's extra labor that her white colleagues don't have to do in a workplace that is white by default. The problem is not a lack of diversity; it's an excess of privilege and advantage bestowed upon white dancers because they are white. And it exacts a toll—in time, money, mental and emotional energy, and long-term professional sustainability—on their colleagues of color.

And of course Black dancers, especially those with darker complexions, are made aware constantly that, on a stage full of white dancers, their skin makes them a magnet for attention and scrutiny. Boodoo says that in her previous position at Pennsylvania Ballet, she was explicitly told that she needed to perform better than her white counterparts in the corps de ballet. The director, Angel Corella, who is white, told her she "needed to work even harder because [she] stood out so much." Boodoo understood his concern, but says that there was an obvious solution: "Maybe if you had more girls that looked like me, then I wouldn't stand out so much."

Multiple dancers who identified as Black or mixed told me that they had had to fight to stay in ballet even as white teachers pushed them out of it, urging them to audition for contemporary dance companies instead of classical ones.

Almost every Black dancer I interviewed said they'd been encouraged to audition for Alvin Ailey American Dance Theater or its school, where they'd perform contemporary choreography surrounded by other dancers of color, most of them Black. Ailey's dancers all have excellent classical ballet training, but the company does not perform classical choreography. Others said they'd been encouraged to audition for Alonzo King LINES Ballet in San Francisco or Hubbard Street Dance Chicago. The former places an emphasis on contemporary ballet and has a notably racially diverse cast of dancers, and the latter performs modern dance, not classical ballet.

"One teacher in the [Washington Ballet] school came up to me and was like, 'You know, I think you would really be interested in going to Alonzo King LINES,'" Boodoo remembers. "And it was only my first couple of months at the Washington Ballet. . . . I didn't know how to take it, but I assumed it was because she thought it'd be a good fit." Boodoo had come to Washington by way of Joffrey Academy of Dance and Dance Theatre of Harlem School, where she acquired an excellent classical ballet training. She is and was a classical ballet dancer.

"It just makes me harder, I guess?" Boodoo says of working in a field in which white bodies are the default and the ideal against which all other bodies are measured. "Because it's just like, I have to keep proving people wrong. Sometimes it gets to be a little bit too much."

Aesha Ash found that it was too much as well. Ash, who is forty-two, graduated from the School of American Ballet in 1996 and won a prestigious prize for promising student dancers on her way from the school into the corps of New York City Ballet. She was the only Black woman in the company at the time, and that remained the case throughout her seven-year tenure with City Ballet.

Ash grew up in Rochester, New York, and started ballet on the late side at age eleven, after excelling in jazz and tap classes and competitions. That late start, combined with her only-ness in the company, made for a difficult and isolating experience. She felt like she was working "120 percent every day," she told me in a 2019 interview.

Once she joined the company, Ash felt othered and excluded: as Nardia Boodoo found with her tights, Ash found that while the company provided white dancers with a full supply of performance makeup, she was only given lipstick. Ballet critics singled her out for criticism of her body; one called it "distracting." "That is not talking about missing a turn or being overweight or that your hair is out of place," Ash told the *New York Times* in 2020. "That's talking to who you are. That chips away at your identity and your self-worth as a young adolescent coming into yourself."[16]

While she was in the company, her sister died of pancreatic cancer, and soon after, her father died of colon cancer. "And so it started to become very hard" to keep working, as the maxim goes, twice as hard to get half as far. "And I started to ask why—'What is this all for?'"

("When Aesha left," says current New York City Ballet soloist Georgina Pazcoguin, whose father is Filipino and whose mother is Italian, "I went into all of Aesha's corps spots. So there's one. It's not the first time or the last time that I've been the token or been made to feel like the token." Pazcoguin is the only woman of color in the upper ranks of City Ballet.)

Ash retired from ballet early, at thirty. "I had a good number of years left in me as a dancer," she said in 2019. After leaving City Ballet, she danced for Alonzo King LINES Ballet and then in a well-respected contemporary ballet company in Switzerland (where one young dancer admitted to her that he had been afraid to talk to her for the first year she was there "because all the images [he] ever saw of Black American women seemed so scary and intimidating, and [he] just assumed they were all like that").

And it took her a long time to come back to ballet, first as a community activist through her organization the Swan Dreams Project and then as a guest ballet teacher. In 2020, she became the School of American Ballet's first full-time Black woman faculty member, "an incredible full-circle moment" and also "this tremendous responsibility because it is a first."[17]

Wilmara Manuel remembers the first time her daughter Sasha had a Black ballet teacher, at a summer intensive in California. Wilmara picked her up at the end of the day, "and she kind of whispered, 'Mom, my teacher was Black.'"

"I don't think she even realized the magnitude of what she was saying," Wilmara says. "But to be able to see a Black ballerina who was successful and had done it all, that's huge. . . . It's growth. It's making sure that they'll achieve. It's making them aware of those little things that pertain strictly to what a dancer of color has to deal with. Those things are monumental." That teacher? It was Aesha Ash.

⁓

It is tempting, when thinking about race or racism and ballet, to focus on dancers of color, the exceptions to the rule. Indeed, the initial version of this chapter was about just that: the history of dancers of color, especially Black dancers, and the challenges they have faced in an overwhelmingly white art form.

Those stories are important, to be sure. But it is just as important to understand the rules as it is to study their exceptions. That is, those of us who care about ballet's overwhelming whiteness and wish to change it must look directly at that whiteness, not merely at the exceptions to it. Until we understand why ballet is so white and how that whiteness is enforced, we cannot change it. This is particularly important for those of us who fit the ballet ideal of white womanhood. As we've already seen, it's true that women and girls in ballet wield far less power than boys and men. But the power of being the default body, the ideal body, should not be underestimated. Women might be devalued in ballet, but white womanhood is not.

Racial equity in ballet is a matter of fairness and justice; it is simply not right that the biases of ballet's gatekeepers should cut short the careers and stifle the dreams of dancers of color. It is also a deep failure of imagination on the part of the white ballet establishment—of ballet teachers, artistic directors, board members, and audience members—that ballet remains so stubbornly synonymous with whiteness.

It is also a failure to grasp the diversity among dancers of all races and ethnicities. As Howard notes, there are Black dancers—like Fentroy, Boodoo, and Ash—with long, slender limbs and high arches, and "there are white girls with booties and thighs; there are white girls with flat feet." Ballet gatekeepers "don't necessarily associate that with their race, it's just the body they have," Howard tells me. As she has said for years, the Black body is not problematic. "What's problematic are the implicit biases against the Black body."

And it is a misunderstanding of ballet's history, which is one of constant and at times revolutionary change, to believe that there is one correct ballet body or that the correct ballet body is not always evolving. It is. There is no good reason—no moral or historically accurate eason—why ballet must stay the same and, in doing so, exclude so many talented and deserving dancers.

Finally, it is a matter of survival. "The companies that don't embrace this now will fail," says Aubrey Lynch, the chief officer of education and creative programs at Harlem School of the Arts Dance. "Because in twenty years the majority of the country will be of color, and they're not gonna want to go see a white ballet company with no Black people in it."

For companies to have well-trained dancers, ballet schools—the vast and teeming lifeblood of the ballet ecosystem—must prioritize racial equity. This doesn't only mean ensuring that their classes are open and affordable for students of all backgrounds. It also means ensuring that when students of color come to class, they are taught by teachers whose artistic vision is not clouded by a biased view of what a good ballet body looks like or the assumption that only white dancers can achieve that body.

Many of the dancers I interviewed said that well-meaning teachers had encouraged them to shift their aspirations away from classical ballet and toward modern and contemporary dance, where Black dancers have long been far more welcome. This is, some would say, a rational response to an irrational situation: until classical ballet companies are more diverse, teachers who do this are acting in their students' best interests. But of course, this rational advice fuels a vicious cycle: as long as Black dancers are not training for positions in a classical ballet company, classical ballet companies will say there are no Black dancers to fill their open positions. And they will be partly right.

But the absence of Black dancers on America's ballet stages is ultimately not a failure of talent or training but a failure of leadership. Artistic directors and the boards of directors they answer to—the creative leaders at the top of the food chain in ballet's ecosystem—have the most power to fix this decades-old problem.

"The directors have a lot of antiquated ideas about ballet," Nardia Boodoo says. "Who gets to do ballet, and what ballet is . . . Everyone's still in love and married to their old ideas that just don't work. Then they turn around and want to know why no one wants to come to the ballet. It doesn't represent society anymore."

If ballet is to represent society, it will take more than putting dancers of color onstage. As underrepresented as racial and ethnic minorities are in front of the curtain, they are even less likely to hold administrative and artistic power. If ballet is to survive, it will need Black and brown and Asian American ballet masters and mistresses, repetiteurs, choreographers, composers, costume designers, set designers, and, most crucially, artistic directors. Ballet will not be relevant and will not survive if it becomes a white power structure that uses racialized bodies to realize an unchanged, and unchanging, artistic vision. As dance scholar Lester Tomé has noted, "The display of different bodies may be where diversity starts but not where it should end."[18]

"If you want ballet to be accessible, you have to embrace the different hues of skin tone and body dissimilarity," says Lynch. "And if you don't, you die. Anybody who's not embracing diversity will perish. Any company or organization that's not embracing where the world's going—diversity and openness and empathy—is gonna perish."

CHAPTER 6

DANCE LIKE A MAN

Ballet in the popular mind boils down to the feminine. What the "jock" is to masculinity in America, so the ballerina is to femininity, a distillation of ideas about traditional gender identity carried to their extreme.

LYNN GARAFOLA

Patrick Frenette grew up in west Vancouver, in a small and somewhat conservative town where "boys did hockey and girls got good grades. This is just how things were." Frenette didn't want to play hockey. He tried, but he wasn't built for it. He was small for his age, underdeveloped and scrawny. On the ice, he looked like Bambi, he remembers. "I was the shame of Canada on the ice. So obviously hockey was not an option."

What Frenette wanted to do was dance. At three years old, he had watched his older sister Emma in her dance classes and couldn't stop himself from joining in. It was partly the lure of the music, and partly the desire to be near his sister. For boys, this is a common path into ballet: where big sister goes, little brother follows.

"I would sort of make these rude interruptions into her ballet classes," he remembers, "and I kept getting escorted out because the teachers were like, 'Oh, he's so young, he can't really do anything yet, but bring him back next year.'"

By the time he was seven and Emma was nine, their parents had taken them out of the local recreational dance school where they'd started, and where they'd learned a number of dance styles, and placed them in a ballet-only academy that sent its graduates to professional ballet companies all over the world. Patrick went from being the only boy in his dance school to having a cadre of advanced teen boy students he could look up to.

"I may have been one of a few younger boys in my class, but I had this roster of nine or ten older guys in their mid-to-late teens to idolize and watch and learn from every single day," says Frenette, who is white. "And my choice of maybe three different male instructors as well."

As his ballet training got more serious, so did the bullying he faced at school. It started as curiosity—kids asking questions—but curiosity soon gave way to cruelty.

"Before it was bullying, it was always a lot of questions, like, 'Why do you do ballet? Ballet's for girls, it's for sissies,'" he says. "Before it was name-calling and exclusion, it was always just the questions. . . . 'Why can't you just be normal? Go play hockey, go play soccer.'"

By the time he was eight, he was a social outcast. His classmates excluded him from birthday parties and after-school play dates. "It was me and me alone."

His family had his back, and he felt supported by his ballet teachers. He had friends at ballet school, but none of them went to public school with him. The hours he spent in ballet class after school became a refuge, but the "six hours that I was at public school [were] becoming increasingly difficult to bear."

Some of the bullying was misogynistic—"Ballet's for sissies"—and some of it was explicitly homophobic. And it was difficult for the school administration to help him because his bullies had the support of their parents, too. The school assigned him a counselor, and Frenette remembers a meeting with the counselor, his mother, his most hateful bully, and the bully's mother. "And we were trying to get to the root of the problem, and the mom blurts out, 'Well, my son hates Patrick because he does ballet and he's gay, and I respect that.'"

Once, after gym class, one of his bullies stole his street clothes from his locker, so he showed up to ballet class in smelly, baggy clothes he'd pulled from the lost and found. And every year the bullying got worse. Frenette started to get into physical fights with his tormentors, and soon he was showing up to ballet classes with black eyes and bruises.

His grades fell because he was no longer interested in going to school and wasn't paying attention to class when he was there. One day, in fifth grade, Frenette ran away from campus. "I just knew," he says, "that I could not spend another day in that school."

And his miserable school situation began to take a toll on his time in the ballet studio. His classmates there noticed that he seemed unlike himself, depressed. He started thinking about quitting, wondering if the bullies were right: "He's doing ballet! He's the target! If he would just stop, then this would just all go away."

"It's so hard to get up and have to go to school for six hours and have to face this on a daily basis, and then somehow find the motivation to go to ballet," Frenette remembers. "It was becoming unbearable."

He told some of the older boys at the ballet school that he was thinking of quitting, and they were sympathetic but steadfast: that wasn't an option. If you quit, they told him, the bullies win. It helped, he says. "It really gave me a sort of battle cry, or like a rallying cause to keep [it] up."

It also helped that Frenette could see a clear path from his elite ballet school to a career as a professional ballet dancer. "I wasn't at some regional dance school where kids would just go to college," he says. "I was at a school where, when kids graduated, they had jobs." This wasn't just an extracurricular activity; it could be a job. Watching the teenage boys he'd admired from the studio door win prestigious ballet competitions and secure contracts with top US companies made him believe that, if he could endure the bullying, he'd be doubly rewarded: he'd get to keep doing something he loved, and one day he'd earn a living doing it.

"That, more than anything, helped me put aside the bullying that I endured and focus instead on getting myself to become the best dancer I could be and seeing this job through as far as I can."

But it was clear that if he was going to stick with ballet, something else in his life had to change. When he was thirteen, the entire family moved to Southern California so that he and Emma could attend a new ballet school, and Patrick didn't enroll in the local public school. Instead, he started taking online classes at home.

The flexible, self-directed schedule was ideal for someone who was spending more and more time in the ballet studio; he could pack all his schooling into the first few days of the week and then spend all day Thursday, Friday, and Saturday at ballet. But homeschooling was also a way to insulate himself from the homophobia and hostility he believed awaited him in high school.

"I was a ninth grader at thirteen, and other ninth graders in my class were fifteen, so I was so young and still so small. . . . There was nothing that I was ever gonna be able to do. I just remember going through the scenarios, like, 'Okay, it's gonna be me, the dancer, versus the entire Orange County football team. I'll get eaten alive.'"

Patrick Frenette is now twenty-five and a member of the corps de ballet at American Ballet Theatre, which he joined at eighteen after spending a year at the School of American Ballet. His experience of relentless bullying is a startlingly common one among his peers: while boys, as we've already seen, generally have an easier time than girls inside the ballet studio, many of them face harassment and bullying outside of it, complicating the privilege they enjoy within the ballet world.

Almost every professional male dancer I interviewed, and almost every parent of a male ballet student I interviewed, had a story to tell about bullying. There were stories about social exclusion at school and snide remarks from grandfathers at home. There were memories of concealing ballet lessons from sports coaches and school friends. And there was a sense of loneliness and confusion among boys who, at a very young age, found themselves stuck between a subculture in which they were prized and precious, and a larger culture in which they were pariahs.

The statistics on bullying and boys who take ballet are alarming: in one survey conducted by Wayne State University dance professor Doug Risner, 93 percent of boy ballet students said they experienced "teasing and name calling" and 68 percent reported "verbal or physical harassment." Eleven percent reported physical violence at the hands of people who targeted them because they take ballet.[1]

In the last decade, thanks to activism and media coverage, awareness of the true psychological and emotional toll of bullying has increased. Bullying has been recognized as a genuine threat to the health and well-being of young people, especially young LGBTQ people. The rate of bullying that Risner found in his study dwarfs that in the general population. "If this were not the arts," Risner told me in 2017, "it would be considered a child health crisis."[2]

At the core of the bullying these boys experience lies the belief that ballet is unsuitable for boys because it's so very suitable for girls. It is a feminine activity, both in that it's mostly done by girls and in that, in the US, so many of the hallmarks of ballet—physical grace and flexibility, affinity for classical music, even the act of displaying one's body onstage—are coded as feminine.

Because ballet is "for girls," boys who choose to do it are understood to be deviant. In enjoying something that girls enjoy, they're failing at masculinity, and because, in this worldview, heterosexuality is a mandatory part of masculinity—of being a "real" or "normal" man—there's a strong cultural association between men who dance and homosexuality. In short, even as many sports once reserved for boys and men, like soccer and basketball, have become "normal" for girls, it is still not considered normal, in most places in the United States, for boys to dance. That's especially true if the kind of dance they choose is classical ballet.

"The bullying stemmed from a root of this constant misunderstanding as to why a boy would want to pursue ballet," Frenette says. "And people always are fearful of what they do not understand. . . . When there's just something they can't accept, that makes them hostile towards what is making them question their understanding of normal."

Risner says that the popular conception of bullying is as a series of incidents—a boy is stuffed into a locker, or his clothes are stolen during gym class—but that in focusing only on these visible and discrete examples, observers miss a great deal of the psychological and emotional experience of bullying.

"The experience of being bullied and harassed is far more complicated than we think," Risner says. "Oftentimes we think about teasing and bullying as something overt that we can see and immediately recognize." But as Frenette experienced, sometimes bullying manifests as exclusion and ostracism. And, Risner says, over time, the targets of bullying can start to "assimilate the bullying they received" and modify their behavior in what he calls "auto-oppression."

"Those boys internalize those experiences to such an extent that they actually begin believing them," he says. They believe that they aren't man enough, that they aren't tough enough, that they do not deserve the status that is usually granted to straight men. "All of those deficiencies that they've heard," Risner explains. "They begin to believe they deserve and can expect harassment, bullying, and teasing."

Several of the professional male dancers I interviewed said they'd considered quitting ballet because of the bullying they faced. Jared Allen Brunson, a Black dancer from Florida who performed with Ballet Memphis before joining Complexions Contemporary Ballet in New York City, quit dancing for a year in middle school and went on a manliness kick, switching from dance classes to martial arts classes. "I was really trying to 'be a boy,' you know?" When his dance classmates, his dance community, heard that he wasn't planning on coming back to dancing, they pushed him to change his mind. "It was just an outpouring. . . . It was like that whole community thing."

Like Frenette, Brunson found that having a role model, someone who had stuck with dance and made a career out of it, made it easier for him to keep dancing. For Brunson, it was Danny Tidwell, the classically trained commercial dancer who became an early star of *So You*

Think You Can Dance. Tidwell, who died in a car accident in 2020, was Brunson's "absolute hero, my favorite dancer. . . . I was like, 'Dang'—I saw myself in him, you know? A lot of people said we looked alike. So I was like, 'This can't really be it.'" He went back to ballet.

For boys like Frenette and Brunson, the community and culture they find in the ballet studio becomes a refuge from the bullying they face at school. American Ballet Theatre principal dancer David Hallberg, one of the blond danseurs noble mentioned in Chapter 5, was born in South Dakota and grew up in Phoenix, Arizona, where he endured years of homophobic and misogynistic abuse, which that he documented in his memoir *A Body of Work: Dancing to the Edge and Back*. Hallberg remembers dreading his walk to the bus stop every morning because "the teasing started and ended there every day."[3]

But at his dance studio, he was normal. He had friends who loved dancing as much as he did, "who saw me as the person and the dancer I was, not as someone who was weird. . . . I wasn't the girl or the freak faggot. I was free." Dance, Hallberg wrote, became his escape and salvation.[4]

Parents whose sons dance today are watching as their children navigate the fraught space in which the love of ballet collides and conflicts with the desire to be "normal" among their peers. Ty Schalter, who lives in Lansing, Michigan, put his son in dance classes at the age of three or four (as was the case for the Frenette siblings, Schalter's son followed his older sister into the dance studio). "He saw it and he took to it," Schalter says. "And he really enjoyed dancing, and he tried tap and jazz and other stuff, but he really liked ballet best."

But by third grade, he had figured out that he'd be asking for trouble if he told people that he took ballet and enjoyed it. Already he could sense that the people around him—children and adults alike—were on high alert for deviations from a hypermasculine norm, ready to police anyone who failed to perform masculinity properly. He grew out his hair long, and his ice hockey coaches told him to cut it. Once, he was playing with his sister and painted his nails, and his coaches told him, "Don't do that. Hockey players don't paint their nails."

"And going into third grade, [the students] made an 'about me' poster," Schalter remembers, "and he put 'hockey,' 'ballet,' and some kids were like, 'What? Ballet? What the heck?'" And so, even though Schalter's son believed that ballet was making him a better hockey player, he decided it wouldn't be a good idea to tell his coaches about his other extracurricular passion.

Hiding that they take ballet classes, or at least not advertising it, is a common coping mechanism for boys hoping to avoid bullying, Risner says. "Many boys and male adolescents conceal as best they can that they study dance—living almost double lives."

But of course there are some people from whom boys cannot hide their love of dance. Most heartbreaking in Risner's research are the stories of boys who are bullied in their own homes, by men in their own families, for violating the rigid rules of masculinity. "It's horrible for these young boys," Risner said in 2017. "They report their fathers, their male siblings, uncles, stepfathers, are the least supportive. And in fact are almost a barrier to their dancing."[5] John Lam, a principal dancer at Boston Ballet, faced enormous opposition from his parents, Vietnamese immigrants to California who wanted their youngest son to choose a more stable and "normal" career path, and who also feared that ballet would make him gay.

"I think a major thing for . . . my dad and my mom was that they didn't want me to be exposed to other gay boys," Lam says. "That was very, very apparent." By the time he was fourteen, Lam was a promising ballet student whose teachers were encouraging him to go to an elite residential school where he could prepare for a life as a professional dancer. The school he got into was in Toronto. He also knew he was gay. His father, in particular, didn't want him to go.

"He said, 'You have to stay home. I don't want you to be gay,'" Lam said in 2017. "So I said, 'Okay, I won't be gay. And I just lied in front of my parents.'"[6]

Evan MacBeth, who lives outside Charlottesville, Virginia, says that his nine-year-old son Henry is forthcoming with his peers. "It's a known thing that Henry does dance," MacBeth says. "He doesn't talk about it a lot at school, but it's not like he doesn't talk about it. 'What are you doing Wednesday night?' 'I'm going to dance class.' It's just something that he does. I don't think it's a big deal at nine, which is fantastic." (Then again, MacBeth also says, "We'll see what happens in middle school.")

At the beginning, at least, Henry's grandfather was less than encouraging of his grandson's dance classes. It took an appeal to Henry's future presumed heterosexuality—"You should want your grandson to dance, if only because all a girl wants in high school is a boy who will dance with her"—to placate his grandfather. The result, MacBeth says, is that Henry "definitely perceives dance as something he's not necessarily supposed to like."

Henry doesn't even take ballet classes. He takes hip-hop and jazz, and next year, his father says, he'll likely take lyrical or contemporary classes. "I'm pretty confident he'll love that." But ballet, which his sister loves, has been a nonstarter.

Lyrical and contemporary are as close to ballet as Henry's likely to get, his father predicts. "He's not taking any ballet. He's received a lot of gender bias about it from the world," MacBeth says. "We've talked to him and . . . I don't think we're going to get him into a ballet class."

Some of the boys we met in Chapter 2 had to be coaxed, and their families compensated, to get them into ballet class. And some boys, like Henry, can be convinced to take dance classes—hip-hop, jazz, musical theater, tap—but will not agree to ballet classes. It is not just the tights, or the classical music, or the loneliness of being the only boy in a class full of girls. It is that ballet is a bridge too far into femininity, an intolerable deviation from masculinity. Musical theater or tap, while suspiciously feminine, are tolerable, and hip-hop, with its roots in Black American culture and its associations with a stereotypical, hypervirile Black masculinity, might even be considered cool. Ballet is simply too deviant. What kind of boy would enjoy something so feminine, and what kind of parent would encourage it?

Aubrey Lynch, the chief officer of education and creative programs at Harlem School of the Arts Dance, says that if he wants boys to take ballet classes, he has to ease them into it by teaching them other styles first, sprinkling ballet steps into the all-boys creative movement classes he teaches to five-year-olds. These classes are specifically designed to recruit boys into dance, and from there, "I recruit hip-hop to ballet," he says.

But the best way to get boys into ballet classes, Lynch says, is to let them perform. "I put them in a show. Put a kid in a show and you got him." When Lynch puts on these shows, he invites his young hip-hop dancers to perform, "and they see the teen boys and other dancer boys and ballet boys dance. And ultimately they come in and stand in there and watch and [say], 'I'm gonna try it.'"

Lynch's method confirms Risner's research on what draws boys and young men to ballet, which is the opportunity to express themselves and to put on a show. "Artistic expression, self-discovery, and creativity," Risner says. These are, by and large, the same reasons girls are attracted to ballet, though for girls ballet comes with the additional satisfaction of fulfilling—or at least trying to fulfill—a hyperfeminine ideal.

"My research shows that it's clearly the same for boys and girls," Risner says. "They aren't attracted to dance for different, gendered reasons. . . . 'I am more like myself than I am anywhere when I'm dancing.' And that's the way we should pinpoint recruitment and enlarging the field, [by going] after what we know brings people to dancing."

Unfortunately, that is often not the way ballet attempts to recruit boys or, more broadly, how it justifies its value and existence. Instead, those hoping to appeal to boys (and their parents) stress that ballet is extremely athletic—more athletic, even, than the kinds of sports that boys receive social validation for doing.

This tendency has a long history, from 1950s press coverage that emphasized that New York City Ballet star dancer Edward Villella had once been a boxer to coverage of NFL player Lynn Swann and bodybuilding-era Arnold Schwarzenegger taking ballet classes. It was on full display in the summer of 2019 when an anchor on ABC's *Good*

Morning America made fun of a then-six-year-old Prince George for taking ballet classes and scoffed at the suggestion that any boy would enjoy such a thing.

In a short segment that would go surprisingly viral, *GMA* host Lara Spencer walked her fellow hosts and the audience through the curriculum that the heir to the British throne would be taking in second grade. It included computer programming, poetry, and ballet (this last one was not in fact a new development; Prince William had told the press the previous year that his son had been enjoying weekly ballet classes).[7]

"Prince William says Prince George absolutely loves ballet," Spencer said, barely suppressing a laugh. "I have news for you, Prince William. We'll see how long that lasts."[8] Next to her, George Stephanopoulos scoffed, echoing Spencer's skepticism: no normal boy, once he knows his own mind, would ever enjoy ballet. It was an act of public bullying of a child, and a clear message to American boys who take and enjoy ballet: *There's something wrong with you.* Viewers, many of them mothers of sons, were invited to scoff with him.

"It was rather triggering," Frenette said, "because it wasn't her remarks that stung so much—it was the fact that she said something and then there was a room of people around her that joined in on the laughter. And that's what always got me as a kid."

In response, professional ballet dancers, especially men, used their social media platforms to push back against the derision and cruelty in Spencer's words and, as Jared Allen Brunson put it on Instagram, "drag" her. Some called for her to be fired, and others for her to issue an apology or air a follow-up segment about boys who dance and the bullying they face (the following week, *GMA* did just that).[9]

Other dancers used the moment as an opportunity to share messages of encouragement to boys who dance, urging them to keep doing what they love and to persevere in the face of ignorance and unkindness.

Some were explicit about the misogyny and homophobia that lie at the core of Spencer's joke and of so much discomfort with the idea of boys taking (and enjoying) ballet classes. "It's all due to gender stereotypes and toxic masculinity," wrote Washington Ballet dancer Cory Landolt, who said he was subjected to homophobic taunts and physical violence for several years in middle school.

"Just for dancing ballet. Because it's seen as something only girls do. Boys should be playing sports and the arts are for girls. . . . The bullying didn't stop until one day when I was 14. I'd had enough from the wrestling team captain. He pushed my head into a locker and I snapped and beat him up. We became friends after, but I shouldn't have had to beat up a kid to prove my worth and masculinity."[10]

But many responses played into the very same gender stereotypes that Spencer's comments did—that in order for ballet to be a legitimate pursuit for boys and men, it must be proven to be appropriately manly. Alexandre Hammoudi, a French-born soloist at American Ballet Theatre, posted a slideshow of tough guys—Schwarzenegger, James Dean, Patrick Swayze—taking ballet classes. The official account of Pacific Northwest Ballet posted a photo of its male corps dancers mid-leap during a performance of Jerome Robbins's *West Side Story Suite*, in which men perform not in tights but in jeans and sneakers, with a caption about the "high level of physical and mental stamina" that ballet requires and the "physical strength" it bestows on those who practice it (along with "personal growth," "friendship," and "a lifelong appreciation for music and movement").[11]

The outpouring of protest from the dance world and the resounding show of support for boys who dance demonstrated one of the advantages of social media: signal-boosting a positive message all over the world and showing strength in numbers. (But of course, the flip side of this in an era of social media saturation is that for boys who do ballet, bullying no longer stops when school lets out. Frenette says he's grateful that he had transitioned to homeschooling by the time the internet became an easily accessible platform for his bullies, "before there were Facebook groups and private chat rooms and all of these horrible things that kids have to go through now. Because once something's on the internet, it's never going away. . . . I feel for them for having to deal with this new kind of bullying.")

Nearly all the response posts mentioned strength, usually physical and sometimes mental, as one of the hallmarks of male ballet dancers. Few mentioned elegance, beauty, and self-expression as reasons to value ballet and for boys to study it.

The implication of these defenses is that ballet is legitimate because it's not so different from sports—it might even be more athletic than the kinds of sports that boys and men are encouraged to do. Ballet inculcates the same attributes that make sports synonymous with manhood: a strong body and strong fraternal bonds. Men who dance ballet are just as strong as football players and other hypermasculine athletes, in this argument—in fact, bodybuilders-cum-action-stars and rebels without a cause turn to ballet to make themselves *even manlier*. These defenses, well intentioned as they were, affirmed the misogyny inherent in the suggestion that real men and normal boys don't do or enjoy ballet.

High-profile ballerinas, in a well-intentioned attempt to defend their colleagues, also emphasized how physically strong male ballet dancers are and how that strength is used to reinforce the weightless, otherworldly femininity of ballerinas. New York City Ballet principal dancer Tiler Peck posted a photo of herself coaching a young male dancer with a caption that exemplified this line of argument.

"It takes discipline, strength, and so much to be a dancer," Peck wrote. "I am forever grateful to all of the men who lift me up and partner me on a daily basis . . . for allowing me to go beyond the capacity of what my body can do alone and be able to float and walk on air. This feeling is a gift I wish every human was able to experience!"[12]

(Li Cunxin, a former star dancer who is now the artistic director of the Queensland Ballet in Australia, was even more explicit about this gendered performance. "Boys don't know what they are missing," he told ABC News in early 2020. "There are so many beautiful girls to dance with them, to move around them, and boys often feel like they are kings.")[13]

Sometimes the attempt to prove how manly ballet dancers are verges on the comical: a desperate, repeated attempt to distance men who dance from anything resembling femininity by playing up the athleticism of dancing and playing down its artistic side. In one BBC video, a ballet dancer from Northern Ireland named Ruaidhri Maguire assures viewers that "ballet isn't just about being dainty and looking pretty." The video featured footage of him rehearsing and shots of him rolling out his muscles with a foam roller. "It's really a sport with an artistic side to it," he tells the interviewer. "There's a true strength to it and there's a true rawness . . . a true athleticism."[14]

Maguire "is currently a soloist with the Baltic Opera Ballet in Poland," the video text says, "but"—but!—"he spends hours in the gym every day to keep up with training." He lifts, bro. Maguire goes on to tell the interviewer that he goes to the gym six days a week to cross-train because male dancers "aren't just there to look pretty." The video then shows stills of him doing difficult overhead lifts with his pas de deux partners, which, he says, is "strenuous," "energetic," and "athletic." It's not subtle.

Of course, it is true that ballet requires exceptional physical strength and mental discipline and that many male dancers do extra work in the gym to achieve both the strength and the appearance of strength that ballet demands of them. It is also true that ballet requires grace and elegance, and self-expression and musicality, all things that are coded feminine and are rarely associated with sports like football and baseball. Ballet, unlike sports, prizes something that men are not supposed to want for themselves: beauty.

Masculinity permits men to be consumers of beauty, to look at it and appreciate it, to be subjects of beauty while women are objects. It discourages them from being beautiful themselves, and in the US, men who spend "too much" time or pay "too much" attention to how they look are viewed with suspicion. Ballet asks men to *be* beautiful, to move beautifully, and to dedicate a great deal of time and attention to those goals.

What if boys and men who dance didn't have to justify their choices with assurances about how traditionally masculine ballet is? What if they didn't feel the need to shore up their masculinity, and for many, their heterosexuality, by emphasizing the bravura leaps and turns that ballet demands of them in addition to all that beauty? What if they were allowed to be dainty and pretty—what if they were allowed to be feminine—without apology? As one Atlanta Ballet dancer asked me in 2017, "Why can't ballet just be ballet? Why do we have to super-masculinize it? Why do we have to compare it to football? There's no need to compare us; we're a fine art, not a sport."[15]

The reality, an uncomfortable one for many, is that beauty and performance draw boys to ballet, just as they draw girls. Only 2 percent of boys in Risner's studies said they participated in team sports, and 8 percent believed that "if their teachers made dance more like sports, it would increase male participation." Efforts to recruit more boys into dancing by comparing ballet to acceptably masculine sports—it's basically soccer, but with tights and a piano!—"those are just wrongheaded assumptions that deny boys what it is they like about dancing."[16]

Risner says that these efforts do have one positive effect: they make it easier for skeptical or resistant parents to get on board with their sons' dancing. "Parents—primarily fathers—may be less inclined to tease, taunt, or, in some cases, forbid their sons from taking dance classes," he concedes. But that's only if the son in question is taking recreational ballet classes, that is, if it "isn't viewed as serious . . . but instead is perceived to be athletic, 'good exercise,' or will help improve his athletic ability (i.e., [help him] jump higher)."

But "for boys and young males pursuing professional dance study, there's minimal value in attempting to make dance more like sports or utilizing sports analogies." For boys and young men pursuing professional dance study, the reassuring familiarity of "real" manliness doesn't help.

Increasing the number of boys and men in ballet and making their experiences outside the ballet studio less emotionally traumatic will require work. It will mean expanding the mainstream understanding of what boys and men are allowed to be so as to include some things we currently understand to be feminine.

It simply isn't accurate, or effective, to insist that ballet is just as athletic as football and that it's therefore as valid a pursuit for boys and men. The reality is that ballet is dainty and pretty, and what of it?

⁓

Because of the significant obstacles to boys' participation in ballet, there has been, as Risner suggests, a concerted effort to recruit boys into ballet training. As we saw in Chapter 2, that can take the form of scholarships or heavily subsidized tuition. Other structural efforts include boys-only classes, many of which are taught by male teachers. This way, boys have peers and older role models, and they have a better chance at feeling "normal" than if they take classes in which they're vastly outnumbered by girls and which are overseen by a woman teacher, who might not be able to empathize with their experiences in and outside of the ballet studio.

At Boston Ballet School, which is affiliated with the Boston Ballet company, all-boys classes are the norm beginning when students are just eight years old. That's unusual; at many American schools, where there might not be enough boys to assemble an all-boys class anyway, gender segregation starts at eleven or twelve, when girls start dancing on pointe.

Adrienne Kisner, who put her now-nine-year-old son into classes at Boston Ballet School at a very young age, says that being in a class with half a dozen other boys, taught by male teachers, has been "essential" to his sticking with ballet "because it's very social for him, and because there's other little boys there," she says. "I think he's just really found his people. And if it were all girls, I don't know if it would be the same thing."

Other institutions use the ballet calendar and the popularity of summer intensive training programs to assemble short-term all-boys classes. Patrick Frenette's sister Emma is a cofounder—along with their mother and the director of a North Carolina ballet school—of a summer intensive training program that's for boys only. The Boys Ballet Summer Intensive, where Patrick is a regular teacher, has seen increased demand since it began five years ago with about twenty boys. "The need for the program stemmed from wanting to provide a space for boys to train that I would've benefited from when I was their age," he says.

"These kids need to be with each other and interact with each other and make friends with each other, and have a positive experience from engaging in dance," says Robert Fox, the cofounder of another all-boys summer program, this one in Sydney, Australia. The Boys' Summer School has convened boys from all over the country since 2007, and Fox believes it's especially valuable for boys from rural areas, who are more likely to be the only boys in their ballet classes and perhaps their entire ballet schools. At the Summer School, they can spend time with like-minded peers, even if it's only a week a year.

Like the Frenettes, Fox has seen enormous growth in interest in the program, which began with fewer than thirty boys and now hosts almost a hundred every year. Unsurprisingly, the Summer School also stresses that dance is on par with men's sports. Its program ambassador is Australian ballet dancer Alexander Campbell, who is a principal dancer with the Royal Ballet in London. "He could have chosen cricket," Fox tells me. "He was a top cricket player when he was in his teens, and he chose ballet."

Campbell is also affiliated with the Royal Academy of Dance's Project B initiative, a three-year program that launched in 2017 with the goal of increasing boys' participation in ballet (and girls' participation in cricket). "The campaign aims to break down stereotypes to show that dance is just as physical and demanding as many sports," its website says, "and is not something that only girls can do." One way it envisioned doing that was to "fire boys' imaginations with new dance partnerships inspired by sports and superheroes." It also offered boys-only workshops and financial support to help more boys afford dance training and more men afford teacher training.[17]

These structural efforts are surely a good thing, provided that they don't reinforce the very misogyny and homophobia that makes them necessary. But the urgent need to recruit and retain more boys in ballet can warp the culture of the ballet world into one in which boys become vastly more valuable than girls. It also sends a clear message to boys that, *within* their ranks, there's a hierarchy in which heterosexual or traditionally masculine boys and men are better for ballet's public image than queer men or men who present or dance in a more feminine way.

While the ballet studio is, for many queer and questioning boys and men, a refuge from an inhospitable larger culture, ballet doesn't necessary embrace those boys with wholehearted enthusiasm. While boys of all sexualities might have a place in ballet, it's made clear that all boys are expected to dance "like men."

"In the ballet world that I grew up in, there was a lot of signaling about, 'Don't dance like a girl. This is how men dance,'" says Avichai Scher, who trained at the School of American Ballet for eight years. "There are a lot of comments from students I remember and from teachers about 'Don't be effeminate.'" Scher, who is white and gay, remembers that he even got that message from his gay and out teachers. "[Former New York City Ballet principal] Jock Soto, who is gay and was out, sometimes would say things like, 'Don't be too feminine; dance like a man.'"

That hierarchy shows up in casting and promotions for professional dancers, too. "There's a built-in sort of patriarchy, I guess you could say," says Jared Allen Brunson, who is straight. "There's this delineation between who are the men and who are the boys, and it seems like the boys, which are the least respected, are going to be the feminine types." Those dancers, Brunson says, are slim and flexible—"flimsy, if you will"—and have "beautiful feet and hyperextension." But to be a principal dancer, you have to be able to partner a woman. You have to be able to lift her, and you have to be able to project heterosexual masculinity as you do. "You have to have great partnering techniques. . . . To be a principal dancer, you're not going to get there just because you're flexible or you can turn."

Scher agrees. "I think in certain roles, people would say, 'He can't be the prince; he'd go out there and people would think he's a woman, [that he] dances like a woman.'"

In other words, men in ballet are rewarded for performing a very specific kind of masculinity, one that codes as straight. And just as both queer and straight boys are given more leeway in ballet than girls are, men who can deliver that performance of straightness are granted allowances. If you have a great partnering technique, you can get away with being less flexible, less gifted at turning, Brunson says, alluding to "your macho men who only know how to partner, who are not great technicians and don't really have great lines."

Boys who dance ballet live in the tension between two truths: they have it very easy and also very hard. Because ballet is synonymous with femininity, the choice to study ballet makes boys a target for misogynistic and homophobic bullying at school and sometimes in their own homes. Because they choose to deviate from acceptably masculine activities like sports and, like Prince George, have the temerity to enjoy that deviation, their masculinity is questioned by a culture that views femininity as inherently inferior to masculinity.

At the same time, within the subculture of ballet, boys are rare and precious, sought after and recruited with scholarships and special programming. They are held to lower standards of talent and behavior—they're even excused from wearing standard-issue ballet gear if it will keep them from quitting. While girls learn early that they are dispensable and disposable, boys—especially those boys and men who best conform to the larger culture's understanding of masculinity—learn that they are untouchable. As Stoner Winslett, founder and artistic director of Richmond Ballet, neatly summarizes it, boys "get the bullying outside [the dance studio], but the girls get the bullying inside."

Sometimes, Avi Scher says, the homophobic and misogynistic bullying he endured came from his male classmates at SAB. "Because they had their own hang-ups about being there . . . they had to assert their masculinity." And as we'll see in Chapter 7, that need to prove and perform aggressive masculinity can have disastrous consequences for the men involved and, more importantly, for the women around them.

CHAPTER 7

PRINCES AND PREDATORS

A ballerina's belief in her power is reflected in her body. She spends her life—often from the age of three or four—navigating the world physically.

LUCY GRAY

Alexandra Waterbury had been dating Chase Finlay for about two years when she found the horrifying cache on his laptop. She was alone in his apartment and, hoping to check her email, logged into his computer, which was synced to his cell phone. A flood of text messages popped up from men whose names she recognized: like Finlay, two of them were principal dancers at New York City Ballet. One was a donor who had given about $12,000 to the company over the course of six years.[1] Another was, like Waterbury, a former student at the School of American Ballet, the school affiliated with City Ballet.

The sexually explicit, misogynistic text messages were gut-churning enough, but then there were the images. There were photos, and videos, too, taken during sex or while the men's sexual partners were undressed. Waterbury saw a video of herself there, as well as photos of other women dancers. She hadn't consented to those videos and photos being taken, and she certainly hadn't consented to their being shared with anyone, let alone with men who might have one day become her coworkers.

In a civil lawsuit she filed against New York City Ballet, the School of American Ballet, the three dancers, and the donor, Waterbury said the company permitted "a fraternity-like atmosphere" to fester, a culture in which male employees came to understand that they could commit sexual harassment, and worse, with impunity.

In the September 2018 suit, Waterbury alleged that this culture came from and was condoned by those at the top, and that the company's leadership had made it clear to the male dancers that as long as they danced well, such behavior would be ignored or even tacitly encouraged.

Finlay had already been suspended once that year, after he showed up for a performance in Paris "apparently hungover . . . raising concerns for the safety of his dance partners." And before that, in an incident mentioned in Waterbury's suit, he had been given a warning for damaging a hotel room in Washington, DC, when the company was on tour. But damage to the hotel's plumbing wasn't the worst of it: in that hotel room, Waterbury alleged, company members threw a party and invited underage girls, whom they "plied with drugs and alcohol." The total bill for the damage to the hotel room was $150,000, which the party hosts were made to pay—but there was no punishment for their other behavior. "Instead, they were simply advised to confine such behavior to New York City, where 'it would be easier to control.'"[2]

Men dancers, especially the principals, who were so valuable to the company, "could degrade, demean, mistreat and abuse, assault, and batter women without consequence," the suit read. That culture, Waterbury alleged, "permeates the Ballet and its dancers and emboldens them to disregard the law and violate the basic rights of women."[3]

The suit certainly made a persuasive case. It reproduced the text logs between Finlay and the other two dancers, Zachary Catazaro and Amar Ramasar, in which Finlay sent photos of Waterbury in a state of undress to the other two and urged them to reciprocate with photos of their own ballerina conquests. "You have any pictures of girls you've fucked?" Finlay wrote to the other men, sending a photo of Waterbury naked. "I'll send you some [of] ballerina girls I've made scream and squirt."[4] They thanked him for what he sent ("OMG I love you") and returned the favor.

With the donor, Jared Longhitano, Finlay texted back and forth in terms that recalled the backstage bourgeois horse-trading of the Paris Opera Ballet two hundred years earlier, and that seemed to support Waterbury's allegation that the company was "a breeding ground for sexual exploitation."

The two men exchanged messages in which they discussed dancers from American Ballet Theatre in disturbingly violent and misogynistic terms. "Just violate them," Longhitano proposed in texts that were included in the suit. "I bet we could tie some of them up and just abuse them like farm animals."

"Or like the sluts they are," Finlay replied.

"I want them to watch me destroy one of their friends," Longhitano wrote, "and they know they're next. I bet we could triple team."

Longhitano resigned from his volunteer role in City Ballet's Young Patrons Circle. In early 2020, his lawyer argued that the suit should be dismissed, saying that while his client's texts had been "obnoxious" "sexist," "uncouth," "immature," and "gruesome," he had not himself done Waterbury any harm.[5] The company, for its part, insists that it bears no responsibility for the men's actions because they took place outside of work hours, off company property.

Finlay resigned from the company shortly before news of Water-bury's lawsuit broke. Catazaro and Ramasar were initially suspended without pay for the rest of the year and then were fired. But they appealed this decision with the help of the American Guild of Musical Artists (AGMA), the union that represents ballet dancers, and the company was compelled to reinstate them. Catazaro chose not to return and now performs as a guest artist with ballet companies in Europe. Ramasar did return to performing with City Ballet, saying he regretted his actions and had undergone counseling. But he soon took a leave of absence to perform in the Broadway revival of *West Side Story*; Waterbury led a well-publicized campaign to get him fired from the show. Waterbury, who was already working as a model and attending college when she filed the suit, has no more aspirations to be a professional ballet dancer—and even if she did, she told me in early 2019, she knew that coming forward with her allegations would have made that impossible.

By fall 2020, all parties except Finlay had been dropped from the suit, and all but one of Waterbury's claims against him (including assault and intentional infliction of emotional distress) had been dismissed, although the judge in the case described his actions as "deplorable." In October 2020, Finlay responded to Waterbury's allegations in court filings, sticking to a familiar script that depicts women who allege sexual misconduct as unstable opportunists: he claimed that she had been emotionally volatile and even abusive during their relationship and accused her of staging a "public relations campaign" around her lawsuit in order to "financially profit and promote herself." Finlay also claimed that she consented to his taking the photos and that though he shared them with his friends "under the influence of alcohol or a controlled substance," he did so not to inflict harm on Waterbury but to "titillate" and "brag" to his friends.[6]

The entire Finlay fiasco is the ugly and utterly predictable outcome of ballet culture, a culture that views women's bodies as malleable and disposable and discourages them from voicing dissent, even as it regards men's ability and willingness to dance as precious gifts to be preserved at any cost. At the same time, outside the ballet world, those men have had their manhood and their heterosexuality questioned at every turn. And, as we'll see in the next chapter, the vast majority of institutional power at the highest levels of ballet—especially the power to choreograph and to run ballet companies—is wielded by men. In ballet, the best women are obedient and the best men can do what they please, so long as they don't quit dancing. It is a near-perfect recipe for the kinds of transgressions that occurred in the Finlay case.

To read the text messages that Finlay and his friends exchanged is to eavesdrop on a group of men who are desperate to prove their own masculinity, to themselves and to each other, and who have learned to use the domination of women's bodies and boundaries to do it. This desire is not unique to ballet, of course: the conversation that unfolded in that text chain has unfolded among football players and *Access Hollywood* guests a thousand times over. But the gendered power dynamics of ballet, and the unique blend of privilege and persecution that boys and men who dance experience, makes it especially poisonous, and entirely predictable.

In 2017, a movement that had sparked in Hollywood began to burn across other industries, exposing all kinds of men, from high-profile chefs to supervisors at Ford assembly plants, as having abused their power over their women coworkers.[7] #MeToo came for the news anchors, the boy band stars, and the stand-up comedians. Slowly—too slowly and far too late—it came for the ballet teachers, choreographers, and artistic directors.

In late 2017, a respected Delaware ballet teacher was arrested and eventually pleaded guilty to illegal sexual contact with a minor; a few days after his arrest was reported, a dancer in Pennsylvania told police that the teacher had molested him over a period of two years beginning when the student was 15. The teacher was convicted of indecent assault, unlawful contact with a minor, corruption of minors, and endangering the welfare of children in Pennsylvania in early 2020. In early 2018, a "revered" California ballet teacher was accused of sexually assaulting at least two of his students, one of them repeatedly. Both girls were under fourteen at the time of the alleged assaults (the California case, in which the former teacher denied the allegations, resulted in a mistrial).[8]

In late 2018, a former Royal Ballet principal dancer pleaded guilty to sexually abusing three students during private lessons between 1997 and 2010. In a separate case, in August 2019 the Royal Ballet's resident choreographer, Liam Scarlett, the "choreographic wonder boy of British ballet," was accused of soliciting nude photos of male student dancers at that company's feeder school and rewarding those who complied with better roles. The company suspended Scarlett when the allegations were made, and Scarlett and the company "parted ways" after a seven-month investigation "found there were no matters to pursue in relation to alleged contact with students of the Royal Ballet School."[9]

In early 2020, a former English National Ballet principal dancer was charged with assaulting three girls, all over the age of sixteen, at a London ballet school. That summer, a prestigious Scottish ballet school closed after more than sixty girls and women alleged that the vice principal had groomed and harassed them; the allegations, which he has denied, spanned at least fourteen years.[10]

And in July 2020, a group of male dancers, all of them Black and all of them alumni of the Ailey School, said that Troy Powell, the former artistic director of the second company Ailey II and a former teacher at the school, had sexually harassed them in their late teens. All said they were over 18 when the alleged harassment occurred, claiming that Powell sent them inappropriate messages and, in some cases, crossed the line into nonconsensual groping. He allegedly promised professional opportunities to those who accepted his advances—and yanked them away from those who refused. "My name was written on the cast list," one of Powell's accusers told CNN. After he rebuffed Powell, though, "it was scratched off." Powell was placed on a leave of absence during an investigation into the allegations, commissioned by the Ailey organization. The investigation found that Powell "engaged in inappropriate communications with adults enrolled in the School," and that "his conduct was inconsistent with the standards expected of Ailey's staff," the organization said in a statement announcing his termination. Powell allegedly abused his position as a gatekeeper by proposing mentorship—a precious thing for Black men in ballet—and dangling the possibility of a job in front of the young men he targeted.[11] As we've seen, many boys who dance are bullied *because* they dance, and it's possible that this makes them uniquely vulnerable targets for predators who find them in what is supposed to be their safe haven: the dance studio.[12]

But the two highest-profile cases of abuse of power in American ballet, by far, both happened at New York City Ballet. At the beginning of 2018, a few months before Alexandra Waterbury discovered explicit images and texts on her boyfriend's computer, his boss, former City Ballet principal dancer turned artistic director and ballet master in chief Peter Martins, had retired from the post he had held for more than thirty years under a cloud of controversy.

Martins, who had taken the reins of the company from George Balanchine, was accused of physically assaulting, sexually harassing, and verbally abusing dancers at City Ballet and, in one case, a student at the School of American Ballet who was twelve at the time of the alleged physical abuse, which occurred during a rehearsal. "He assaulted me onstage in front of the whole cast," the former student, a man, told the *New York Times*.[13]

A former City Ballet dancer said that in 1989, Martins came up behind her in the hallway of the theater, put his hands around her neck and screamed, "You fucking bitch, why can't you listen to what I have to say? I need to break your spirit." Martins, Kelly Cass Boal told the *Washington Post*, "was definitely trying to hurt me. I'd never seen him this crazy before." Wilhelmina Frankfurt, who danced at City Ballet in the 1980s, described the atmosphere at the company at that time as "a deviant alcoholic culture" and alleged in 2017 that Martins exposed himself to her in a dressing room in the middle of a performance, and she alluded to another incident that is "so big I don't think I can talk about it."[14]

And lest this all be written off as a few 1980s excesses, one current City Ballet dancer, speaking anonymously out of fear of retribution, told the *Times* that they had "the visual of him standing over me with a fist clenched two weeks before he promoted me." In 2017, taking a leave of absence from both City Ballet and SAB, where he was also the artistic director, Martins denied all the contemporary allegations of wrongdoing. An internal company investigation, which was not released to the public, found that the allegations could not be corroborated.

Martins resigned from City Ballet and is now a member of the George Balanchine Trust, a role in which he licenses and stages Balanchine ballets for companies around the world. City Ballet still performs the ballets he choreographed there. And even after he retired he reportedly had some control over who was cast in the dances he choreographed; in early 2019, one principal dancer claimed she had been removed from the opening night cast of *The Sleeping Beauty* as retaliation for calling the company "a leaderless state" that allowed Finlay's, Catazaro's, and Ramasar's alleged abuse to "fester."[15]

To those who knew Martins's record, none of these accusations should have come as a surprise. In her controversial 1986 memoir *Dancing on My Grave*, former New York City Ballet principal Gelsey Kirkland dancer describes a fraught romantic relationship with Martins, then her colleague, and his violent relationship with another City Ballet principal dancer, Heather Watts. Kirkland recalls Martins dragging Watts up and down a flight of stairs at a party. Kirkland's colleague, John Clifford, remembers seeing Martins "pick [Watts] up and slam her into a cement wall" in a dressing room.[16]

And in 1992, Martins was arrested for physically abusing his wife, Darci Kistler, then also a City Ballet dancer and Martins's employee. Kistler accused him of hitting and slapping her, leaving her with cuts and bruises on her legs and arms. She dropped the charges a few days later, and an SAB board member called the domestic violence charges "a personal matter" that "had nothing to do with [Martins's] competency or his support in the ballet community."[17] With all this in mind, it is hard to escape the conclusion that Waterbury made in her lawsuit: that the culture of mistreating women came from the top.

"This culture was set up for it to happen," Waterbury told me in early 2020. "The older men set the example and then the younger men are learning from them."

"These guys . . . they grew up going to SAB looking up to people like Peter, and then they end up working under Peter," she said. "And Peter this entire time is setting the example of what not only a straight male successful dancer looks like, but also somebody who ends up coming into a lot of power and more money . . . setting the example for these boys, their entire lives. And so, they follow in his footsteps."

Describing the dance world as "cyclical" and "insular," Waterbury noted that, just as Martins progressed from dancing to choreographing to running the company—imitating Balanchine's mercurial management style and habit of dating his employees as he did so—any of the three men in that text chain could have been handpicked by Martins to take over when he retired. (Christine Cox, the cofounder and artistic director of BalletX, calls this hiring model—"where really great dancers are offered directorship, roles as directors, so we're plucking people who are not really sure they know how to run multimillion-dollar organizations"—both "odd" and "archaic.")

"Had I not come forward," Waterbury told me, "maybe one of them would have taken over the company one day, and then they would have set that same example for everybody that was coming after them."

"It's like Balanchine is like a god," she told the *Guardian* in a 2018 interview. "It's like a cult." Boal—the dancer Martins allegedly attacked from behind—told the paper she had been trying to raise the alarm about Martins for years. But it wasn't until the #MeToo movement expanded the public's understanding of what abuse of power by powerful men looks like, and how institutional complicity can crush the women who allege wrongdoing, that her stories finally found a receptive audience. "Someone finally asked," she said, "and someone cared."[18]

These cases, of course, are only the ones that made the news, the ones in which reports were made and charges pressed. As it is everywhere, harassment—sexual and otherwise—is underreported in ballet, in part because it can be so hard to establish a clear line between a necessary physical adjustment of a student or employee and an inappropriate touch, between a demanding teacher and an emotionally or verbally abusive one. "The lines are very blurred when it comes to sexual harassment and what's appropriate and what's not appropriate," says Washington Ballet corps de ballet member Nardia Boodoo.

That blurriness serves predators and the institutions that would prefer not to hold them accountable, and it makes it extremely difficult for their victims to know when something is wrong and to convince people to take their concerns seriously.

As we've already seen, ballet students begin learning the importance of following directions, and following them immediately and without question, at an early age. For girls in particular, the hidden curriculum teaches that success in ballet requires obedience to adults with authority, even when they feel emotional discomfort or physical pain. Several dancers and former dancers told stories about incidents that occurred during their training that struck them as strange or made them uncomfortable at the time, and that they now realize were unacceptable transgressions. At the time, they felt a silent pressure to accept them.

"A lot of stuff that I thought was weird but normal at the time turned out to be kind of creepy," says Grace Segers, who trained seriously at a suburban New York ballet academy as a teenager before being sidelined by illness and mental health issues. "Weird but normal" sounds like a contradiction, but it is in fact a perfect way to capture the sense that even if something a teacher says or does feels to a student like it crossed a line, objecting aloud won't make any sense to the people around them. "As in, 'That made me uncomfortable,'" says Segers, who is now twenty-five, "'but it's probably just how things are done.'" It is easy to doubt your own instincts when no one else seems to share your discomfort, and it is hard to speak up when you are young and have spent years practicing complying with authority figures.

One "weird but normal" incident that stands out in Segers's memory occurred when she was cast as a maid in the party scene in her school's annual production of *The Nutcracker*. As is common in school productions, the parents in the party scene, who do very little actual dancing, were played by actual parents of ballet students, "and at one point they had the maids do a little dance for the dads [onstage]. . . . It was like a cheeky, French maid kind of dance." She was fourteen, and the men in question were her classmates' fathers.

"I felt uncomfortable at the time, but I was like, 'Okay, whatever,'" Segers says. "And now, looking back, that was really weird and someone should have said something." Did anyone? I asked her. "No, not that I know of." As far as fourteen-year-old Grace knew, her class-mates thought it was fine and their parents thought it was acceptable. And her teachers said it was mandatory. She did what ballet students are taught to do: she obeyed their instructions and didn't question their authority. It was weird but normal.

Ja'Malik is a former dancer who now runs Ballet Boy Productions in New York City; he is fifteen years older than Segers and danced professionally with several companies, including Ballet Hispánico and BalletX. Ja'Malik, who goes by his first name only, says that he can't remember seeing sexual harassment in the studio or experiencing it himself, but that ballet's "blurred lines" permit other forms of mistreat-ment, too. "I have seen emotional cruelty in abundance," he says. "And it happens way more frequently than people want to talk about. That's actually the bigger part. The sexual part, I didn't see as much, but the emotional abuse is way bigger. And I think [it's] just as detrimental to the person."

Because ballet demands so much of a young person's time, such a narrowing of their world, it can be hard for them to identify and resist abuses of power from teachers and then from bosses, he says. "We're young when we get in these ballet companies. I think I was sixteen when I joined Cleveland Ballet. . . . We're still teenagers joining these companies, and we're professional dancers. And the mental and verbal abuse is just crazy. And at that age, you don't really understand it, so you can't fight against it." For a child to be yanked around onstage by the artistic director is clearly over the line. But to be yelled at in front of your colleagues in rehearsal as a young adult? That likely falls into the "weird but normal" category.

Ja'Malik echoes Segers's sentiment that, even as students, dancers are trained to tolerate behavior from authority figures that is borderline or even over the line. They practice accepting it, albeit less consciously than they practice their pliés and pirouettes.

"You just kind of accept it, and then the technique is kind of built where you just listen and you take in; you don't really talk that much," he says. And if you do talk, there are real risks, just as there are in other workplaces. "If you are vocal about it," he says, "then you have a very hard time in your profession."

Sometimes the transgressions are far more obvious but far less public, and while they never make the news, they filter through the whisper network of the insular professional ballet world. "I have very close friends who were sexually assaulted by their teachers," Boodoo tells me. In fact, these stories never make the news *because* the ballet world is so insular: because almost everyone knows almost everyone, there's a strong disincentive against coming forward about even obvious abuses of power. "Nothing ever happened" to those teachers, Boodoo says, because their victims "were so scared, and they felt like it would affect their dance career if they spoke up about it."

"Stuff like this has been going on, as we know in the ballet world, for years," Ja'Malik says. "For *years*." But as Boal told the *Guardian*, it's still too risky for many women to come forward, in part because even after they retire from dancing, many ballerinas stay in the insular ballet world as teachers. Telling the truth would put their new careers at risk.[19]

While many of the dancers I spoke to were not surprised by Waterbury's allegations about City Ballet—many had heard stories and rumors about the culture she described—they were surprised at the response from their own institutions. One might imagine that City Ballet's peer institutions would leap into action to ensure that their own dancers were being treated lawfully and respectfully by their colleagues and that they knew their rights at work, if only to protect their own reputations. That does not seem to have been the case.

"Nothing was said to us," says Miami City Ballet principal soloist Lauren Fadeley Veyette, at least not right away. Two of the men in Finlay's text conversations had been involved with the company shortly before the lawsuit: Amar Ramasar had coached MCB dancers to prepare them to perform works that had originated at City Ballet, and Finlay himself had performed with the company as a guest artist. "I was a little shocked that we were never spoken to, like, 'I know you guys have all seen these allegations, [and] if you have seen anything, ever, if you have ever been made to feel uncomfortable by these people, please let us know,'" Fadeley Veyette says. Instead, the dancers got a talking-to about how to conduct themselves appropriately on social media.

In 2019, Fadeley Veyette says, there was a mandatory meeting about sexual harassment for the first time since she joined the company in 2016. "It was very serious and it was mandatory," she says, "and I do believe that they are trying to take action to rectify things."

One of Fadeley Veyette's colleagues, corps de ballet dancer Eric Trope, says a member of the company's HR department and a harassment attorney led the meeting, which he calls "a good first step . . . to acknowledge [and] not to ignore what was going on in the ballet world, and to acknowledge that it was something that was happening." But, Trope says, the one-hour meeting wasn't specifically about sexual harassment, and the lawyer focused on how to avoid making jokes "that could be taken the wrong way."

"I think she understands we're all friends . . . but she made it very clear where that line is, how to avoid offending someone or doing something of that nature," Trope says. "I thought that was a good response from the company." Considering that some dancers I interviewed said their company did not mention or even allude to the sexual harassment scandal roiling one of the premier institutions in their industry, perhaps this is a relatively good response. But it hardly displays an accurate understanding of sexual harassment, which is not a matter of jokes gone awry but of abuse of power. And it is certainly not a full-throated statement that sexual harassment and other abuses of power will not be tolerated.

Still, it was more than some companies did. One member of the Washington Ballet says that there was no mention of sexual harassment at the time. "There was an email sent about the Washington Ballet being a place that doesn't tolerate those types of behaviors, but that was at the top of the season, so it wasn't following that situation at all," they say. The company doesn't have an HR department. If a dancer were to be harassed or otherwise mistreated by a colleague, a member of the artistic staff, or a visiting choreographer, it's "unclear where we would go" within the company. "I mean, we don't ever have conversations like this."

Of course, that dancer acknowledged, they could go to the union. The dancers of the Washington Ballet, like those in many major ballet companies (though, notably, not in Miami City Ballet), are represented by the American Guild of Musical Artists (AGMA), and, absent a company employee to report to, they can go to their union rep.

But in the case of New York City Ballet, the union prioritized the needs and rights not of alleged sexual harassment victims but of the men alleged to have committed the harassment. When Ramasar and Catazaro were fired, they appealed through AGMA, and through an arbitration process, the company was ordered to offer them their jobs back.

Less than two weeks after the two men had been dismissed, their once and future colleagues gathered on the stage at Lincoln Center and, before a packed house at the opening of the fall season, did something unusual: they talked. Teresa Reichlen, a principal dancer, took the microphone and, surrounded by dozens of City Ballet dancers, read a statement she cowrote with fellow principal Adrian Danchig-Waring.

"We will not put art before common decency or allow talent to sway our moral compass," Reichlen said, promising that "we the dancers" would adhere to "the high moral standards that were instilled in us when we decided to become professional dancers."[20]

"Each of us standing here tonight," she said, "is inspired by the values essential to our art form: dignity, integrity, and honor."[21] Not even seven months later, Catazaro and Ramasar were offered their jobs back.

The company had defended the dismissals, saying that although the texts had allegedly been "personal," and were sent "off-hours and off-site," the men had violated the company's "norms of conduct."[22] But the independent arbitrator found that in firing the two men, City Ballet had violated the terms of their employment contracts.

"This was a complicated situation," the union said in the statement. "We pursued this case because it's important to us that your employer is prevented from taking extreme and potentially career-ending action based on non-criminal activity in your private life."[23]

In a statement responding to the arbitrator's decision, Catazaro said he was "grateful and relieved that the arbitrator has found the New York City Ballet's abrupt termination of my contract to be wrongful and unjust." Ramasar, announcing his intention to return to City Ballet after a brief stint in mandatory counseling, said, "As I move forward, learning, and evolving, I am eager to once again dance amongst the colleagues I respect, doing the ballets I have held close to my heart for the past 18 years."[24]

The reaction inside City Ballet was mixed, with several women dancers, who understandably did not want their names used in the press, expressing disappointment and dismay that, in their view, the union had advocated for the two men's rights over the rights of dozens of their women colleagues.[25] Though the company's response to Waterbury's suit had been to wash its hands of responsibility by emphasizing that whatever the men allegedly did, they did outside of work hours and away from company property, the institution had at least listened to the concerns of the women who said they would be uncomfortable continuing to work with Catazaro and Ramasar.

Those who could sign their names to their sentiments were far more forthcoming. "In deciding to advocate for these two dancers, AGMA has not only sided with alleged offenders in multiple serious cases of degradation and sexual harassment, but has also sent a clear message to the whole dance community that the redemptive narrative of these male dancers is more important than the trust and safety of their female colleagues," wrote dancer and choreographer Kosta Karakashyan in an op-ed in *Dance Magazine*.

"Even if the women they were texting about were not fellow company members"—and one of them, Waterbury alleges, was and still is—"it is hard to imagine their female partners feeling safe dancing with them, knowing what they've been accused of. The union has given these male dancers a seemingly free pass to privately demean and harass women."[26]

"We asked ourselves these same hard questions before taking action," the associate executive director of AGMA responded in a statement.

"As a union, we are legally obligated to represent our members when their contractual rights have been violated."[27]

Given what we know about the relative value of boys and girls, of men and women, in ballet, it might come as a surprise that in this case, the ballet company deemed women's rights in the workplace a priority. Considering it was under intense public scrutiny and already reeling from the controversial departure of its longtime leader, its reaction makes sense. So, too, does the union's focus on the men's right to remain employed in the absence of a contractually valid reason to fire them.

But given the intimacy of the workplace to which those men were being restored and the "blurred lines" that abound in ballet, there is simply no way to resolve the conflict in a way that respects the rights of every party. There is no moving the men to a different department where they won't come into frequent contact with the women who are uncomfortable working with them. In a company that is smaller than City Ballet, which has almost one hundred dancers, there would be almost no way to avoid casting one of those women with one of those men, meaning they would spend hours in rehearsal together and be expected to perform perfectly on the same stage.

In short, there is little recourse for women who are harassed by their colleagues in a ballet company. Even if women are able to cut through the disorienting fog of "weird but normal" and are willing to risk their careers by making allegations of sexual harassment or other abuses of power, they come up against this roadblock: the system, as AGMA and the women of City Ballet discovered, is ill equipped to handle an extremely common problem.

In other ways, unionization has been essential to dancers. With the exception of Miami City Ballet, all ballet companies in the US with annual budgets over $10 million are unionized and, according to Griff Braun, a former ballet dancer and the director of organizing and outreach at AGMA, most of the companies with budgets between $5 million and $10 million are, too.

Smaller and regional civic companies tend not to be unionized, though many adhere to the general contours of an AGMA contract in order to attract the best dancers. ("They stick to them until they don't," Braun says, "and that's really the major difference. . . . There may be comprehensive terms and conditions for the workplace, but the employer doesn't necessarily have to follow them").

A ballet union contract has plenty of familiar features, like minimum weekly pay, benefits, and retirement contributions. With or without those protections, dancers are spectacularly underpaid. A full-time company member in Birmingham, Alabama, reported in 2018 that they made $16,000 a year. In New York, one full-time corps de ballet member with ten years of company experience reported making $21,350. Another New York company member, this one with twenty years of experience, was making $60,000. One full-time dancer in California with twelve years under their belt made $18,000, and another, with eight years, made $7,000.[28]

The low wages and high competition for jobs cannot be separated from the abuses of power that dancers often experience, and the echoes of the abonnés of the 1830s are loud and clear nearly two hundred years later. The precarity of dancers' lives makes them targets for those outside the dance world, too: when convicted sex offender Jeffrey Epstein went prowling for young victims, he used the New York City dance scene as his hunting grounds. In September 2019, a woman alleged that when she was seventeen, she was lured to Epstein's Manhattan home after a fellow dancer approached her after ballet class and offered her a position as Epstein's personal trainer.[29]

The first time they met, the woman says, "Mr. Epstein quizzed her on her dance aspirations, promised to buy her new pointe shoes and asked her to take part in several sexually charged stretching activities." A few visits later, he asked her to give him a massage, "during which he assaulted her with a sex toy and masturbated, the complaint said. He implied [her] dance career would be over if she did not go along."[30] Then he urged her to recruit more dancers for him.

It was an ingenious, evil form of opportunism: find an insular industry that is full of girls who are young, obedient, and eager to succeed— and exploit their precarity.

"Unless you are contracted with a major company in New York City," wrote *Pointe* magazine editor Amy Brandt the day the allegations against Epstein were reported, "it can be very difficult to make a living, much less pay for daily class and pointe shoes. . . . I was a freelance dancer in New York for ten years and I was frequently broke. Most of my gigs came through word of mouth. If someone had approached me with a lucrative side job, *especially* if that person was a fellow dancer, I would have at least looked into it."[31]

Dancers who are lucky enough to have stable employment need unions to ensure that their artistic efforts are repaid with more than poverty wages, especially when doing their jobs well requires so much more work and so much more time than is seen in the dance studio and onstage. By one estimate, 2018, the median salary for a ballet dancer in the US, combining full-time and part-time dancers at union and nonunion companies, was $30,000. In a 2020 Department of Labor analysis, dancer—of all kinds, not only ballet—was ranked as the most physically demanding job, above firefighter, roofer, professional athlete, and oil rig operator (choreographer was ranked ninth, just above reinforcing iron and rebar worker). The mean annual wage was listed as $43,056.[32]

There are some elements of a ballet union contract that are unique to dancing. For example, a contract might specify what kinds of floors dancers can be required to rehearse and perform on, forcing companies to provide sprung floors or the not-too-sticky, not-too-slick dance mat known as marley. Some contracts lay out a range of acceptable temperatures for rehearsal studios and theaters. Others cap the number of shows a dancer can be required to dance each week. There are provisions about the maximum hours of rehearsal and maximum contiguous hours, and these limits vary during performance weeks. Dancers are paid overtime if rehearsals run over.

While the number of hours each company agrees to vary, "those kinds of rules are common across all the ballet company contracts," Braun says. "For the protection of their bodies and their minds, there need to be some limitations around that." Similarly, each contract guarantees dancers a certain number of weeks of paid work per year. The most guaranteed weeks of work any US ballet company offers is forty-four, at Houston Ballet; most guarantee forty weeks or less.

Braun notes, rightly, that these pauses in rehearsal and performance are necessary. "A ballet dancer would not want to be working fifty or fifty-two weeks a year—it would kill them," he says. "But at the same time, it would also be better if they were paid fifty-two weeks a year." They're not: during "layoffs," dancers go without pay unless their company has a stipend, funded by deductions from their regular paychecks, to help them bridge the gap. Many dancers file for unemployment benefits with the state to get them through their unpaid leave, during which they are required to stay in decent dancing shape; it is a break, but it is hardly a total vacation. While some contracts provide a "health maintenance" stipend that can be used to cover a gym membership or Pilates, gyrotonics, or similar classes, companies don't generally subsidize ballet classes their dancers might take during a layoff (though some are contractually required to provide free classes for the last week or the last two weeks of a layoff so that dancers can come back to work in acceptable shape).

Fewer weeks of paid rehearsal time means that dancers find themselves going onstage with less preparation than they might like, with no change in expectations for the quality of their performance. In other words, barely rehearsing is no excuse for a subpar performance. "You're always underrehearsed," former American Ballet Theatre soloist Sascha Radetsky told me. "You kinda go out there and that's part of the magic, the spontaneity."

But that's not how it should be, Braun says. "Artists should feel prepared to go onstage. When you get to a certain point in your career, there's a little bit of pride in the ability to [have] almost no rehearsal and go out there and still do a decent show." Dancers are responsible for ensuring that they are performance-ready, and with so many of them on one-year contracts, the stakes of a bad performance are high.

"I know from personal experience," says Braun, who danced with American Ballet Theatre, Complexions Contemporary Dance, and several other companies, "that companies rely on their dancers to be able to get things together in a short amount of time, and often largely on their own, to just make things happen at the last second and create a sort of miracle on opening night. Dancers do it, but they shouldn't have to."

Even during their limited weeks of paid work, dancers do an enormous amount of work to keep their bodies in dancing shape, and that all happens outside of the rehearsal time that's covered by their contracts. Daily company class, which is about ninety minutes long, isn't included in your daily hours. It's technically voluntary, but as Braun says, "voluntary is with some quotes"—that is, it's not contractually part of the workday, but few dancers would dare skip showing their face in company class.

Then there's all the nondancing work that is unpaid but eats up a dancer's time and energy all the same. "The work the dancers are doing in the studio is a fraction—I mean, it's a considerable fraction, but [it's] a fraction of the work they do to be able to do their job," Braun says. "There's all the preparation before class and the physical therapy and the cross-training that everyone does now." For women, there's more work on top of that. "I mean, the amount of hours that the women spend prepping pointe shoes is unbelievable."

There's another shift dancers are compelled to work for which they may or may not be compensated: the social media shift. Even when dancers are not at work, they are on the Instagram clock, under pressure to create content that will boost their personal brands and thereby give them a chance to attract endorsement deals and other work to supplement their meager salaries. There is no guarantee these efforts will pay off, but that doesn't stop dancers from filling their Instagram feeds with ballet and ballet-adjacent content in the attempt. There is no layoff from the Instagram hustle; indeed, if dancers do go on vacation, they keep posting photos of themselves holding arabesques on mountaintops and doing pointe work on boats. *Here I am doing a grand jeté in a national park, without warming up, attempted a dozen times before we got the shot right.* The work never stops, not even when work actually stops: when the pandemic sent hundreds of dancers home from work, many of them without pay and no sense of when they'd be back in the studio or onstage, the hustle continued, and my Instagram feed was full of dancers doing barre in their kitchens and battements on their balconies.

Unions also offer protections for early-career dancers, who are cheaper to hire and put onstage than more senior ones. Some contracts regulate how companies can employ and cast corps de ballet members and apprentices, who are no longer students but are not full company members, either, and who usually dance corps de ballet roles. Apprentices are paid very little; some are paid nothing at all, and in some companies they in fact pay for their positions.

While Braun notes that there is "some real variation" in how unionized companies are allowed to use apprentices, the most important regulations are the ones that limit how long apprenticeships can last. For smaller companies, apprenticeships can last two years; for larger ones, it's just one year.

"Our experience has been that where there aren't some parameters," Braun says, "companies will keep people as apprentices for years, and dancers will agree to it sometimes." Of course they will; they have worked so hard and beat such tough odds to make it even to the bottom rung of the professional ballet ladder. Of course they feel enormous pressure to do whatever it takes, to take whatever shabby deal they're offered, in order to hang on to that ladder. These union-imposed time limits, Braun says, ensure that they don't get stuck on that bottom rung, that companies must either promote them to full members of the company or release them to audition for other companies.

There are restrictions on how apprentices can be cast, too, which are designed to protect more senior dancers and ensure that they are given the performance opportunities they have earned. Some companies are only allowed to cast apprentices in corps de ballet roles; if they want to cast them in soloist roles, they have to promote them and pay them accordingly. And if they want to borrow dancers from their affiliated schools, as is often the case for ballets with large casts and long runs, like *The Nutcracker*, they have to pay those students as they'd pay an AGMA dancer. (The protections vary by company, Braun says, but they're all meant to make sure that "the dancers onstage are being paid appropriately, and that the audience is seeing a company of professional dancers.")

Understandably, not all early-career dancers appreciate these restrictions. Ballet careers are short, and many dancers want to perform as much and as prominently as they can while they still can. Isabella Corridon, nineteen, is a first-year member of Ballet West II, Ballet West's second company, based in Salt Lake City. Second companies, which are generally smaller than main companies, provide early-career dancers with their first paid dance jobs—though the pay is essentially an honorarium; in 2018, a second company member in Washington, DC, reported an annual salary of $12,000 and another in Philadelphia reported one of $8,000.[33]

Ballet West is unionized, but as a second company member, Corridon does not belong to the union. She is, however, affected by union rules: the main company is only allowed to supplement its casting with a certain number of second company members, which means Corridon doesn't get to perform as often as she'd like. And as a second company member, she can only dance certain roles.

"We can only perform snow, flowers, we can be a party parent and do the Arabian corps" in *The Nutcracker*, Corridon offers as examples. She concedes that the rules are in place to safeguard the meatier and more prestigious roles for first company members, "but it also protects us because they could be making us do so much more but we wouldn't be paid enough to do that." Still, when she looks up the ladder—from second company member to first company apprentice to corps de ballet and so on—she sees a lot of union rules blocking her from dancing the roles she dreams of.

"It frustrates me because I feel I have already gone through my training, so at this point I feel like I want to dance," she says, but "even if I get into the corps for three years, at Ballet West [the progression is] apprentice I, apprentice II, then artist, then corps. To not be able to dance all the roles I would like to for three years is so frustrating."

Given the choice, Corridon says, she'd join a company without a union over a company with one.

Braun understands her frustration. Ballet careers are short and tenuous, and early-career dancers want to dance while they can. But of course, so do more established dancers, and the union regulations make it harder for companies to push them offstage in favor of their younger and cheaper colleagues. If Corridon is fortunate enough to have a full career—to progress out of the second company and up the ranks of a main company—she might one day find herself grateful for those very same regulations.

Still, as the Finlay case demonstrates, there are some problems in the ballet world that unions cannot, or have not yet figured out how to, solve. Unions are necessary to repair a great deal of ballet's brokenness, but they are not sufficient—especially because, as we have seen, ballet's skewed and easily abused power dynamics begin long before a dancer signs her first employment contract.

Unions alone cannot fix a subculture that, like the larger culture in which it is nested, values the careers and livelihoods of one or two men over the safety and dignity of dozens of women. They cannot create more dance jobs or force governments to prioritize arts funding so that dancers are not constantly in desperate competition and under pressure to accept poor pay, overwork, and other exploitations and abuses simply so they can stay employed in their field.

They cannot undo decades of men in leadership positions using their workforces as a dating pool or repair a ballet training culture in which boys are taught that they are irreplaceable and girls are expendable. They certainly cannot sharpen ballet's blurred lines and erect clear boundaries between rigorous coaching and abuse, or teach young students that what feels weird is not normal. That is a job for the field's institutional and artistic leaders—the teachers, company directors, and choreographers—and unfortunately, as we'll see in the next chapter, far too many of those leaders are men.

CHAPTER 8

A NEW STORY

There is the famous quote from Balanchine: "Ballet is Woman." Well, it's a woman made by a man.

Pam Tanowitz

Claudia Schreier choreographed her first dance, a solo for her summer camp talent show, when she was twelve years old. In her sophomore year of high school, she did it again, choreographing a pas de deux for herself and her best friend, Kaitlyn, which they danced as the school orchestra played music from *Swan Lake*. The year after that she made a solo and performed it with the accompaniment of the school jazz band. By college, she was making ballets not just for herself and her best friends but for larger groups of dancers, and they consisted of a mix of classical and contemporary movement that reflected her own training.

Schreier, who grew up in Stamford, Connecticut, with a Jamaican mother and a white Jewish father, remembers feeling a compulsion to move to music when she was a child.

"My parents will tell stories of when we were growing up, it'd be time to sit down for dinner and I would be spinning in the kitchen," she says. "I just was too restless to sit down. I'd be doing pirouettes by the dinner table."

It's a familiar story among dancers, but Schreier didn't only want to move. "For me, it was beyond just the dancing," she says. "It was the idea of wanting to create movement that felt like something outside of myself. That's really what I remember the most, this compulsion to make movement and not just move."

Schreier, thirty-four, is now a full-time choreographer, and has made ballets for Miami City Ballet, Dance Theatre of Harlem, the Joffrey Ballet, Atlanta Ballet, and American Ballet Theatre's second company. Her path into ballet choreography, and her presence in it, are both unusual.

For one thing, Schreier was never a professional dancer. As a teenager, she was prone to injuries: bone spurs that led to severe tendinitis in both ankles, problems with the ligaments in her shoulders, and repeated strains in her hip adductors. "PT was just a regular thing for me growing up," she says, "and I think it was in large part due to the fact that I was trying to get my body to do things it was never meant to do." Her knees didn't straighten all the way, and she wanted hyperextended knees, the kind with a slight curve at the back of the leg to emphasize the opposite curve of the pointed foot.

"I was surrounded by long-legged ladies with hyperextended legs, high arches, flexible backs, arms on the right way," she says, and she tried all kinds of tricks to make her body more like theirs. "I tried to bend my knees backwards, to make them hyperextended. And so I would put my knees through things that they should never be put through to try to elongate the lines. . . . I put myself through hell."

By the time she was preparing to graduate from high school, it had become clear, she says, that she wasn't meant to be a classical ballet dancer. Injuries aside, she'd been told over and over again that her body was wrong for ballet. Her feet didn't point enough; her legs didn't straighten enough; she had a swayback and, by ballet standards, a prominent backside. "It was always a point of reference or conversation" with her teachers, she remembers. "Always."

But she loved classical ballet, even if it didn't love her back. "I couldn't imagine doing anything else." When a teacher encouraged her to audition for the contemporary dance program at Juilliard, she was insulted. In hindsight, she concedes, she had no reason to be—it was an excellent program and she had very little contemporary training. "That's something I would gladly take now and was not even remotely interested in at the time," she says, "because to me it represented a failure on my part . . . a failure to achieve the look of the idealized ballet dancer."

At the age of eighteen, Schreier stepped off the path that would have been mostly likely to lead to a career as a dancer: instead of enrolling in a college dance program or auditioning for full-time preprofessional ballet schools like Joffrey Ballet School, she enrolled at Harvard, where she could only minor in dance. She majored in sociology.

There isn't much of a clear or formalized path to becoming a ballet choreographer, but to the extent that one exists, this is not it. Most ballet choreographers were once professional ballet dancers, usually full-time at a company, and sometimes that company is the first place where they are paid to make dances. After college, Schreier did go to work for a dance company, but in the office, not the studio. For seven years she worked in the marketing department at Alvin Ailey American Dance Theater, juggling a full-time arts administration job with what was, at the beginning at least, a side hustle in choreography.

Every spare second was devoted to choreographing and rehearsing a small company of dancers for performances of her work. "I would work during the day at my desk and then I would throw on my garbage pants and go downstairs to the studio and set [a] ballet until nine, ten o'clock at night, whatever it was," she remembers. In her off-hours, she could use Ailey's studio spaces at a discount, so she spent all of her paid vacation days in the same building where she'd usually go to work.

"I took my two weeks of rehearsal vacation to stay in the building," she says. "I went back into my office building every day, putting on my other hat. [I'd go] past my coworkers and then take a left and go to the studio." It was exhausting and unsustainable. "I was wearing myself out. I was waking up way too early, going home way too late. Every single lunch break, every free minute, every moment I had I was trying to split the difference."

Choreographing, like all other creative pursuits, requires time and space. Rehearsing dances requires a very specific kind of space, and staging them requires another; neither of those spaces is free or even inexpensive, especially not in New York or other major cities. And of course, while choreography can be done alone, you will eventually require dancers, who need to be paid for their time and labor. Choreographing, like all creative pursuits, can start to look less like a career path and more like a luxury for those who have alternative sources of income or wealth.

After almost a decade of splitting the difference, well after her side hustle had become its own nearly full-time gig, Schreier received a choreography fellowship that allowed her to quit her office job and focus all of her energy on making dances. She had the time and the space she needed, as well as access to dancers, and didn't have to maintain a full-time job in order to subsidize her art. At last, choreographing was no longer in the seams of her life but in the center of it.

Schreier is unusual not only because of her path from aspiring ballet choreographer to full-time dance maker. She's also a woman of color in a line of work that has traditionally been inhospitable to women and to people of color. In the 2018–2019 season, 81 percent of the works performed by American ballet company companies were choreographed by men. Of the world premieres that were performed that same season, 65 percent were choreographed by men. New York City Ballet, one of the nation's oldest ballet companies, has more than four hundred works in its repertory; only ten were choreographed or co-choreographed by Black artists.[1]

In 2020, among companies that had installed resident choreographers—"one of the most secure opportunities for the otherwise freelance choreographer" because it provides "a steady salary, the possibility of benefits, a group of dancers with whom to work-shop, time, access to set, costume, lighting designers and a regular audience"—76 percent of companies worldwide had a man in the posi-tion.[2] In early 2020, Schreier was appointed to a three-year term as the resident choreographer for Atlanta Ballet.

The question of why there are so few women making dances for bal-let companies is not a new one. In 2005, dance historian Lynn Garafola noted the dearth of women in the current ranks of ballet choreogra-phers and also argued that the apparently slim contributions women have made over time were a matter not of fact but of historiography. It was not that women did not choreograph, she argued, but that they were barred from choreographing for the most prestigious ballet com-panies and theaters. And because of ballet's fixation on the elite, those dances—and the women who made them—have largely been written out of ballet's history.

"Viewing the ballet past as a succession of individuals of genius," she wrote, "consigns most of ballet history to the dustbin. Yet it is here, in the now invisible crannies of the popular, the forgotten, and the second-rate, in the everyday chronicle of the ballet past as opposed to the se-lective chronicle of its most privileged institutions, that women made dances." Garafola recounts finding traces of these women—Louise Vi-rard, Adelina Gedda, Rita Papurello—almost by accident, calling them "turn-of-the-century ghosts . . . invisible to history although they had worked in the theater for years."[3]

In other cases, the dances women made have remained on record, but the women have not been credited for their contributions. Women have always choreographed, Garafola wrote, but theirs were rarely the names in the programs—or, because the programs were not printed for the most revered theaters in town, they were never saved and placed in an archive to be fished out and dusted off by dance historians who were writing the story of ballet.

Women, Garafola wrote, "were seldom entrusted with entire pro-ductions: indeed, because their choreography usually took the form of isolated dances within a larger work (dances, moreover, that they themselves often performed), their contribution rarely was acknowledged."[4] Instead, the story of ballet has been written as one in which women dance and men make dances. The dancers die, but the dances are written down, passed down in notation and in dancers' bodies from one generation to the next, almost always with a man's name attached to them. Men create ballets on women, but the women fade away. The ballets make the men immortal.

The disappearance of women's choreographic contributions from the historical record means that women who aspire to make ballets don't look like the "succession of individuals of genius" that come to mind when the ballet world collectively pictures a choreographer. That succession—Jules Perrot, Jean-Georges Noverre, Marius Petipa, Sergei Diaghilev, Kenneth MacMillan, Frederick Ashton, George Balanchine, and Jerome Robbins—is a centuries-long line of white men, with brief appearances by white women like Bronislava Nijinska and Agnes de Mille. Whether or not the mental image is historically accurate, this is what the ballet world thinks a choreographer looks like.

This bias adds yet another obstacle to the already hard road for aspiring women choreographers, even those who enjoy advantages Schreier did not. Even for white women who belong, or have belonged, to ballet companies, there are structural barriers to entry. The first will be unsurprising by now, given all we've learned about how girls and women are valued and trained in ballet. Choreography requires creativity; ballet teaches girls the importance of conformity. Choreographing requires finding and using your voice; ballet rewards girls and women for silence. Choreography is a form of leadership; ballet punishes girls and women who aren't obedient. From their earliest days, girls in ballet learn that what is valuable about them is not their mind or their creative spirit but their body and their ability to follow instructions.

Boys, as we've seen, are encouraged—or at least permitted—to think and speak for themselves. Rebellion is tolerated and individuality is cultivated. Boys are the center of attention and sometimes the center of the formation, dancing onstage surrounded by girls because they're the only boy in their class. This is lonely, and boys suffer in their own ways; they also become accustomed to the ideas of nonconformity and leadership. These are not skills so much as they are part of a mindset, and equipped with this mindset, boys who grow up in ballet have clear head start over their female peers.

Then there's the matter of time. As Griff Braun noted in the previous chapter, professional ballet dancers have very little spare time on their hands once they've taken company class, rehearsed for upcoming performances, finished costume fittings, and gone to physical therapy and cross-training. And the women have even less time than the men, not just because preparing their pointe shoes and doing their hair and makeup for performances eats up time that men don't have to spend. It's also because women in many companies spend more time onstage, and therefore more time in rehearsal, than men do.

"You put on a ballet like [Balanchine's] *Walpurgisnacht Ballet* and there's one guy and, like, twenty women," New York City Ballet principal dancer and choreographer Ashley Bouder told me in 2017 (in fact, the ballet requires twenty-four women). "Even if there are guys who are on every night, there are women who are on in three ballets every night. Which means more rehearsal time, too, during the day. Which means less creative time."[5]

When she was a new company member dancing in the corps, Bouder remembered, "I was onstage every night and then I had to go home and sew my pointe shoes." Because Bouder is white, her pointe shoes match her skin tone—for dancers of color who want to wear shoes that match their legs, there are limited retail options, and until very recently there were almost none. Dancers whose companies permitted them to wear matching shoes had to "pancake" them: paint them the correct color using foundation or special pointe shoe paint. It's an extra cost, in both time and money, that white dancers don't pay. "You're just preoccupied," Bouder said of life at the bottom rung of a company, which is where most dancers spend their careers.[6]

"A lot of choreographers . . . come out of the corps or the soloist position with so much [choreographic] talent that they don't really make it" to the principal rank, Bouder said in a 2019 interview, "because their focus is elsewhere. And as a corps member a female ballerina spends hours sewing pointe shoes, in their pointe classes—more classes than the men when they're training—and putting on stage makeup. It takes so long to put your hair up in that perfect bun and pin on the tiara and put the false eyelashes on. And I know some men that take quite a long time with their makeup, but for the most part you can dash on some eyeliner and some pancake and you're good to go."[7] Creativity requires time, and in ballet, men have more of that than women do.

Next, there is the question of opportunity. New choreographers must be tapped, nurtured, encouraged, and then employed. Choreography is a skill that must be honed; simply having been a dancer does not make one a dance maker. But women dancers who do become choreographers need to first imagine themselves in that role—something that's harder to do if you've spent your ballet career dancing works by men—and they need to have that vision validated by the artistic director and other gatekeepers around them. They need to be given the opportunity to hone their skill, the space and time to practice and fail and improve, and then they need to be given the chance to stage their work with a company.

And just as it can be hard for women to imagine themselves "at the front of the room"—where choreographers, teachers, and artistic directors stand, wielding power over dancers—it can be hard for ballet's gatekeepers to see women as artistic leaders of any kind.

"When I was young," Bouder said in 2019, "I remember telling a male authority figure in the dance world that I wanted to be a director, and he literally tapped me on the head and said, 'Good for you.' So that early experience really colored how I viewed my career and what I could do. It made me feel like a little girl." As Alexandra Waterbury noted in the previous chapter, the path from dancer to choreographer to artistic director is well trodden for men; in the US, that same path has very few women's footprints on it. In 2016 and 2017, 75 percent of America's top fifty companies had male artistic directors. In 2019, it was 74 percent.[8]

"At that point I was young and definitely not capable of being a director," Bouder went on, "but it was a goal. And it made me feel like my goal was not achievable or valid."

Employing any new choreographer is a risk for a ballet company. Each year, every company presents a mix of pieces; usually it's a blend of works created by the artistic director or resident choreographer, existing and new dances by outside choreographers, and ballets made by beloved and long-dead masters. In each season, there are few slots for new work.

The question of why men are so staggeringly overrepresented in ballet choreography is not a new one, but it is one that has been asked with increased volume and urgency in recent years. In 2014, New York City Ballet staged a program called 21st Century Choreographers, with black-and-white headshots of the dance makers in question peering out thoughtfully from the promotional poster. All five of them were white men.

The contrast between the paleness and maleness of the poster and its claims to cutting-edge modernity drew immediate criticism. "They are all white men, and their pieces start off a season of revivals by more white men," one journalist wrote in *Dance Magazine*. In an interview with the *New York Times*, Ballet Master in Chief Peter Martins patted himself on the back for his purported daring and courage. "What can I say, I'm gutsy," Martins said. "I liked the idea of having all these people in their twenties, making new work. It shows the art form is really alive." But in the twenty-first century, what is gutsy about continuing the ballet's lamentable track record of telling stories from the perspective of one small group of people? What's brave about a cycle in which the white men who run ballet companies mentor the next generation of white male choreographers, investing their time and lending their credibility to people who look just like them? "How," Lauren Wingenroth asked in *Dance*, "can an art form be alive when it excludes so many?"[9]

Commissioning new ballets is a costly business: the choreographer must be paid, and the dancers need more time to rehearse than they might for a ballet they've danced before (if the ballet uses live music, the orchestra will need additional rehearsal time, too). There's the cost of designing and making new costumes, sets, and lighting.

The artistic leadership of a company takes a risk with every new ballet it commissions. Their audience might not buy tickets to see the new work or like it if they do. Ideally the audience will love it, and it will become a reliable earner in subsequent years, paying for itself several times over. There is no guarantee.

It is little wonder, then, that companies might make conservative choices, commissioning safe works from tried and tested choreographers—artists with existing track records rather than new and untested voices whose names the audience might not recognize. It is little wonder that they choose men.

The 2014 cycle of the "where are the women choreographers?" debate did make an impact on some of the country's biggest ballet companies. In 2016, American Ballet Theatre launched the Women's Movement program "to support the creation, exploration and staging of new works by female choreographers for American Ballet Theatre and the ABT Studio Company." It committed to supporting at least three women choreographers in creating new works each year, one for the main company; one for the Studio Company; and a third "work-in-process workshop for ABT or Studio Company dancers." Several of the choreographers supported by the program were current or former company dancers, either at ABT or City Ballet, who were on the dancer-to-choreographer path that so many of their male peers had been encouraged to take.[10]

In 2017, Tulsa Ballet staged an entire new works program "dedicated to the power of the female voice" that showcased "three female choreographers who [were] at the height of their creative careers," one white, one Latina, and one Asian. Cincinnati Ballet staged a similar program in 2016 and Pacific Northwest Ballet in Seattle followed suit in 2017, and in 2018, all the ballets performed in ABT's annual fall gala were choreographed by women, Claudia Schreier among them.[11]

In 2018, Boston Ballet launched the ChoreograpHER program, which encouraged aspiring women choreographers to begin even earlier, holding choreographic workshops for students at Boston Ballet School. It also committed to three years' worth of annual performances "dedicated to amplifying the voices of emerging female choreographers." And for the 2020–2021 season, the company planned a performance program "dedicated to female artists in creative fields including choreography, music, design, and visual art." In the fall of 2020, the company announced that the 2021 ChoreograpHER program would be performed live, but before an audience at 50 percent capacity to minimize coronavirus transmission risk. It would feature five world premieres, including one by Schreier. "Five of the six choreographers are women; three of the six are black," Boston Ballet artistic director Mikko Nissinen told the *Patriot Ledger.*[12]

All this "dedication" is, of course, a welcome development. But unlike in some other industries, where gatekeepers have come under pressure to include at least token minority voices in panels and programming, ballet gatekeepers continue to stage seasons in which audiences can go an entire evening without seeing a ballet made by a woman. In the 2018–2019 season, 70 percent of the programs staged by the top fifty US companies were made up entirely of ballets choreographed by men. In the same season, performances in which all the ballets were made only by women made up just 4 percent of programming. And in the 2019–2020 season, a truncated one thanks to the pandemic, the numbers had improved but were still dismal: 62 percent of all ballet programs exclusively featured works choreographed by men, while performances entirely created by women accounted for 6 percent of programs.[13]

In other words, an all-men evening is a just normal night at the ballet, at which no one bats an eye. An all-women evening is a special event, a showcase, a diversity push. It happens very, very rarely, and never without a press release. For example, in 2016 the English National Ballet, led by artistic director and principal dancer Tamara Rojo, started staging evenings of works all choreographed by women and called the program She Said. In 2019, the program returned, expanded and now called She Persisted.

"The thing that drives me crazy is when these companies in general say that they're doing [an] all-female choreographer program," says Kyle

Abraham, an award-winning choreographer who has made works for prestigious contemporary companies as well as for New York City Ballet. After winning a MacArthur "genius grant" in 2013, Abraham saw an opportunity to leverage his power to make more room for choreographers who have been shut out of opportunities, and he implemented a policy of requiring his work to be performed alongside the work of women choreographers or not at all. At the beginning, he says, he had to specify that those women still be alive, and he had to provide artistic directors with a list of choreographers they might consider; they said they didn't know any.

Abraham says he worries that the all-women programs feel like gimmicks or stunts and signal that commissioning and performing work by women is somehow special rather than simply how things should be. "If you're only putting them in this one program, I don't really know if you're really listening and doing what you're supposed to be doing," he says. "Are you saying that they're not good enough to be in the mixed-bill program with other choreographers? Will these works last more than one season, since you lumped them all together in an oddly segregated way?"

On the other hand, in late 2019, press coverage noted that every work in the Royal New Zealand Ballet's 2020 season would be choreographed by a woman. Its new artistic director, Patricia Barker, dismissed the newsworthiness of her decision: "It's just as easy to hire a female choreographer as a male one," she told *Pointe*.[14]

That's certainly true. But it's not as easy to succeed as a woman choreographer. For one thing, as in other industries, when women are given the opportunity and the resources to create, they're shortchanged. As in Hollywood, women choreographers struggle to attract the kind of investment that men get, meaning that they're more likely to make short or one-act ballets rather than long and expensive three-act works. It is exceedingly rare for a ballet company to take the financial risk of a full-length ballet made by a woman: a staggering 83 percent of the new full-length works performed in the 2019–2020 season were choreographed by men.[15] In 2016, British choreographer Cathy Marston was tapped to make a full-length ballet version of *Jane Eyre*, and as American Ballet Theatre principal dancer Isabella Boylston was preparing to perform the title role in 2019, she said it was the first time in her entire career that she had danced a full-length ballet made by a woman.

And often, the opportunity to make full-length works can only be found in Europe, where government support of the arts is far more robust than it is in the United States. American choreographer Helen Pickett, one of the three women featured in Tulsa Ballet's 2017 all-women program, waited more than a decade to make her first full-length work.

Then there's the question of what a lifetime in ballet does to the creative spirits of women, particularly women of color, and most especially Black women. Abraham remembers watching a dance choreographed by a white man whose work he admires, and marveling at its quality. "But the thing was, I was realizing, they're moving with so much freedom. There's not a lick of insecurity here, because they were never told or made to feel like less than," he tells me.

"If you have experienced freedom throughout the majority of your life," Abraham theorizes, "you're probably going to move that way too." If, on the other hand, you've spent a lifetime in ballet being made to feel insecure about your feet, Abraham says, "you're probably not going to make the most amazing petit allegro. You know what I mean?" For Abraham, racist stereotypes about Black dancers' bodies have left him a physical legacy, and a creative one. "There's so many insecurities about my feet, or about these things that I was told I wasn't good at. . . . That lack of encouragement puts a weight on the way in which I move that kind of can lock up certain possibilities for movement."

Finally, in another dynamic that persists in other industries where white men are overrepresented, women choreographers are permitted precious little room for error. One poor (or poorly received) ballet can mean the end of opportunity, whereas overrepresented choreographers are permitted the occasional mediocre work or critical or commercial flop. This was Ashley Bouder's experience when she first ventured into choreographing: after her poorly received first try, she didn't try again for years. Where male choreographers are granted room to fail and to grow, women are expected to be perfect the first time and every subsequent time.

If ballet is to be and stay a living and evolving art form, the choreographic ambitions of men of color and of women of all ethnicities must be encouraged and nurtured. As students, dancers of all genders should learn choreography by choreographers of color, including women, so that their understanding of what a choreographer looks like, of whose choreographic potential matters, is not limited to the same tiny sliver of the ballet world.

Ballet companies must commit to taking chances on not only new choreographers who aren't white men but also the choreographers who already have a body of work to prove their talent and potential. "Emerging" choreographers are essential; so too are those choreographers who have already emerged, who are established and experienced in spite of the many cultural and systemic challenges they have faced. Granting opportunities to midcareer choreographers who might already be well known and widely performed if not for the roadblocks detailed here is just as important as finding and amplifying new choreographic voices. In the case of women, they have, as Garafola noted almost a generation ago, always choreographed. It is unjust to exclude the older ones from ballet's new interest in gender equity, and it does the ballet world no good to have a robust younger generation if those choreographers will not have mentors or role models they can look to for guidance.

And if companies are going to tout their investments in emerging choreographers, they must make those commitments long-term ones. One of the advantages of the resident choreographer position is that the dance maker has some leeway to create a critical or commercial flop without endangering her job security. But there are few resident choreographer positions in the US because many companies don't have them. Given that reality, artistic directors should commission multiple ballets at once from a new choreographer so that if their first or second attempt is deemed a failure, it will not be their last. This is the unspoken, informal freedom that has long existed for emerging white male choreographers—the freedom to fail from time to time and get another shot anyway—and companies should codify it and extend it to new choreographic voices of all genders. If white male choreographers are going to be permitted occasional mediocrity, then all choreographers should be.

For centuries, the most iconic stories in the classical ballet canon, the meaty three-act ballets that audiences know and love and that dancers, especially ballerinas, aspire to dance, have been stories about women, told by men. This is true of *Giselle*, *The Sleeping Beauty*, *Romeo and Juliet*, *La Sylphide*, and *Don Quixote*; all but the last are stories about women who die, some young and tragically. (Aurora of *The Sleeping Beauty* doesn't die, thanks to a fairy-brokered compromise. She is merely knocked out for a century and then wakes up just in time to get married.)

Let's consider the most iconic of ballerina roles, *Swan Lake*'s Odette/Odile. *Swan Lake* premiered in Moscow in 1877 and, despite its cool reception, has survived for almost 150 years, and a great deal of the 1895 revival choreography, by Marius Petipa and Lev Ivanov, is intact in contemporary productions.

The details of the plot vary from production to production, but the general outlines are the same: Odette, a beautiful maiden (in some productions a princess), is cursed by an evil sorcerer to spend her days as a swan while at night she regains her human form. The curse can only be lifted if a man who has never been in love before promises to love her faithfully forever. She is nearly hunted as a swan by Prince Siegfried, who is under pressure from his family to pick a bride but who would rather marry for love; she tells the prince her story and they fall in love. On the night Siegfried is supposed to choose a wife, the sorcerer arrives at the castle with his daughter Odile, whom he has bewitched to look just like Odette. She seduces Siegfried into declaring his love for her, dooming Odette to permanent, round-the-clock swanhood. Realizing his mistake, Siegfried rushes to the lake to find Odette and apologize. She forgives him, but the spell can't be broken, and in her despair she throws herself into the lake and drowns. In some productions, he follows her; in others, she remains a swan forever and Siegfried lives.

Swan Lake is a story about a woman whose body is violated by a man she does not know and whose trust is then violated by a man she does. Ultimately, what breaks Odette—what kills her—is not the first violation but the second. For nearly 150 years, this story has been told almost entirely by men choreographers who have used women's bodies as their medium. While women have danced the steps, it is the men who made them. It is also the men who have made choices about the plot, about whether Odette and Siegfried will both die or whether Odette will forgive Siegfried's betrayal before her life ends. Some of these men have performed that job commendably.

But surely, after a century and a half, we have heard enough from men about what it means for a woman to be violated and betrayed. Surely there are women choreographers who could bring a crucial and missing perspective to this story, who might find new rage in Odette and new nuances in Odile, who is both victim and villain. Perhaps, in a woman's hands, this very old story about a woman's bottomless forgiveness of male inconstancy might become one about her rebellion and freedom. There is nothing inherent to women choreographers that equips them to do this, of course, just as there is nothing inherent to men choreographers that prevents them. But after 150 years, surely there are ballerinas who are tired of performing a man's idea of a woman's experience, who would relish the opportunity to dance both Odette and Odile as a woman might envision them.

Consider what it looked like when one woman took another beloved (and even older) ballet story and told it differently. In 2019, Black South African choreographer Dada Masilo reimagined *Giselle*, transforming the story just as she had *Swan Lake* several years earlier (in her *Swan Lake*, Odette and Siegfried get married even though Siegfried is in love with Odile, who is a man).[16]

Giselle, which was first performed in Paris in 1841, was choreographed by two men and has a story written by a man (based on an account of a German folktale also written by a man). Giselle is a teen-age German peasant who loves to dance and whose mother would pre-fer that she didn't because she has a weak heart. Giselle is in love with a man she believes to be a fellow peasant, Loys, but Loys is in fact a nobleman named Albrecht in disguise. Only Hilarion, the local game-keeper, who, like Albrecht, is in love with Giselle, discovers his secret identity. He reveals it to the town with some help from Albrecht's noble fiancée Bathilde, who shows up in the town square during a hunting trip and is understandably perplexed to find Albrecht there dressed as a vineyard worker. Giselle, devastated by Albrecht's betrayal, goes mad and dies of a broken heart at the end of the first act (in some produc-tions, she stabs herself with Albrecht's sword).

The second act finds both Albrecht and Hilarion at Giselle's grave in the woods, distraught with grief and guilt. Giselle appears, newly initiated into the Wilis, the ghosts of women who died before their wedding day after being abandoned or betrayed by their intended. The Wilis take their revenge by trapping men who pass through the woods and forcing them to dance until they collapse and die. They seize on Hilarion and kill him, but Giselle, who still loves Albrecht and has forgiven his betrayal, pleads with their leader, Myrtha, to spare him. They do, and as dawn arrives, Giselle disappears back into the woods and Albrecht is left to grieve her all over again. (In some productions, he marries Bathilde as the curtain falls.)

There are multiple ways to read *Giselle*: as a story about the aristoc-racy mistreating the peasant class, a story about true love thwarted by rigid class barriers, a story about a love so strong it can overcome death. No matter which of those readings you choose, *Giselle*, like *Swan Lake*, is also a story about a woman who is mortally wounded by a man's be-trayal. The setting and the choreography of *Giselle* have changed over time; one choreographer set the second act in a mental asylum, and another turned the villagers into migrant sweatshop workers in "ghostly abandoned factories" and blended kathak dance with ballet steps to make the Wilis "part animal, part ghost, part woman" and depict their attacks on men as "not about vengeance but about grief and mourning." One choreographer has reimagined the ballet as *@giselle*, a production that uses projections and digital effects to examine "the ways social media has leveraged an unexpected change on the nature of modern love." In the hands of the many men choreographers who have retold the story since 1841 (and the few women, including former Australian Ballet director Maina Gielgud), one thing is constant: Giselle forgives Albrecht and saves his life.[17]

But in Dada Masilo's hands, she doesn't. In Masilo's 2018 production, which blends classical ballet choreography with South African dance steps and remixes the conventional score by Adolphe Adam with South African rhythms, Giselle doesn't beg Myrtha for mercy. She watches as her ghost sisters—played by both men and women and led by Myrtha, who is played by a man—dance Hilarion to his death. Then she looks on as they do exactly the same to Albrecht. As the ballet ends, she steps over his dead body, literally, and slowly walks off the stage toward a bright light.

Masilo's production stunned me. It had never occurred to me that Giselle could make this choice, that she could be something other than an endlessly understanding, bottomlessly forgiving martyr to love. Maybe Myrtha had been right all along, and I—like all the other choreographers who'd told me this story, most of them men—had never seen the truth: Albrecht didn't deserve her forgiveness, and he didn't deserve to live.

Albrecht is often performed beautifully by men who capture his tortured grief and his lifelong guilt at having betrayed Giselle and caused her death. Sometimes, like Siegfried, Albrecht is danced as a restless soul who yearns for freedom beyond the strictures of royal life; sometimes he is a careless and carefree cad who falls in love and is changed by it. But in every version of *Giselle* besides Masilo's, there is this constant: Giselle dies and, thanks to her posthumous forgiveness and pleading, Albrecht does not.

What might the story of *Giselle* look like if it were told and retold by women instead? What kind of righteous rage might those choreographers find in the girl who was mistreated by the man she loved? What kind of grief might they find in her mother, whom we watch weep over her daughter's dead body as the curtain closes on the first act and then never see again? What might they reveal about Myrtha and how she became the steely and ruthless leader of a cadre of vengeful virgin ghost brides who hunt men for sport? Truly, what kind of masculine betrayal does it take to make you the Queen of the Wilis?

It is not simply a question of new insights into very old ballet stories: when women are given the rare opportunity to make full-length narrative ballets, they do the essential work of adapting stories that have never or rarely been made into ballets. Helen Pickett, an American choreographer who creates a great deal of work with European ballet companies, turned Tennessee Williams's play *Camino Real* into a ballet for Atlanta Ballet in 2015, and in 2019, she created a critically acclaimed ballet interpretation of Arthur Miller's *The Crucible* for the Scottish Ballet. "I'm looking for stories where the women don't have to kill themselves," Pickett told *Dance Magazine*. "They are on their feet, on the earth with hard decisions to make. It's the man who gives up his life in *The Crucible*."[18]

Annabelle Lopez Ochoa, a Colombian-Belgian choreographer based in Amsterdam, has created works for many American ballet companies, including Dance Theatre of Harlem, the Joffrey Ballet, San Francisco Ballet, and New York City Ballet. A small number of these have been full-length narrative ballets: in 2012, Lopez Ochoa choreographed *A Streetcar Named Desire* for the Scottish Ballet, and in 2019 she made *The Little Prince* for BalletX, a contemporary ballet company in Philadelphia.[19]

In 2016, Lopez Ochoa ventured beyond adapting plays and novels to create a ballet based on the life and art of Frida Kahlo. *Frida* began as *Broken Wings*, a one-act work created for English National Ballet's 2016 She Said program, and was then expanded to a full-length ballet that was premiered by the same company in 2020. "I'm sure Frida would have wanted a woman to tell her story," Lopez Ochoa told *Dance Magazine*. Women, she said, "can expose more layers—sometimes we know we are breaking inside, but we have to keep strong on the outside—and we can be nuanced instead of using clichés." At English National Ballet, artistic director and principal dancer Tamara Rojo has made a practice of commissioning stories about women, choreographed by women: in 2019, the company's associate choreographer Stina Quagebeur created *Nora*, based on Ibsen's *A Doll's House*.[20] It, too, is a one-act work—for now.

Cathy Marston, the English choreographer whose 2019 full-length ballet of *Jane Eyre* was the latest in a long line of story ballets she choreographed (her previous works included *Lolita*, *Wuthering Heights*, and *Lady Chatterley's Lover*), was, like Lopez Ochoa, drawn to the biography of a fellow artist. *The Cellist*, a one-act story ballet about the life and art of Jacqueline du Pré, explored the title character's relationship with her husband and with her own ailing body (du Pré's career was cut short by multiple sclerosis in her late twenties, and she died of the disease at forty-two). It also explores her most intimate relationship: the one she had with the cello itself, which in Marston's production is played by a male dancer. This choice means that the woman playing du Pré often lifts and supports her partner, a twist on the traditional ballet pas de deux. "It is so important for me to express women as sharers of weight, not just givers of weight," Marston told *Dance Magazine*. "They don't always need to be lifted and carried around."[21]

All but one of these women choreographers are white, and most of the ballets they are creating are about white women, in part because many are based on works from the Western literary canon. Consider what stories ballet is missing by extending the chance to choreograph story ballets to mostly white men and a few white women. Certainly, by telling and retelling the same handful of stories, the ballet world repeats and entrenches racist stereotypes about the people and cultures considered "exotic" and "other" by the European choreographers and librettists who first created these ballets.

A prime example of this phenomenon is *La Bayadère*, a ballet first performed in Russia in the late 1870s and a staple in American ballet since it was revived for American Ballet Theatre by the Soviet ballet star Natalia Makarova in 1980. The ballet is set in "the Royal India of the past," though in truth the setting is the Orientalist imaginings of the original choreographer Marius Petipa and his Russian collaborators 150 years ago.[22]

The events of the ballet take place in and around a temple (*la bayadère* means "the temple dancer") and feature a warrior, a rajah, and a dancing golden idol. The costumes vary from production to production, but often the lead women (who are called Nikiya and Gamzatti, not names you'd call authentically Indian) wear billowy pants and bejeweled cropped tops. In many productions, the warrior Solor often wears a turban with a feather sticking out of it. Then there is the choreography, which, like the racist and caricature-ish steps still performed in *Nutcracker* productions all over the country, features a lot of bowing and hand gestures that certainly resonated with Russian audiences in the 1870s but do little to make Asian audiences feel represented and welcome at the ballet today.

"Some participants can simply enjoy fantasy portrayals of 'other' cultures and revel in the feeling of ballet history being reenacted in front of their eyes," wrote anti-yellowface activist and former dancer Phil Chan in his book *Final Bow for Yellowface*. "But the usual caricatured portrayals suggest to minority audience members that ballet isn't *for* them, though it sometimes pretends to be *about* them. Some of us don't have the privilege of ignoring how we as a people are seen in this society."[23]

British choreographer Shobana Jeyasingh was more blunt. "When I first saw *La Bayadère* it made me squirm," she told the *Guardian* in 2020. "It was an embarrassing portrait of India. No matter how many explanatory notes you have in the programme, you experience dance when the lights go down and something moving hits your eye. . . . I'm offended as a British Asian to sit in an audience and see supposedly Indian holy men [the fakirs] move like servile monkeys."[24]

La Bayadère, much like another beloved classic, *Le Corsaire* (The Pirate), is also an Orientalist fever dream. "If the glitzy depiction of human trafficking doesn't make you cringe," wrote a *Washington Post* reviewer of the Mariinsky Ballet's production of *Le Corsaire* in 2019, "how about its parade of deplorable ethnic stereotypes, starting with turbaned Turks ogling female captives at a slave market?"[25] Yet these ballets are not entirely without value; some of the choreography is enormously difficult and beautiful and gives ballet companies the chance to showcase the technical skill of their dancers. *La Bayadère*'s iconic Kingdom of the Shades scene, in which two dozen women of the corps de ballet (clad—inexplicably, given that they're supposed to be in India—in white tutus) descend "from the Himalayas" in a series of perfectly synchronized arabesques. It is a stunning exercise in endurance, but narratively, it happens because Solor is having an opium dream.

Many of ballet's "classics," most of which date from the late nineteenth century, include imitations and approximations of national folk dances: *Swan Lake* features displays by visiting "Neapolitan" and "Hungarian" emissaries, and *The Nutcracker*'s Land of Sweets is inhabited by a veritable United Nations of candy, including Spanish chocolate and, of course, Chinese tea and Arabian coffee. For more than a decade, American ballet companies have been wrestling with how to rework these short dances, especially "Tea (Chinese Dance)," to make them less offensive. Some companies have stopped putting their dancers in yellowface makeup and have removed the caricature-ish pointed fingers and shuffling steps; others have rechoreographed the sections entirely to more closely mimic traditional Chinese dance styles.

But it's harder to update a classic when the entire ballet is set in "Royal India of the past." One 2020 attempt, at Pennsylvania Ballet, enlisted Phil Chan and Pallabi Chakravorty, an anthropologist and choreographer of kathak dance. Chakravorty helped replace some of the less accurate movements in the traditional ballet choreography—the bows, for example. But small tweaks to beloved classics cannot solve the larger problem: as one reviewer noted of Pennsylvania Ballet's production, "The ballet would need a larger overhaul to truly remove the Orientalism."[26]

Chan is now at work on his own overhauled and modernized *La Bayadère*, and Jeyasingh choreographed her own version, too. Meanwhile, the choreographer Jeremy McQueen, founder of the dance organization Black Iris Project, has created ballets about the Middle Passage, the grief of Black mothers, and the life of Nelson Mandela.

Even progress on this front can highlight how dismal the status quo is. In September 2020, American Ballet Theatre announced a digital season of short ballet films made during the pandemic in place of the company's regular season.[27] It marked the first time in almost two decades the company had commissioned new work from an Asian choreographer.

"I can count on one hand the Asian choreographers who have made work for a major company," Chan said in a May 2020 interview with Edwaard Liang, a former New York City Ballet dancer who is now a choreographer and, as artistic director of BalletMet in Columbus, Ohio, the first Chinese American artistic director of a US ballet company. "And you're one of them, and the others are mostly dead."[28]

"We have more Asian dancers onstage, but where are the Asian choreographers? The ones telling the stories?" Chan asked. "Your experience with your Asian parents, the way you've had that Asian relationship with them—when you depict a mother-child relationship onstage, it might look slightly different from when [Russian choreographer Alexei] Ratmansky does it. . . . And I think there is value to giving oxygen to your way of doing it." Liang agreed.

What other transformations of the beloved old story ballets might we see if more choreographers of color were given the chance to remake them? And what if we stopped nibbling around the edges of the classics and created new, inclusive, and innovative story ballets? What new stories—what novels and plays beyond the overwhelmingly white Western canon—might we see adapted into ballets?

"Part of our mission," says Tulsa Ballet's artistic director Marcello Angelini, "is keeping alive the classics. . . . But then at least two or three times a year, two or three programs a year have to be dedicated to innovation." Preserving the classics is important, but it can't be used as a pretext for reproducing racist depictions of racial and ethnic groups that are underrepresented both on ballet stages and in ballet audiences. And, Angelini asks, "if we don't create new works that talk about who we are today, how are future generations going to know who we were and how we thought and our social environment?"

"If you go and see *Giselle* or you go and see *Swan Lake* or you go and see *La Sylphide*," Angelini says, "those works take you back in time, and now those are the classics. But they are the classics because somebody decided to write the music and choreograph the ballet, commission the ballet. . . . But in order to create the classics for the twenty-second century, we need to make them now."

While most dancers' first exposure to an authority figure in ballet is a woman teacher, the power to make sweeping cultural change rests, for the most part, with men. That's because change comes, in part, from the top, and there aren't nearly enough women at the top of the American ballet ecosystem. Roughly three-quarters of the country's top fifty ballet companies by budget are run by men, but that number doesn't tell the whole story. Men leaders are disproportionately distributed in the companies with the largest budgets: of the nation's top ten companies by annual budget, nine are currently helmed by men.[29] Fewer than ten of the top fifty companies are run by a person of color.

Put another way, some women have been entrusted with leading the country's top ballet institutions, but only the ones with smaller budgets and less power to effect change throughout the ecosystem. The most equitable distribution of power is in the bottom half of the top fifty companies, where 65 percent of companies are helmed by a man. And, predictably, women artistic directors are paid less than their male counterparts; in 2020, the Dance Data Project found that women artistic directors earn sixty-three cents for every dollar a man earns in the same job. The one woman who runs a top-ten company makes $325,000 a year; the average salary among her nine male counterparts is just over $455,000.[30]

It is important to recognize that simply installing women at the top of more ballet companies will not solve the many problems that threaten the ballet world. They are cultural and systemic problems with deep historical roots, and simply hiring more women to run companies will not eliminate them. Women have founded and run ballet companies for decades—American Ballet Theatre was cofounded by a woman, as were Atlanta Ballet and Houston Ballet—and the art form's racism and sexism have persisted.

For decades, ABT cofounder Lucia Chase had what one dancer described as a "mandate" against hiring Black dancers.[31] And the women artistic directors I interviewed told me that in their roles as leaders, they uphold ballet's body standards, its literally narrow ideas of what a ballet dancer looks like, just like their male counterparts do. As Christine Cox, the cofounder and artistic director of BalletX, told me, "There are male directors that lead with integrity and grace, and there are male directors that don't. There are female directors that lead with integrity and grace and female directors that don't." Installing one leader in place of another cannot by itself solve ballet's many problems; without wholesale, transformative change, a change in leadership will only put a new pretty face on an old and ugly problem.

Still, if story ballets are to survive as more than museum pieces or reheated and re-embroidered replicas of something created in Russia in the 1800s, the distribution of power at the top has to become more equitable, by both gender and race.[32] There is simply no good reason for eight of the top ten ballet companies in the country to be led by white men. And the white men who will remain in control of ballet companies must earn that privilege by committing themselves to commissioning new classics and amplifying new voices, as well as to retiring the racist and outdated elements of old classics that make dancers and audiences feel unwelcome in the ballet world.

As for shorter, nonnarrative works, the kinds that were presented on that all-male 21st Century Choreographers program in 2014, it should no longer be acceptable for a company to stage an evening of ballet that includes zero contributions from women choreographers or choreographers of color. Choreographers themselves can exert pressure on artistic directors to make better programming choices: just as some men have adopted a policy of not appearing on panels where there are no women present and some white women have adopted a policy of not appearing on all-white panels, choreographers can do what Kyle Abraham has done and stipulate that their work shall not appear on homogenous programs. This involves sacrifice, of course, a willingness to risk a company no longer performing your work, but if those choreographers are genuinely committed to the survival of their art form, it is a risk they should be willing to take.

Ballet as we know it could not exist without women's bodies. Women's bodies are the materials with which centuries' worth of choreographers, most of them men, have told stories about the world as it was, is, and could be. But if ballet companies want to survive in the twenty-first century, if they want to be able to restage the new classics in the twenty-second, the absence of women's voices cannot continue. Ballet cannot continue to tell the same old stories and expect to cultivate new audiences. It cannot keep amplifying the same voices and expect to find something original to say. And it cannot go on using women's bodies to tell stories that are not their own. This centuries-old art form must evolve, quickly and radically, or it will die, taking the dreams of millions of people with it.

CHAPTER 9

I KEEP DANCING ON MY OWN

*This is important. There was this kind of global uproar
for a reason, and it's not enough to just acknowledge that
we've talked about it. The work has to continue.*

Claudia Schreier

Katy Pyle spent the summer of 2020 dancing outside. Ballez had been
awarded a residency at the Flatiron dance studio where I'd taken
class with Pyle at the start of that year, and the company was supposed
to use it to rehearse Ballez's latest production, *Giselle of Loneliness*, a reimagining of that ballet that asked the audience to grapple with how
ballet makes women suffer—and how ballet audiences are complicit in
that suffering. Performances were scheduled for the Joyce Theater in
Chelsea in the last week of June, and the residency began on the thir-
teenth of March.

"[The residency] had been something I had applied for seven years in
a row," Pyle told me in August. "Finally got it, got together this really
stellar cast to come into the studio with me."

On the first day, two days after the NBA suspended its season, Pyle and their dancers went into the studio, sat six feet apart from each other, and talked about whether there was still a way to create and rehearse the second act of the show. Perhaps in small groups in the large rehearsal space?

"I had already built the first act of my show. . . . I was in this perpetual state of trying to create the second act, which was supposed to be about community and togetherness and this sort of healing relief from the torture and suffering of ballet, which is really what the first act put up," Pyle told me. The first act of *Giselle of Loneliness* is a series of solo dances (including one by Alexandra Waterbury, in a rare professional dance performance), but the second act "is supposed to be a community coming together, touching, being close to each other."

Or, as Pyle put it, "literally all the things that you can't do."

When the city shut down, Pyle left the studio as it was, wigs and costumes still in the space. They tried to keep rehearsals running from isolation, helping dancers practice their solos over Zoom, but they didn't have enough money to pay dancers for their work, and "things just started to really fall apart. People had friends getting sick; my stage manager knew someone that had died." Pyle and their partner both came down with COVID-19 (they have since made full recoveries). Ballez's show, along with every other dance performance in the city and the country, was canceled.

Because they perform live and indoors, ballet dancers were some of the first workers to be pulled off the job, and they are likely to be among the last to go back. Outdoor performances are an option in parts of the country where the climate permits, but taking classes and rehearsing outside is a challenge, especially for those who dance on pointe and require stable and even specialized flooring. And as it became clear that the pandemic was going to be prolonged and worsened by a policy response that was patchwork at best and lethally negligent at worst, companies and schools began to pivot their performances and teaching toward digital offerings.

As I write this, in the late fall of 2020, many US public schools are back in session using a hybrid online–in person model, or with reduced in-person class sizes and masks. In Europe and Canada, ballet companies are slowly getting back to work, and some are even staging live performances again. But in the US, where schools and companies would usually be entering the final stage of rehearsals for their most beloved and lucrative production of the year, they are instead staring down the barrel of a *Nutcracker*-less Christmas. While some schools and companies have cobbled together digital, live-streamed, or limited-capacity *Nutcracker*s, or have staged pop-up live performances outside, most will go without their most important production this year.

Pyle found that Ballez was better prepared than many other dance schools and companies to meet the sudden demand for online instruction: Ballez's digital class, *Ballez Class Everywhere*, had been posted on YouTube in April 2019, proof of Pyle's belief that people who didn't live in New York should have access to gender-inclusive teaching, too.

"Suddenly everyone needs videos and all of our viewings spiked and people started thinking about that stuff," they said. "So I was very happy that I had done that project and that those were out there." They taught live online classes as well, from their living room, requesting optional donations in exchange. And once it was safe to go outside, they started teaching *en plein air*, on basketball courts and in parks.

And because Pyle had long functioned outside of ballet's mainstream, without much institutional support to speak of, they found that they were also quite well positioned to adapt to the instability and uncertainty wrought by the crisis. They had always bemoaned the lack of institutional support, they told me, the lack of roots—"I feel like an air plant in this whole thing, you know what I mean?" Ballez didn't have a rehearsal space to call home or a proper board, and Pyle never had anyone to answer to except themselves and their community. So they just kept answering to them.

That meant that, a few times throughout the summer, Pyle canceled Ballez classes and urged their would-be students to go and protest in defense of Black lives, or encouraged them to donate their class fees to racial justice organizations instead of to Ballez.

"I hope you are all safe and well as we collectively rise up and follow the leaders of the movement for Black lives," Pyle wrote in an email to students on June 7, a week after George Floyd was killed in police custody in Minneapolis. "I hope and trust that you are all taking care of yourself, each other, and doing what you think best to create the world that supports LIFE, aka, one where we dismantle white supremacist culture, defund the police, and abolish prisons, as a start."

Ten days later, Pyle canceled class "for the vigil for Oluwatoyin Salau," the nineteen-year-old Black Tallahasseean who disappeared shortly after tweeting about her sexual assault and was later found dead. Pyle told students that if they wanted to take a previously recorded class on that day, Pyle would send the link in exchange for a screenshot of a donation to the organization Justice for Black Girls.

Though Pyle considers themselves outside of the elite classical ballet world, they've watched as the mainstreaming of Black Lives Matter protests pushed institutions inside of it to respond publicly to the protests, often for the first time.

In the summer of 2020, as the protest arm of the movement saw a resurgence in the US and around the world, ballet companies and schools made public statements in support of racial justice and made public commitments to racial equity. For years, ballet institutions had been able to get away with vague and gauzy statements about diversity, with safe and donor-friendly initiatives that promised gradual and unthreatening change. Not anymore. In the summer of 2020, polling showed that white Americans were more likely than not to support the Black Lives Matter movement, with 31 percent of them telling Pew they "strongly supported" it,[1] and by year's end, Black Lives Matter was the largest protest movement in US history. Under pressure both from dancers and community members, and emboldened by the growing white acceptance of the movement, school and companies were more explicit than ever about racism in ballet, and about their plans to eliminate it.

Pyle is cautiously optimistic about the potential for systemic, rather than cosmetic, change—but not because so many institutions were finally willing to post a black square on Instagram and say the words "Black Lives Matter."

"I feel like typically what happens is kind of like a tokenizing, you know, 'Let's just try to hire some more forward-facing people to put a Band-Aid on this situation,'" Pyle said. "The thing that's super exciting about this moment is that young people are not going to accept that. That's my sense, that young people are going to continue to really push and demand more."

~

The way Pyle sees it, the pandemic put Ballez on something of an even footing with all the vaunted institutions in ballet's mainstream. "Everyone's put on that same level of not having access to the supposed thing that you have to have in order to be able to dance in these exclusive places," they told me. "But actually, you can do ballet in a handball court, which is what I've been doing with people. You can do ballet in your living room. You can do it on your roof. The kind of privatization of space and access is over. So I think it's a really radical moment of awakening."

And Pyle believes that the pandemic has revealed a truth about ballet: that it's about relationships, not institutions. "We have an illusion of structure, we have an illusion of these kinds of institutions that are gonna be there and are gonna last forever," they told me in August. "That's not true, and we have seen all of those things crumble and fall apart in the past four or five months."

So what's left of ballet when the theaters and studios and structures disappear? For Pyle, what's left is the relationship between individuals and their community, and their relationship to their own dancing.

"And that is not something that can be owned by anyone. It can't be privatized. It has [appeared to be] privatized and made hierarchical and made extremely exclusive, but that's an illusion."

The radical moment of awakening occasioned by the pandemic has come at a steep cost for Pyle. They and their partner have both recovered from COVID-19, but as Pyle's paid work has dried up, they haven't had the funds to pay their dancers, and they've had to stop creating new work except what they can make on their own. They received a surprise grant from the Lewis Center for the Arts at Princeton University, designed to support emerging artists so they can keep creating through the pandemic, but they're using that money to live. Performances of *Giselle of Loneliness* have been rescheduled for June 2021, but Pyle knows how many things have to go right in order for those performances to go ahead. "We don't know if any of these institutions are going to survive this," they warn.

In the meantime, they're dancing outside as much as they can, experimenting with sneakers to find the pair that best supports their feet on the concrete. They note that hip-hop has been practiced and performed outside for as long as it has existed, and tens of thousands of people run marathons every year. We have the technology to support bodies dancing on concrete. "I think that the way we use our feet, the way that we use our timing and rhythms are in relationship to the surfaces we're on—so there do need to be things that change," they concede, "but it's not impossible to do a whole bunch of things in a different space." In late September, the company premiered a new ballet that was performed in sneakers on a Brooklyn basketball court, captured on camera, and posted on Instagram.

And if staging *Giselle of Loneliness* isn't safe inside, they say, they can see it happening outside. "Maybe the show's gonna happen in a cemetery," they muse. "Or just in nature, because the Wilis are of nature, right?"

⌒

When the pandemic caused the suspension of in-person ballet classes at her Virginia ballet school on March 17, Danya Walker was disappointed. She'd just barely started dancing on pointe. Over winter break, her mother, Anisha, had taken Danya for a momentous, thrilling trip to the dancewear store so that she could be fitted for her first pair of pointe shoes, a rite of passage Danya had spent years waiting and working for.

Danya really wanted a pair of shoes that would match her skin tone, but that wasn't to be, Anisha said. At her fitting, none of the shoes in her skin tone fit properly, and the shoes that fit her feet best, a design called Ava made by the American brand Capezio, don't come in her skin tone.

"So we're stuck with pink. Unless we paint them," Anisha told me in August. "I mean, I'm not opposed to painting the shoes, but I do wish that all brands kinda came that way."

A pair of "petal pink" Avas costs ninety dollars, and Anisha just bought Danya's second pair, and Capezio does not make pointe shoe paint. The leading brand of paint, Pointe People, comes in colors like "Macadamia," "Darjeeling," and "Garam Masala" and costs twelve dollars per bottle, which will cover one pair of shoes. Even in well-lit press photos, satin that has been modified with the paint looks mottled and uneven, not like the pristine brown satin of a ready-made pointe shoe. Danya could buy from the English brand Freed, which in late 2018 released a line of brown and bronze pointe shoes in collaboration with UK dance company Ballet Black, but only if their shoes fit her.[2]

In June 2020, responding to a petition signed by over three hundred thousand people, Capezio promised to make pointe shoes available in more shades in the fall of that year. Bloch, an Australian brand that now sells dancewear around the world and has a significant presence in the US pointe shoe market, made the same promise—but noted that "development was severely slowed down" by the pandemic.[3] It also promised to "address" its color names, presumably a reference to the many light-pink garments that it had heretofore labeled "nude."

As the Black Lives Matter movement moved toward the mainstream—that is, as it became socially acceptable and even socially expected for more white people to engage with it and participate in BLM protests—Danya's dance school introduced a new policy on flesh-tone dancewear.

At a meeting with parents conducted via Zoom, the studio director, a white woman, said "'something along the lines of, 'As always, you can always choose the shoes in your child's particular skin tone.'" Danya was the only Black mom in the meeting, and the "as always" part of that statement was news to her.

"That definitely has not always been the case," she told me. "It's definitely always been ballet pink as far as tights and the shoes, but I guess she wanted to feel good about herself in that moment, so I just let her have it. But I know that the studio, the website, and what she has always said before, has been pink tights and pink shoes."

Anisha thought that the massive protests prompted some reflection from the studio owner about "how she's been running things, her studio, without actually realizing it. . . . I think she's trying." So far, that's meant reminding the parents repeatedly that their children are allowed to wear ballet gear that matches their skin tone. Danya is the only African American ballet student in her age group and one of just a few in the entire school. The school has one Black instructor, and he teaches hip-hop.

Still, Anisha was heartened—if a little surprised—by the school's response. "It's been great for us," she said. "[The director's] been a lot more in tune with it than I kind of expected her to be."

When the school stopped in-person classes because of the pandemic, Danya did what so many other students across the country and the world did: she learned to take classes on Zoom. The Walkers set her up in a room in their house where she could dance on a hardwood floor and bought her a ballet barre. She didn't especially enjoy taking digital classes, but she didn't want to miss out on dance, either.

Rather than ask parents to pay for these digital classes, the dance studio ran them for free, and it also gave the Walkers a credit for future tuition, taking into account the fees they'd already paid for competitions and recitals that were now canceled. Toward the end of July, the studio reopened for private lessons and then launched a summer camp with small classes of five dancers or fewer, and Anisha spent some of her credit on those. They cost sixty dollars an hour.

As we saw in Chapter 2, ballet runs on moms, who do the bulk of the childcare work that makes it possible for kids to get to and from ballet class with secure buns in their hair, clean tights on their legs, and the right color leotard in their dance bag. As the pandemic shifted millions of school-age children to online instruction and the moms who could work from home did, it felt as though the country was increasingly running on moms, too, as though swathes of the economy and the national fabric were being held together by white-collar women's ability to supervise homeschooling, dial in to Zoom meetings, serve lunch, and stitch DIY face masks—all at the same time.

Women who were raising children with men were already doing more than their share of housework and childcare work before the pandemic closed childcare facilities, schools, and summer programs. Once the kids were home, moms added far more childcare work to their already-longer list of chores than men did. Those women took on an extra thirty hours a week in domestic work. As workplaces began to reopen, many childcare centers didn't (some had been shuttered entirely), and as many schools stayed online or switched to a hybrid model, women were left with a choice that wasn't really one: their kids or their job. Women had already lost jobs at a higher rate than men, and now, even more women were being pushed out of their employment. The combined phenomena threatened to wipe out years of progress toward closing the gender and race wage gaps and increasing women's representation in the workforce.[4]

Anisha was relatively lucky: she had a job she can do from home and her employer was flexible, so she started working remotely full-time in mid-March. Still, she said, "it was definitely challenging trying to manage the last quarter of school for the kids and still having to get my work done." She didn't have to supervise Danya's remote ballet classes—at most, she said, she'd set up the laptop and then leave the room, and sometimes she'd simply text Danya the Zoom password and let her daughter do the rest.

Anisha thought the time away from the studio, where Danya had been dancing multiple times a week for eight years, made her daughter appreciate the in-person experience of dancing more. "Privates were great for her, but I think she enjoyed the semi-privates in a small class size, too, because she was back dancing with people. It's hard to dance [when] everybody else is in their own computer screen box."

The future of Danya's dance studio, like that of so many others around the country, is unclear. It has not committed to classes for the entire 2020–2021 academic year, promising parents instruction from September to December only. The school hasn't entered any teams into competitions for the foreseeable future, not wanting to commit entry fees and other funds to competitions that could easily be canceled by a fresh outbreak. And, of course, there will be no *Nutcracker* this year.

Danya had danced in *The Nutcracker* every year since she joined the school at the age of four. Anisha said that when Danya found out that the production was canceled, she handled it pretty well—but as the holiday season approaches, she might remember what she's missing out on. She had been looking forward to her first opportunity to dance a *Nutcracker* role on pointe.

"But there's always maybe next year," Anisha said. Always maybe.

⁓

Mark had planned to spend the summer of 2020 on tour in Europe: eight weeks of traveling and performing with his small contemporary ballet company. Instead, he spent it at home in the southern state where he grew up, unemployed except for teaching the occasional Zoom dance class, and unsure when his company would call him back to work.

He had never been happier.

"I have taken this time to actually not dance, believe it or not," he told me in August. "I love to dance, but I've been wanting a break for so long and my body has been needing to heal for so long, so I've actually just been letting my body rest."

The company was on tour in mid-March when companies began canceling their performances and telling their dancers to stay home from work. Mark doesn't get paid if he doesn't perform: when the tour was canceled, Mark's income vanished with it. He found someone to sublet his New York City apartment, went home, and applied for unemployment. (The dancer who took over his apartment was a cruise ship dancer who had contracted COVID on the ship, and Mark had friends who performed on cruises and found themselves stranded in Japan for months.) The pandemic overwhelmed his state's unemployment insurance system, and with *Nutcracker*s all over the country canceled, there were few ballet schools looking to hire a freelance *Nutcracker* Prince come December.

Still, he said, he felt great. The groin tear and ankle injury that had disrupted earlier performance seasons were now fully healed, and while he was staying active—riding his bike, lifting weights, and dancing a little in order to teach his classes—he didn't feel the need to stay in performance shape when it was clear there weren't going to be any performances for a very long time.

It's easy to understand why so many dancers wanted to stay in top form: they wanted to be ready to head back to work the second their companies resumed rehearsals, and they wanted to be in perfect shape when they got there. Some no doubt felt pressure to be seen working hard, even when they didn't have a job to go to. And for many dancers, the daily rhythm of class and rehearsal brings comforting, necessary structure to their days.

But if his injuries had taught Mark anything, it's that rest is good for the body. "I think that notion of taking a break as something to be risky or to be afraid of, that's an old way of thinking. That's archaic," he said. "I personally know, 'cause I've done it before, that you can take some time off, a year even, and come back stronger sometimes, depending on how you take care of yourself."

So as his fellow dancers filled their social media feeds with videos of jury-rigged dance studios in cramped New York City kitchens and balcony barre exercises, he took a break from Facebook and Instagram.

"I just felt this overwhelming pressure to partake in this frantic display of dance love, you know? But I am taking this time to actually search inward and [be a] recluse a little bit."

Slowing down physically meant moving out of crisis mode, or sprint mode, and into a healthier routine. He was eating better, drinking more water. "When you're on the go," he said of tour and performance life, "it's like, just throw something in your mouth . . . and now that everything's slowed down I'm taking the time to actually develop a schedule, develop a way of eating and all that stuff. So my body feels great."

He also spent time working on his education: after he was pulled off the tour, he applied for a masters in fine arts in the dance program at the University of the Arts in Philadelphia and was accepted soon after. It has been a revelation.

"Whew, it changed my life," he said in August, after the first six weeks of classes. "Changed my entire life. It changed the way I think and speak about dance." He was taking political theory and queer theory classes, and learning to see dance in everything, "like everything from marches, people marching—how is that dance? How do you dress—how is that dance?" Because Mark went straight from high school into a dance career, he didn't go to college, and now he was back in the classroom. It helped him to understand some of the pressures that dance company administrators are under and inspired him to think about what kind of an artistic leader he would be, if he were to become one.

"I do understand more about what a company is right now and why it is the way it is and what capitalism has done to dance. . . . It makes me want to leave [ballet], but it makes me want to leave only to restart something better. Maybe in the future, but I want to be a catalyst for maybe the new way of dance."

The downtime has left him with a renewed sense of longevity in dance. Before the pandemic, he had been planning his exit from ballet; the injuries were stacking up, and he was exhausted. Now, he said, he felt well enough to get back onstage for "high-octane" dance, if and when his company called him back to work.

But he knew his days of thirty-seven-city tours were numbered. He still wanted to perform and was eyeing a move to Broadway whenever the theaters reopened. Life as a Broadway dancer is far from easy, but it's good, consistent money, without a frantic tour schedule. There are replacement dancers to cover you if you get injured. For the first time in his career, he'd be in a union. He'd have employer-provided health insurance.

If he makes the move to Broadway, he'll be following the path laid out for him by other Black dancers who found that musical theater was a more hospitable environment than classical ballet. When the uprisings for racial justice began in May, and as their demands for reckoning spilled over into every industry, including ballet, Mark found himself in an Instagram group with 150 other Black dancers from around the country and the world. They started strategizing about how to hold their companies accountable for the racism each of those dancers had experienced on the job.

"Every company's different, every company has its own problems, so that's the thing—not everything can be attacked in the same way," he said. "There's been a lot to handle there, but [companies including ABT], they've stepped up their game, San Francisco, Boston. . . . The companies have reached out to their dancers and are working with us." Mark was optimistic about that.

But the most noticeable change, he said, was in the dancers themselves. He saw his fellow Black dancers view themselves for the first time as leaders and potential leaders in this art form. And he saw in his fellow dancers a new sense that they were entitled to work at a company that takes racial justice seriously.

"So regardless of whether these institutions change or not, our attitude is changing. And what's gonna have to happen is that they're going to have to match what we have to offer, and if not, we are now at a place where we're going to say something," he said. "That fear of saying something is gone. Now that that is gone, there is a charge ahead, and that's what I'm optimistic about."

⌒

At first, being sent home from the Royal Ballet School felt to Sasha Manuel like a break or a vacation. The school closed in mid-March as the pandemic began to hit Europe to catastrophic effect, and Sasha's mother, Wilmara, got her on a plane home to the US the very next day, driving from Indianapolis to Chicago to pick her up at the airport.

Sasha came home in exceptionally good shape: she had been rehearsing hard for the end-of-semester show that would serve as culmination of Year 11, and she had been preparing to audition for the Royal Ballet School's hyperselective Upper School. If students make it to the Upper School, they move to a new campus for the final years of their ballet education, taking daily classes in Covent Garden, just a short walk from the Royal Opera House and the studios where the Royal Ballet rehearses. They eat lunch in the same canteen as members of the Royal Ballet, who, with any luck, will soon be their coworkers. Only one hundred students in the world make it into each class at the Upper School. Sasha got in.

But then she went home. And stayed there, for far longer than she had anticipated.

"I just kind of assumed I would be going back to school in maybe a few months, and it would all be fine and my dancing would resume," she told me in August, just before the RBS resumed in-person classes. "But I think after the first month I started to realize, 'Well, I'm definitely not coming back now.'"

She started running three times a week and was taking a cardio class recorded by one of her teachers, and then she did what Danya and Katy Pyle's students had also learned to do: she took classes on Zoom.

"I give her credit for having that kind of determination and motivation," Wilmara said, especially since the time difference between London and Indiana meant that several days a week, Sasha was waking up at 4 a.m. to make it to her morning class.

Wilmara and her husband, realizing that Sasha's stay at home was going to last at least a few months, scrambled to set her up to train there as best she could. "We had to quickly create a dance studio at home," Wilmara said. "We sort of turned our family room into a mini dance studio." Through the school, they got a discount on a special dance mat—known to dancers as "marley"—that would allow Sasha to dance without slipping, "and then my husband tried to be creative in terms of getting a subfloor." The total cost of the DIY dance studio was about seven hundred dollars.

Sasha was most concerned about the fact that, even in her new at-home studio, she couldn't jump or complete the center portion of class to her full capacity. "It's just impossible to train at such a high level when you're in your kitchen about to hit the fridge when you do something," she said. Having a barre was essential, but "it's hard to just repeat the same small moves, and [you're] not going to really work up a sweat just standing in place." She lost a lot of the stamina and strength she'd brought home with her.

"You're not able to do jumps and the turns like you normally practice in a variation," Wilmara said. "So really, you're at the barre, doing whatever you can, and everybody has different space up in their houses, so it's hard to gauge who can do what."

After a few months, Sasha was able to go back to her old local dance studio, where she took a summer intensive with a small group of other dancers. Like Danya, she found that first day back in the studio to be an enormous relief after months of dancing alone on Zoom. After weeks of simply trying to maintain her technique, she was now actually improving, progressing.

"I think being able to dance back at my old studio allowed me to find another purpose for dancing, because I was with other people and they were all dancing as well, so it was like there was an energy that I just didn't have when I was dancing in my house."

It was motivating, she said, to dance with other people. "It's like a healthy competition going on, just the fact that you always want to look your best in front of everyone else." She had real music to dance to, not just the tinny reverb through a computer speaker. It was dancing, she said, "where you were meant to be." Other dancers who had spent the first few months of the pandemic dancing alone in their houses expressed this deep sense of relief, too. "It was amazing. I was smiling the whole time," said Ballet Hispánico dancer Dandara Veiga a few days after going back to the studio to dance with her colleagues after months of Zoom classes and trying to do barre in her apartment without disturbing her downstairs neighbors. "I spent the whole week thinking about it, I enjoyed it so much."

By August, Wilmara and Sasha were both back in London: the Royal Ballet School had reconvened in person with some very strict new guidelines. Students were required to complete a two-week quarantine in London before going to the school, and students who didn't live in London had to do that on their own dime (Wilmara and Sasha stayed in a friend's apartment, which happened to be empty).

When school resumed, students were grouped in small bubbles: they would eat, sleep, and take classes with their small cohort, and only that cohort. "For the dorms, eating, even walking to school, they're going to be walking in a bubble," Wilmara said, not long after being briefed by the school at a meeting for parents—held, of course, on Zoom. "They don't want them on public transportation, [and] they will stagger when they leave." Eating in the canteen with the pros would have to wait, too. "With COVID they're not allowed to do that this year, so that's a bummer. So they have to bring their lunch because they can't go out."

The rules were strict, and it was made clear that anyone who broke them would be removed from the school, but Wilmara thought it was worth it for the students to be able to dance in person, together, and without masks. And she suspected that they would comply—willingly if not happily. "These kids are so thrilled that they're going back and will be in a studio and they'll be able to dance," she said. "I do think they'll do whatever it takes."

Other things had changed over the summer, too. As Black Lives Matter became a renewed global phenomenon, the Royal Ballet School—like many other ballet schools and companies—made an effort to make its students of color feel heard and seen.

"They had one of the third-year students create a group chat with all the students of color in the school," Sasha explained, "and asked us how we felt at the school so far, things that we feel are good and things that need to be improved." That information was then conveyed to the school's artistic director and head of pastoral care.

Like at Danya's school in Virginia, the question of shoes and tights came up in these conversations, and the school changed its policy: it now allows students to wear both shoes and tights in their own skin tone. Sasha wears Freed pointe shoes, and two of their four shades work for her; she also sometimes uses Pointe Paint.

"One of the things that Sasha was keenly aware of, and some of the other students of color, is they've never really experienced any racism. . . . But it's those little things that are a little implicit," Wilmara said. She remembered the previous year's performance, when the school had provided students with makeup and undergarments—but didn't account for darker skin tones in either case.

Sasha remembered it well, too, telling a story that sounded eerily like the one Wilmara had told me about rushing around a competition trying to find a nude leotard her daughter could wear and discovering that the on-site retailer had nothing for her.

"At the end of the school year when we're having a show, we get this big bin of makeup to use," Sasha explained.

"All the older students usually use their own makeup, but sometimes you don't have time, so you need to use what Royal gives us, but last year they didn't have my shade. So it was a little last-minute [and] I had to go out and buy some." The same thing happened for performance undergarments: white students were able to wear the school-provided ones, and the students of color had to fend for themselves.

Wilmara said she was encouraged by the actions she'd seen from the school far, but she knew there was a lot more work to be done to shift ballet away from the default of whiteness, a problem that the makeup and undergarment incidents illustrated perfectly.

"I think their eyes are certainly more aware," she said in August. "I mean, I'd like to see a little more urgency, but honestly, there's a lot to be done."

~

Patrick Frenette spent a lot of 2020 trying not to think about what might have been. The twenty-five-year-old American Ballet Theatre corps de ballet dancer had been sent home from work in the second week of March, his spring plans disrupted just like Katy's, Danya's, Mark's, and Sasha's.

Patrick had been preparing for the company's spring season at the Metropolitan Opera House at Lincoln Center, which was meant to feature a farewell performance by beloved veteran principal dancer Stella Abrera and a landmark performance of *Romeo and Juliet* starring Misty Copeland and soloist Calvin Royal III—the first time the company would have had a Black Romeo and a Black Juliet at the same time. Patrick was rehearsing some exciting new roles, a chance to stand out from the crowd of the corps and enjoy the spotlight on the Met stage.

But by the end of March, Patrick found himself doing barre in his mother's North Carolina living room and spending hours on hold with the New York Department of Labor, whose website frequently crashed because of the sudden and overwhelming influx of people filing for unemployment.

To its credit, ABT was able to pay dancers until the end of the scheduled spring season. That was lucky, because when Patrick and I spoke in August, five months after the pandemic began and Patrick started applying for unemployment, Patrick said he'd received just three unemployment checks.

"We were paid full salaries. That was fantastic; it was everything we all needed, especially with what I was going through with the unemployment department. . . . I cannot and will not speak for any other ballet companies, but I know that ABT has definitely stood by its dancers through all of this."

Still, ABT was like every other ballet company in the country: struggling. It canceled its fall season and then its annual *Nutcracker* performances in Orange County, California. It turned its annual gala performance into a fairly uninspiring digital presentation, and later in the summer it hosted a cast reunion of the classic dance movie *Center Stage* as a fundraiser for its Crisis Relief Fund. (The Washington Ballet also rehearsed and streamed a digital gala, after which the artistic director and one dancer tested positive for COVID-19.)[5]

Throughout the summer and early fall, dancers were furloughed and artistic staff had their salaries cut. Large companies like Pacific Northwest Ballet and Houston Ballet placed dancers on extended leave, and smaller regional companies like Colorado Ballet furloughed them. Louisville Ballet furloughed its staff and cut salaries.[6]

At New York City Ballet, dancers resorted to their own fundraiser, independent from the company. "New York City Ballet has made its best efforts to support us throughout this crisis, including the establishment of the NYCB Relief Fund," explained the website for the dancers' fundraising effort. "However, the loss of revenue from multiple canceled seasons means the company still cannot provide us with adequate financial assistance to sustain us through the end of the year." One dancer said that she had hoped to use the break necessitated by the pandemic to take college courses, but in reality, "I can barely afford to keep the roof over my head, let alone pay college tuition. Now my daily focus is on survival."[7]

Patrick was lucky: like Mark, he was able to use the unexpected time away from the studio and the stage to make plans for his life after ballet. ABT gave all its dancers the option to complete its National Training Curriculum for free, and Patrick, who already had some teaching experience, jumped at the chance to get some formal teacher training. The program added some much-needed structure to his day and gave him a valuable credential he'll be able to use when he retires from dancing.

"It was amazing to have a schedule again. I would wake up, I would get myself ready for a Zoom call, I would study," he said. "It was like being in a company and like being in college at the same time. It was exactly what I needed." Almost thirty of his fellow dancers took the course, too, and are now certified ballet teachers.

By July, his teacher training completed, Patrick was able to go dance in a studio at the nearby ballet academy where his sister teaches. Finally he had the space and the proper flooring to jump safely, something he couldn't do in his mother's living room. And once North Carolina permitted it, the boys-only summer intensive held at his sister's school went ahead—with some modifications.

"Everyone was six feet apart, I had a mask on, and it was totally fine," he said. "The mask was not a big deal at all. You just get on with it. You get used to it."

Taking time off from full-on training took a toll on Patrick's body: he wasn't old, but he wasn't as young as he once was, and he felt it. Some of his teenage students, he said, had gone weeks or months without a ballet studio to dance in. They'd been doing at-home barres just like he had, but "they came right back into class, and their bodies just hopped right to it and got the muscle memory back."

Patrick's body, not so much. "I was originally surprised about certain things that departed," he said. He could only pull off half the number of consecutive pirouettes he was usually be able to do. "My center of balance for pirouettes was gone for the first few days," he said with a laugh. "It was a definite shock."

Still, he didn't feel like he was losing time—yet. "If I was in my thirties or on the other side of that," though, "then absolutely I would probably attest to that, as many dancers have. I'm somewhere in the gray area, I would say."

When we spoke in August, ABT had canceled its fall season but had not yet made an announcement about the fate of that year's *Nutcracker* performances, even though peer companies—including New York City Ballet, San Francisco Ballet, and Houston Ballet—had canceled theirs. Patrick remained optimistic about whatever awaited him and his company on the other side of the crisis.

"I'd like to think that when—I don't want to say 'if'—when we get back to work, I am quite confident that my career is going to develop just from where it left off," he told me in mid-August. A few months later, ABT canceled its entire spring 2021 season.

⌒

When Claudia Schreier quit her desk job to be a full-time choreographer, she knew that it was a risk. That her income would be unpredictable and unsteady. That living the creative dream usually means sacrificing the comforts of stability. "I just did it out of the faith that

I would figure it out," she told me late in the summer of 2020, "and I always have."

Still, even an artist who plans on instability couldn't have foreseen a disruption as significant as a global pandemic that shut theaters and put her entire industry on hold for more than six months.

Schreier had had a busy year planned: at the end of 2019, she'd been named choreographer in residence at Atlanta Ballet, a three-year position in which she would create several works for the company, starting with a kid-friendly "family ballet." In the spring of 2020, as coronavirus hit the US, she was supposed to be in New York City, where Dance Theatre of Harlem was going to premiere a dance she had made for the company. Then she was meant to go on to Miami City Ballet to teach them another new work, which they would perform in October. All that, of course, was canceled, postponed, pushed, thrown up in the air.

Now there was a new schedule, a plan for a truncated 2020–2021 season at Atlanta Ballet, with shorter performances and no intermissions in order to limit how many times patrons entered and left the theater, and how long they spent there. It was tentative, of course. "Obviously," Schreier said in August, "that's all TBD."

Choreographers are generally paid like authors: They are paid a portion of their fee up front, when they begin the rehearsal process. They're paid another portion when the work premieres, and the final portion when the run of the performance ends. After that, they're paid royalties any time the ballet is performed. Postponed performances and pushed rehearsal schedules mean lost income for a choreographer like Schreier, and even a relatively stable gig like her choreographer-in-residence position is not salaried. So while the visibility of that prestigious position made her a hot commodity and secured her commissions with other companies, all the income those commissions would provide was in the future—and, for the time being, somewhat theoretical.

"The royalty fees have stopped because there's no performances," she said, "so like many other people, I'm on unemployment right now." She gave up her apartment in New York City, and she and her fiancé went to stay with family. "It's worked out very well for us, luckily. I don't have any significant income coming in right now, but I also have been very careful about the expenses going out. A lot of people don't have the ability to mediate risk like that, so as difficult as things have been, I don't pretend that I have it even close to [as] bad as it could be."

Like Mark, Schreier didn't feel compelled to create in the early days of the pandemic. She didn't feel inspired by dance's pivot to home video, and she didn't feel that she had anything to say, choreographically speaking, about the pandemic.

"I didn't feel this immediate need to reflect and speak to it artistically that some of my peers did," she explained, "and there's no right or wrong answer to that. I think I just didn't feel a need to create in this *Brady Bunch* Zoom atmosphere. It just didn't feel right to me."

It wasn't until Black Lives Matter protests swept over the country demanding justice for George Floyd, Breonna Taylor, and so many other Black people whose lives were snuffed out by state violence, that something was jogged loose for Schreier. "The moment at which I started to feel like I was kind of alive again was when the Black Lives Matter movement resurged," she said, "because I felt like there was actually a purpose to what I was talking about."

She felt a new sense of connection to the Black community, she said, and to the Black experience—and a new sense of grief at the many unconscious ways "that I was kind of squashing my own Black identity for so long. . . . It brought up a lot of really raw feelings."

That realization was the result of a process that had begun several years ago, when she had started working on projects that drew on the part of herself that so much of the ballet world had asked her to suppress. The ballet that Dance Theatre of Harlem was planning to perform at City Center in the spring, *Passage*, was choreographed to be part of a program marking the four hundredth anniversary of the arrival of the first enslaved Africans in what would become the United States, and it "celebrates the fortitude of the human spirit and the enduring will to prevail."[8]

"I feel much more comfortable owning my Blackness and speaking to what it means to me," she said, explaining that new sense of connection. "I no longer feel that sense of apprehension. And just the fact that I felt even apprehensive to begin with says a lot about how Blackness is viewed in the ballet community, and how we have learned to express or suppress it depending on the situation."

And as the protests made their way from the outside world into the ballet world, Schreier was heartened by what she saw. As exhausting as the spring and summer of 2020 were, she said, she saw real interest in making change and a concerted effort to set that change in motion.

"I've had a lot of really hard conversations with a lot of people in all levels, from executive and artistic directors to students to everyone in between," she said. "There is a real reckoning that took place."

Like Mark, Schreier observed a significant shift in herself, and in other Black ballet dancers and creators in the ballet world. Now, she said, there was "a certain permission structure that took hold that we didn't have before. I think there is a level of rawness and sincerity that wasn't really, for lack of a better word, permissible." Despite the horrific nature of the catalyst, that shift was one she was grateful for.

Still, she cautioned, the kinds of systemic and cultural changes ballet needs are "seismic" and won't happen overnight, or without consistent pressure and accountability. The reckoning of 2020 was not, she warned, "just another thing we got through to put on the thumbtack board."

"This is important. There was this kind of global uproar for a reason, and it's not enough to just acknowledge that we've talked about it. The work has to continue, and continue, and continue."

CONCLUSION

HOW BALLET SURVIVES

As I wrote in the introduction, there were two questions people reliably asked when I told them I was writing a book about ballet. First, had I been a professional dancer? No, but I interviewed dozens of them, and many of their fellow inhabitants in the ballet world, in order to write *Turning Pointe*.

Second, was this going to be a book about the history of ballet? No, it's about the future of ballet. And as I write this—in late 2020, staring down the barrel of a Christmas with few in-person *Nutcracker*s, watching dancers take classes on Zoom while their training and their careers stall and their schools and companies struggle to survive—that future looks even more fragile and tenuous than when I began my reporting.

There was a third question, though, one that you the reader have perhaps already wondered as you've heard Katy Pyle's story about being squished into a gender box that made them feel stifled and unseen, or Mark's story about dancing through excruciating injury, or Lauren Fadeley Veyette's story about catching the brass ring and burning out a few months later. My friends and colleagues, and strangers I met in my daily life, asked me this question a lot. *If I had a child, would I let them do ballet?*

To even be able to ask this question of myself is a sign of profound economic privilege. And I want to say yes. I want to imagine a future in which I watch my child move dreamily to music, caught by the rhythm and carried on the swelling sound. I want to take them to a ballet performance and see the awe on their face as they're swept away by the grace and the power, the almost magic of what the human body can do. Would I let my child do ballet? I want the answer to be a resounding, enthusiastic *Of course*. I want to say yes. But here's what I know.

There's so much work to be done to make the ballet ecosystem a place that welcomes all children and takes care of all adult artists. Ballet schools need to prioritize affordability so that families of all classes and races can sign their children up for ballet classes and keep them there even if the child isn't "serious" about dancing, or on an elite track. Some schools already do this by eschewing recitals and competitions, and that is a good start. Schools also need to prioritize a racially diverse teaching workforce. If white students never have a teacher of color, they will assume that white people are the authorities on ballet, an assumption that reinforces the very white supremacy ballet must urgently reject. If students of color never have a teacher of color, they will miss out on valuable role modeling and a learning experience that's attuned to their needs.

Schools need to be ready to welcome and accommodate gender nonconforming dancers of all ages. One way to do that is to normalize cross-gender casting in recitals and teach boys steps that are usually earmarked for girls, and vice versa. This is one way to ensure that boys are not coddled and girls are not constrained. Schools should take care to hold boys to the same behavioral and dancing standards as girls, and to encourage girls to start or keep choreographing from a young age.

And, crucially, schools should require teachers to ask students for permission to touch them when giving corrections—every time. It should be made clear to students, in word and deed, that they are free to decline and that their dance education or standing in the teacher's good graces will not be affected if they refuse to be touched. Where possible, ballet studios should have large windows through which teachers can be observed, and schools must act on the very first allegation of sexual misconduct or inappropriate behavior, quickly and decisively.

Ballet schools should also consider delaying the ascent to pointe; as physical therapist Nick Cutri explains in Chapter 3, it's much easier to damage an immature skeleton than one that's fully grown and hasn't been subjected to unusual stresses in childhood. Cutri's preference—and he recognizes, as I do, that implementing it would reshape ballet training as we know it—is that no one be allowed to dance on pointe before age fifteen. If ballet schools are going to continue to permit their preadolescent dancers to start pointe work, they should prioritize safety over aesthetics and tradition, even if that means an "ugly" shoe that disrupts the line. Unless teachers and their students demand a more foot-forward shoe, there will be no incentive for pointe shoe manufacturers to develop one—and they should. Dancing on pointe may not ever be truly safe, but it can be safer than it currently is, and developing better shoes is one way to make it so.

Additionally, ballet schools should make sure that parents of aspiring pointe students understand the increased risk of snap injuries and repetitive stress injuries that dancing on pointe carries. And, should parents decide against pointe, schools must ensure that there is a route for dancers to continue advancing in their ballet training, instead of an "up or out" model that pushes too many young ballet students out of the art form in their early teens. Ballet dads should attend those pre-pointe meetings rather than replicating a pattern in which moms do the bulk of the labor of ballet parenting. (Ballet dads should read this book, too).

Teachers need to convey to students that there is value in resting and taking breaks is not a matter of morality but of making their muscles stronger. Kathryn Maykish, the pelvic floor physical therapist, encourages teachers and parents to move dance to a seasonal model, with a real off-season. "Every other sport that we put a kid into," she told me, "they're going to play soccer during soccer season, and then they're going to have an off-season. . . . But dance, we have intense season, and then we have less intense season. We never have a time when we're not in class. I think that's a big mistake that we're making for our young dancers: not emphasizing that rest time allows our bodies to heal and allows us to actually get better at what we do."

Teachers also need to break the habit of incentivizing dancing through pain and praising dancers who rush back from injury.

They must also accept that a dancing body has value even if it hasn't achieved—and cannot achieve, and never will achieve—the "perfect" shape or line. Some hip sockets are built for 180-degree turnout and some are not, and achieving that turnout is not worth a lifetime of aches, pains, or pelvic floor dysfunction. Teachers should explain this to their students and should not push them to do things their bodies are not structurally capable of doing safely.

Similarly, teachers should resist ballet's movement towards extreme flexibility and acrobatics, especially in young dancers. Parents of students who are "super bendy" should be encouraged to get them screened for Ehlers-Danlos syndrome and other connective-tissue disorders that can cause hypermobility. Dancers with "good" feet—that is, cavus foot, or high arches—should be warned that their feet are more vulnerable to injuries, even as they are more aesthetically pleasing by ballet's standards. Even more radically, teachers should be willing to reconsider what a "good" foot—indeed, what a "good" ballet body—looks like. Finally, dance educators must be willing to tell the whole story of the Great Men of ballet—the ugly truth of how they treated their dancers as well as the beauty of the choreography they created. The human cost of great art is too high to simply excise it from our telling of ballet history.

Ballet companies, for their part, have a great deal of work to do to make ballet fit for purpose in the twenty-first century. Even as they recover from the crisis wrought by the pandemic, companies would do well to remember that ballet was in crisis before the coronavirus—and that any effort to simply rebuild their old ways of being will, ultimately, be effort wasted. As Sean Aaron Carmon wrote in an Instagram post at the height of 2020's Black Lives Matter protests, "Your normal was our oppression."

For example, if ballet companies, and more specifically artistic directors, only want to hire skinny or extremely skinny dancers, they should be willing to say that explicitly and publicly. Companies and their directors have hidden behind the "standard" and the "aesthetic" and have been permitted to gaslight dancers with talk of "health" and "strength" and "fitness" and "length" for long enough. If an artistic director's vision of ballet requires thin dancers and does not allow for bigger ones, he or she should be willing to say that in public, and be prepared to face the consequences.

Companies must also recognize that the push for diversity and inclusion is an invitation to radically expand an exclusive art form and bring in the talents of dancers of different shapes, sizes, and abilities—as well as a wide range of races and ethnicities. They should embrace opportunities to partner with organizations that make professional dance an option for differently abled people, like Oakland's AXIS Dance Company, which stages spectacular work choreographed and performed by dancers with disabilities.

Similarly, when hiring, companies should not ask dancers to pay to audition in person and should not request in-person auditions from dancers who do not have a genuine chance of being hired into the company—especially when an audition requires interstate or international travel. And unless the work of ballet is better paid, ballet companies will continue to lose out on the talents of artists who simply cannot afford to be full-time dancers.

Ballet companies should also welcome unionization for their dancers: union protections help to keep dancers' bodies healthy and rested, and diminish some of the extreme power imbalances between dancers and management. Unions themselves should recognize their responsibility to support workers who are vulnerable to all kinds of exploitation, including sexual harassment. Companies should be prepared to provide mental health coverage to their dancers, just as they provide physical health care, and should work to destigmatize mental illness in their ranks. Traditionally white companies should recognize that working in a racist environment takes a toll on the mental health of dancers of color and consider racial justice a part of retaining dancers and keeping them healthy.

If ballet companies wish to develop repertory that appeals to a wider audience, if they want to stage ballets that speak to contemporary life, they must stop staging programs in which all the ballets were choreographed by men or by white people. Men choreographers should adopt a policy like Kyle Abraham's and place restrictions on their works that require them to be performed in mixed-gender programs, and white choreographers should require that their work be presented alongside the work of choreographers of color or not at all. Companies should think expansively about what kinds of stories are missing from their stages, what kinds of human experiences they are failing to represent, and which audience members they are excluding as a result.

Companies should continue reaching into their ranks to encourage women of color, white women, and men of color to start or continue choreographing early in their dancing careers, and they should ensure that the women in their ranks truly have the time to develop their choreographic skills. They should commit to staging multiple works from emerging and underrepresented choreographers in order to avoid a pattern in which emerging choreographers must be perfect the first time or never have another shot. They should commission works with gender-neutral casting—Justin Peck's 2017 ballet *The Times Are Racing*, in which one of two central pas de deux can be danced by two men, two women, or a man and a woman, is a fine example. Finally, companies must stop staging ballets that feature yellowface and blackface and overhaul their dated productions of the classics that call for them.

⁓

Ballet cannot afford to succumb to crisis: there are simply too many people who need it. The Black girls and young women I met at that Wednesday matinee performance of *Swan Lake* starring Misty Copeland love ballet, love imagining themselves on that Lincoln Center stage. MJ Markovitz, the young nonbinary dancer we met in Chapter 1, feels at home in their body when they're allowed to dance in a way that matches their gender identity. In the right kind of ballet class, they feel fully seen.

As Phil Chan told me, "If you're having a hard day, you can go to class and you'll feel better." Or, if you're an audience member and not a dancer, "you can go to the ballet and escape. It can reaffirm humanity for you, it can make you just sit out in the dark and cry. . . . It can connect you to another human being just with the space of being in a theater and connecting with a dancer onstage. That's magic." Some people already find that magic in ballet, and everyone deserves it.

Miami City Ballet dancer Eric Trope says that ballet has been a precious source of solace and comfort in tough times; as he's battled with mental illness, ballet has been his "greatest savior," the place where he can find his most authentic self and feel the most joy. "I think at the heart of it is something so beautiful," he told me, "and it's simple and pure and something that can reach so many people, but it's true that it's sometimes hard to see. It's hard to see the light through all the fogginess" of inequity and exclusion and injustice.

"I think the entire world is having a reckoning, not just ballet," New York City Ballet soloist Georgina Pazcoguin said in late 2019. "I think society in general is having a huge reckoning, and I think ballet is late to the game, but at least some of us are trying."

Ballet should be a place where children learn the power, grace, and beauty of their own bodies, and the value of their own minds and creative energies. It should be a place where professionals can make a decent living as they live out their childhood dreams safely and with autonomy. And it should be a place where audience members can feel welcome as they sit in the dark and marvel at what humans can do when they decide, collectively, that something matters.

Ballet began in Europe's royal courts in the seventeenth century. It spread from France and Italy to Russia and England, and then to those countries' many colonies, which is how, hundreds of years later, I came to learn the French terminology of ballet—*plié, tendu, fondu*—from teachers with broad Australian accents. For hundreds of years, people have danced ballet, watched ballet, taught ballet, made equipment for ballet, written and played music for ballet, built stages for ballet, sewn crystals onto costumes for ballet.

Each of those people had to be trained by someone else, and their training had to be subsidized by parents or by governments or by philanthropists who believed it was worth spending money on. In Russia, ballet survived Stalinism because Stalin himself enjoyed watching ballet and decided the art form should be kept alive, albeit in a shape that suited his political needs. In the United States, ballet flourished in part because the Soviets excelled at it, and the US was determined to beat the Communists at their own game.

In other words, ballet has survived for centuries because hundreds of thousands of people decided that it should.

That is what culture is, after all: people deciding, en masse, that something matters. Ballet is the result of almost four hundred years' worth of people all around the world—dancers, set designers, the people who make pointe shoes by hand, and all the people who trained all those people—deciding that this old art form is still worth their time.[1]

If ballet is going to continue to be worth our time, it must evolve. For the sake of "the younger audiences and the ballerinas that are coming up now and training now," Pazcoguin says, "I am not going to stand for the same disrespect that I allowed to happen when I was seventeen. I could never."

"I do think there's a way that ballet can change, and it has to, because it's not going to survive," says New York City Ballet principal dancer Lauren Lovette. "The next generation's too smart. They're too smart. They're not going to sign up for it."

If that's true, if ballet's rising generation will be the one to save it, they will do so on the shoulders of those who came before them, including many of the creators and leaders we have met in this book. It is also true that older generations fail the ones who come after them when they hand off to the young the hard work of overhauling broken systems—especially when they themselves contributed to the brokenness. But a new generation is rising, it is accustomed to repairing the failures of previous generations, and it is ready for the work.

Dancing is an act of connection—to music, to community, to history, to an audience, to one's own body. To dance is to affirm our humanity, to take up space, to revel in our own beauty and power. In moments of crisis—be they political, ecological, or epidemiological—acts of humanity and beauty are precious, essential, life-affirming. Ballet is sometimes described as an ephemeral art, a creation that vanishes as soon as it appears. But the harm it can do, as well as the enormous good, will endure.

ACKNOWLEDGMENTS

In the immortal words of Leslie Knope, no one achieves anything alone. *Turning Pointe* would not exist without the generosity, kindness, expertise, and labor of so many people whose names don't appear on the front cover.

JL Stermer is the best kind of agent: curious, relentless, kind, and deeply knowledgeable. I am grateful to her, and to the entire New Leaf Literary team.

Remy Cawley believed in my voice and my writing from before the very beginning and championed this book in sickness and in health. Ben Platt stepped in with grace and humility and brought his insight and enthusiasm to these pages, making them better in a hundred different ways. Katy O'Donnell and everyone at Bold Type Books, including the copyeditors, fact-checkers, and cover art designers, made me feel like I was always in good hands. When I was alone in the dark of the book cave, the Bold Type motto—"Challenging power, one book at a time"—served as a guiding light.

Theresa Ruth Howard helped me find my lane and stay in it, and I am deeply thankful for her expertise and activism.

The research in this book was made possible by Theresa Mangum and the Obermann Center for Advanced Studies at the University of Iowa, where I was a public scholar in the spring and fall of 2020. The many interviews were transcribed, with efficiency and accuracy, by a remarkable group of women: Laurie Batzel, Paige Cornwell, Kitty Guo, Ashley Patrick, and Catherine Trautwein.

My research was also made possible by the publications and journalists who continue to produce arts coverage in the face of huge challenges, most notably at *Pointe* and *Dance Magazine*, the *New York Times*, and the *New Yorker*. We need more arts coverage in this world, not less, and I am so grateful to the outlets that keep investing in it.

My first readers—Jessalynn Adam, Jessie Daniels, Amanda DeLuise, Alfred Martin, and Rainesford Stauffer—gave me valuable feedback at crucial moments in the drafting process. My newsletter readers kept me company during a long and lonely marathon.

Charlotte Pudlowski and Alex Rapson wrote letters of recommendation for writing residencies. Adam and Brigette Ingersoll gave me a place to write. Amy Aronson, Michael Kimmel, Ellen Gesmer, Miriam Peterson, Nathan Rich, Barbara Littenberg, and Stephen Peterson all gave me a place to stay during reporting trips in New York City. Emily Bufferd made it possible for me to do reporting at the Joffrey Ballet School. Leslie Nolte and Katy Pyle opened their dance schools to me. Vivian Le's photographs made me feel like a real author.

This book was also made possible by the editors who gave me a platform to cover ballet, even when that wasn't the beat I was hired for. I will always be grateful to Katy Brooks, who let me write about ballet for the HuffPost arts desk in 2016 and 2017. Thank you also to Danielle McNally, who said yes to ballet stories at *Marie Claire*. Thank you to Lilly Workneh, Choyce Miller, and Damon Dahlen, with whom I was lucky enough to collaborate on ballet coverage at HuffPost.

Behind every published author, if she's lucky, is a team of friends and loved ones who supported her ambitions and her ideas. I am beyond lucky.

My Iowa Coven—Lyz Lenz, Rachel Yoder, and Kerry Howley—gave me excellent advice and much-needed support, and made me feel at home in my new home. Molly Borowitz and Fannie Bialek have been supporting my dance dreams since that meant sitting in the audience of a college dance show surrounded by drunken frat boys. Jordan Kisner led the way, passed along so much of her hard-earned wisdom, and talked me out of more than one book spiral.

Whitney Williams Skowronski and Greg Skowronski helped me prep for a crucial editor meeting as we drove through Vermont in a tiny rental car. Erica Duke Forsyth's curiosity and compassion kept me afloat. Sylvia Qiu and Ariel Williams made sure I never missed a piece of ballet news in our Ballet Snark group chat. Vanessa Zoltan and I have been on the first-book journey together, and I couldn't have asked for a better travel buddy.

Melanie Gross was always ready to listen, and she and her daughters made me bagels when I finished my first draft. Natalia Temesgen had smart things to say about book covers. Jackie Reger, Terry Wahls, and Zeb Wahls endured many discussions of ballet during weekly family dinners, and Claire and Ian Morgan didn't complain when I somehow managed to make every conversation about ballet.

Lauren Sandler wrote recommendation letters, read draft chapters, pushed me to see the biggest possible metaphors in my reporting, and never let me doubt for a moment that I was up to this daunting task. My work, and my life, are so much better because of her friendship.

Abby Bloom and Robert Angyal encouraged me to pick a stable and sensible career path, and then gave me nothing but encouragement and support when I chose freelance feminist journalism instead. I am so proud to be their daughter.

Zach Wahls has nurtured my ambitions and made my success his priority. He supported me through the book-writing process with patience, enthusiasm, and love. I could not ask for a better partner.

Finally, and most crucially, this book simply would not exist if dozens of members of the ballet world had not trusted me with their stories. Thank you. I am grateful for your courage, and I hope I have done you justice.

SELECTED BIBLIOGRAPHY

Adair, Christy. *Women and Dance: Sylphs and Sirens*. London: Macmillan, 1992.

Burt, Ramsey. *The Male Dancer: Bodies, Spectacle, Sexualities*. New York: Routledge, 2003.

Dunning, Jennifer. *Alvin Ailey: A Life in Dance*. New York: Da Capo, 1998.

Farrell, Suzanne, and Toni Bentley. *Holding On to the Air: An Autobiography*. Gainesville: University Press of Florida, 2002.

Fisher, Jennifer. *Nutcracker Nation: How an Old World Ballet Became a Christmas Tradition in the New World*. New Haven, CT: Yale University Press, 2003.

Fishman, Katharine Davis. *Attitude! Eight Young Dancers Come of Age at the Ailey School*. New York: Jeremy P. Tarcher/Penguin, 2004.

Garafola, Lynn. *Legacies of Twentieth-Century Dance*. Middletown, CT: Wesleyan University Press, 2005.

———. *Rethinking the Sylph: New Perspectives on the Romantic Ballet*. Middletown, CT: Wesleyan University Press, 1997.

Garafola, Lynn, with Eric Foner, eds. *Dance for a City: Fifty Years of the New York City Ballet*. New York: Columbia University Press, 1999.

Gottlieb, Robert, ed. *Reading Dance: A Gathering of Memoirs, Reportage, Criticism, Profiles, Interviews, and Some Uncategorizable Extras*. New York: Pantheon Books, 2008.

Gottschild, Brenda Dixon. *The Black Dancing Body: A Geography from Coon to Cool*. New York: Palgrave Macmillan, 2003.

Gray, Lucy. *Balancing Acts: Three Prima Ballerinas Becoming Mothers*. New York: Princeton Architectural Press, 2015.

Hallberg, David. *A Body of Work: Dancing to the Edge and Back*. New York: Touchstone, 2017.

Hanna, Judith Lynne. *Dance, Sex, and Gender: Signs of Identity, Dominance, Defiance, and Desire*. Chicago: University of Chicago Press, 1988.

Homans, Jennifer. *Apollo's Angels: A History of Ballet*. New York: Random House, 2010.

Jacobs, Laura. *Celestial Bodies: How to Look at Ballet*. New York: Basic Books, 2018.

Jowitt, Deborah. *Jerome Robbins: His Life, His Theatre, His Dance*. New York: Simon and Schuster, 2004.

Kelly, Deirdre. *Ballerina: Sex, Scandal, and Suffering Behind the Symbol of Perfection*. Vancouver: Greystone Books, 2012.

Kent, Allegra. *Once a Dancer: An Autobiography*. Gainesville: University Press of Florida, 2009.

Klapper, Melissa. *Ballet Class: An American History*. New York: Oxford University Press, 2020.

Laurens, Camille. *Little Dancer Aged Fourteen: The True Story Behind Degas's Masterpiece*. New York: Other Press, 2018.

Lee, Carol. *Ballet in Western Culture: A History of Its Origins and Evolution*. New York: Routledge, 2002.

Mazo, Joseph. *Dance Is a Contact Sport*. New York: Da Capo, 1974.

Perron, Wendy. *Through the Eyes of a Dancer: Selected Writings*. Middletown, CT: Wesleyan University Press, 2013.

Stoneley, Peter. *A Queer History of the Ballet*. New York: Routledge, 2017.

SELECTED FILMOGRAPHY

Barba, David, and James Pellerito, dir. *Anatomy of a Male Ballet Dancer.* 2017.

Belle, Anne, and Deborah Dickson, dir. *Dancing for Mr. B: Six Balanchine Ballerinas.* 1989.

Cantor, Steven, dir. *Ballet Now.* 2018.

Geller, Dan, and Dayna Goldfine, dir. *Ballets Russes.* 2005.

George, Nelson, dir. *A Ballerina's Tale.* 2015.

Gormley, Scott, dir. *Danseur.* 2018.

Kargman, Bess, dir. *First Position.* 2011.

Lipes, Jody Lee, dir. *Ballet 422.* 2014.

McElroy, Frances, dir. *Black Ballerina.* 2016.

Saffire, Linda, and Adam Schlesinger, dir. *Restless Creature.* 2016.

Watkin, Douglas, dir. *Ella.* 2014.

NOTES

Introduction

1. Charlotte Graham-McLay, "'All Men for 150 Years': Women Take Centre Stage at Royal New Zealand Ballet," *Guardian*, February 1, 2020, www.theguardian .com/world/2020/feb/01/all-men-for-150-years-women-take-centre-stage-at-royal -new-zealand-ballet.

2. Brenda Dixon Gottschild, *The Black Dancing Body: A Geography from Coon to Cool* (New York: Palgrave Macmillan, 2003), 107.

3. Julia Jacobs, "New York City Ballet Dropped from a Woman's Photo-Sharing Lawsuit," *New York Times*, September 28, 2020, www.nytimes.com/2020/09/28/arts /dance/new-york-city-ballet-lawsuit.html.

4. Julia Jacobs, "No 'Nutcracker' This Year, New York City Ballet Says," *New York Times*, June 18, 2020, www.nytimes.com/2020/06/18/arts/dance/nutcracker -canceled-new-york-city-ballet-virus.html.

5. Lauren Wingenroth, "Are Ballet Companies Making Too Much from 'The Nutcracker'?," *Dance Magazine*, December 17, 2018, www.dancemagazine.com /nutcracker-facts-2623194475.html.

6. Soraya Nadia McDonald, "South African Choreographer Reinterprets 'Giselle' as a Vehicle for Female Rage," Undefeated, April 5, 2018, https://theundefeated .com/features/south-african-choreographer-reinterprets-giselle-as-a-vehicle-for -female-rage/.

7. Lucy Gray, *Balancing Acts: Three Prima Ballerinas Becoming Mothers* (New York: Princeton Architectural Press, 2015), 16.

8. Joseph Mazo, *Dance Is a Contact Sport* (New York: Da Capo, 1974), 76.

9. Carol Lee, *Ballet in Western Culture: A History of Its Origins and Evolution* (New York: Routledge, 2002), 191.

10. Mazo, *Dance Is a Contact Sport*, 259.

Chapter 1

1. "Dance Studios Industry in the US—Market Research Report," IBISWorld, December 30, 2019, www.ibisworld.com/united-states/market-research-reports /dance-studios-industry/.

2. Charlotte Graham-McLay, "'All Men for 150 Years': Women Take Centre Stage at Royal New Zealand Ballet," *Guardian*, February 1 2020, www.theguardian

.com/world/2020/feb/01/all-men-for-150-years-women-take-centre-stage-at-royal
-new-zealand-ballet.

3. Melissa Klapper, *Ballet Class: An American History* (New York: Oxford University Press, 2020), 274.

4. Jennifer Homans, *Apollo's Angels: A History of Ballet* (New York: Random House, 2010), 224.

5. Allegra Kent, "Nijinska," in *Reading Dance: A Gathering of Memoirs, Reportage, Criticism, Profiles, Interviews, and Some Uncategorizable Extras*, ed. Robert Gottlieb (New York: Pantheon Books, 2008), 1223.

6. Susan W. Stinson, "Journey Toward a Feminist Pedagogy for Dance," *Women and Performance* 6, no. 1 (1993): 131–146, https://doi.org/10.1080/07407709308571170.

7. Stinson, "Journey Toward a Feminist Pedagogy."

8. Carol Lee, *Ballet in Western Culture: A History of Its Origins and Evolution* (New York: Routledge, 2002), 193–194.

9. Susan Sontag, "Dancer and the Dance," *London Review of Books*, February 5, 1987.

10. Theresa Ruth Howard, keynote remarks at Positioning Ballet conference, Amsterdam, February 16, 2019, https://mobballet.org/index.php/2019/02/21/positioning
-ballet-conference-2019-hosted-by-dutch-national-ballet-theresa-ruth-howard
-keynote-speech/.

11. Stinson, "Journey Toward a Feminist Pedagogy."

12. Stinson, "Journey Toward a Feminist Pedagogy."

13. Stinson, "Journey Toward a Feminist Pedagogy."

14. Christy Adair, *Women and Dance: Sylphs and Sirens* (London: Macmillan, 1992), 12.

15. Adair, *Women and Dance*, 115.

16. Stinson, "Journey Toward a Feminist Pedagogy."

17. Kathryn Morgan, "Romeo and Juliet Death Scene with Commentary," YouTube video, 13:57, October 19, 2018, www.youtube.com/watch?v=0aZDN-GLukc.

18. "Mission," Ballez, accessed November 17, 2020, www.ballez.org/mission.

19. "The Firebird," Ballez, www.ballez.org/shows/the-firebird/; "Giselle of Loneliness," Ballez, www.ballez.org/shows/giselle-of-loneliness/.

20. "Mission," Ballez.

Chapter 2

1. Katherine Davis Fishman, *Attitude! Eight Young Dancers Come of Age at the Ailey School* (New York: Jeremy P. Tarcher/Penguin, 2004), 12.

2. Deirdre Kelly, *Ballerina: Sex, Scandal, and Suffering Behind the Symbol of Perfection* (Vancouver: Greystone Books, 2012), 6; Jennifer Homans, *Apollo's Angels: A History of Ballet* (New York: Random House, 2010), 12.

3. Peter Stoneley, *A Queer History of the Ballet* (New York: Routledge, 2017), 9.

4. Stoneley, *A Queer History of the Ballet*, 9.

5. Judith Lynne Hanna, *Dance, Sex and Gender: Signs of Identity, Dominance, Defiance, and Desire* (Chicago: University of Chicago Press), 123.

6. Kelly, *Ballerina*, 47.

7. Stoneley, *A Queer History of the Ballet*, 10.

8. Hanna, *Dance, Sex and Gender*, 124, 123, 131.

9. Lynn Garafola, *Legacies of Twentieth-Century Dance* (Middletown, CT: Wesleyan University Press, 2005), 138–139.

10. Stoneley, *A Queer History of the Ballet*, 10–11.

11. Homans, *Apollo's Angels*, 131.

12. Lynn Garafola, *Rethinking the Sylph: New Perspectives on the Romantic Ballet* (Hanover, NH: University Press of New England, 1997), 7.

13. Garafola, *Rethinking the Sylph*, 138.

14. Stoneley, *A Queer History of the Ballet*, 23–24.

15. Homans, *Apollo's Angels*, 145.

16. Kelly, *Ballerina*, 50–51.

17. Stoneley, *A Queer History of the Ballet*, 24; Hanna, *Dance, Sex and Gender*, 124, 125.

18. Garafola, *Legacies of Twentieth-Century Dance*, 142.

19. Garafola, *Legacies of Twentieth-Century Dance*, 140.

20. David Charlton, *The Cambridge Companion to Grand Opera* (Cambridge, UK: Cambridge University Press, 2003), 106; Kelly, *Ballerina*, 55.

21. Camille Laurens, *Little Dancer Aged Fourteen: The True Story Behind Degas's Masterpiece* (New York: Other Press, 2018).

22. Hanna, *Dance, Sex and Gender*, 125.

23. Melissa Klapper, *Ballet Class: An American History* (New York: Oxford University Press, 2020), 131.

24. Eileen Patten, "Racial, Gender Wage Gaps Persist in U.S. Despite Some Progress," Fact Tank, Pew Research Center, July 1, 2016, www.pewresearch.org /fact-tank/2016/07/01/racial-gender-wage-gaps-persist-in-u-s-despite-some -progress/; Angela Hanks, Danyelle Solomon, and Christian E. Weller, "Systematic Inequality: How America's Structural Racism Helped Create the Black-White Wealth Gap," Center for American Progress, February 21, 2018, www.american progress.org/issues/race/reports/2018/02/21/447051/systematic-inequality/; Bohne Silber and Tim Triplett, *A Decade of Arts Engagement: Findings from the Survey of Public Participation in the Arts, 2002–2012*, NEA Research Report #58, National Endowment for the Arts, January 2015, p. 66, www.arts.gov/sites/default/files/2012 -sppa-feb2015.pdf.

25. Doug Risner, "Bullying Victimisation and Social Support of Adolescent Male Dance Students: An Analysis of Findings," *Research in Dance Education* 15, no. 2 (2014): 179–201.

Chapter 3

1. Joseph Mazo, *Dance Is a Contact Sport* (New York: Da Capo, 1974), 25.

2. Brenda Dixon Gottschild, *The Black Dancing Body: A Geography from Coon to Cool* (New York: Palgrave Macmillan, 2003), 11.

3. Victor R. Prisk, Padhraig F. O'Loughlin, and John G. Kennedy, "Forefoot Injuries in Dancers," *Clinics in Sports Medicine* 27, no. 2 (April 2008): 305–320; Joel Schwarz, "Ballet Dancer Injuries as Common, Severe as Athletic Injuries," UW News, University of Washington, October 11, 2000, www.washington.edu /news/2000/10/11/ballet-dancer-injuries-as-common-severe-as-athletic-injuries/.

4. Abi Stafford, "Ache, Throb, Hurt," *Dance Magazine*, December 29, 2016, www .dancemagazine.com/ache-throb-hurt-2307053105.html; Jeffrey A. Russell, "Preventing Dance Injuries: Current Perspectives," *Open Access Journal of Sports Medicine* 2013, no. 4 (September 2013): 199–210, https://doi.org/10.2147/OAJSM.S36529.

5. Prisk, O'Loughlin, and Kennedy, "Forefoot Injuries in Dancers"; Megan Goulart, Martin J. O'Malley, Christopher W. Hodgkins, and Timothy P. Charlton, "Foot

and Ankle Fractures in Dancers," *Clinics in Sports Medicine* 27, no. 2 (April 2008), 295–304.

6. Christopher W. Hodgkins, John G. Kennedy, and Padhraig F. O'Loughlin, "Tendon Injuries in Dance," *Clinics in Sports Medicine* 27, no. 2 (May 2008): 279–288.

7. "Dramatica Stretch Axis Pointe Shoes," Bloch, accessed November 17, 2020, https://us.blochworld.com/products/dramatica-stretch-axis-pointe-shoes-pink-satin.

8. Prisk, O'Loughlin, and Kennedy, "Forefoot Injuries in Dancers."

9. Padhraig F. O'Loughlin, Christopher W. Hodgkins, and John G. Kennedy, "Ankle Sprains and Instability in Dancers," *Clinics in Sports Medicine* 27, no. 2 (April 2008): 247–262.

10. I've used pseudonyms for dancers who were under eighteen at the time I interviewed them, unless I had parental permission to quote them.

11. Megan Goulart, Martin J. O'Malley, Christopher W. Hodgkins, and Timothy P. Charlton, "Foot and Ankle Fractures in Dancers," *Clinics in Sports Medicine* 27, no. 2 (April 2008): 295–304; Russell, "Preventing Dance Injuries."

12. Kevin Conley, "Pointe Counterpointe," *New Yorker*, December 2, 2002.

13. Conley, "Pointe Counterpointe."

14. Deirdre Kelly, *Ballerina: Sex, Scandal, and Suffering Behind the Symbol of Perfection* (Vancouver: Greystone Books, 2012), 84, 85.

15. Kelly, *Ballerina*, 86.

16. Steven B. Weinfeld, Steven L. Haddad, and Mark S. Myerson, "Metatarsal Stress Fractures," *Clinics in Sports Medicine* 16, no. 2 (April 1, 1997): 319–338; O'Loughlin, Hodgkins, and Kennedy, "Ankle Sprains and Instability in Dancers."

17. Pierre A. d'Hemecourt and Anthony Luke, "Sport-Specific Biomechanics of Spinal Injuries in Aesthetic Athletes (Dancers, Gymnasts, and Figure Skaters)," *Clinics in Sports Medicine* 31, no. 3 (July 2007): 397–408.

18. John G. Kennedy and Christopher W. Hodgkins, "Bunions in Dancers," *Clinics in Sports Medicine* 27, no. 2 (April 2008): 321–328.

19. Kennedy and Hodgkins, "Bunions in Dancers."

20. S. Byhring and K. Bø, "Musculoskeletal Injuries in the Norwegian National Ballet: A Prospective Cohort Study," *Scandinavian Journal and Medicine and Science in Sports* 12, no. 6 (December 2002): 365–370; Dennis Caine et al., "A Survey of Injuries Affecting Pre-professional Ballet Dancers," *Journal of Dance Medicine and Science* 20, no. 3 (2016): 115–126.

21. Jennifer Homans, *Apollo's Angels: A History of Ballet* (New York: Random House, 2010), 23, 128.

22. D'Hemecourt and Luke, "Sport-Specific Biomechanics."

23. Renata Veloso Teixeira et al., "Prevalence of Urinary Incontinence in Female Athletes: A Systematic Review with Meta-Analysis," *International Urogynecology Journal* 29 (December 2018): 1717–1725; H. H. Thyssen, L. Clevin, S. Olesen, and G. Lose, "Urinary Incontinence in Elite Female Athletes and Dancers," *International Urogynecology Journal* 13 (March 2002): 15–17.

24. Teixeira, et al., "Prevalence of Urinary Incontinence."

25. Maya Dusenbery, *Doing Harm: The Truth About How Bad Medicine and Lazy Science Leave Women Dismissed, Misdiagnosed, and Sick* (New York: HarperOne, 2018); Abby Norman, *Ask Me About My Uterus: A Quest to Make Doctors Believe in Women's Pain* (New York: Hachette, 2018).

26. Goulart, O'Malley, Hodgkins, and Charlton, "Foot and Ankle Fractures in Dancers."

Chapter 4

1. Jennifer Stahl, "Our Wish List for the Next Decade of Dance," *Dance Magazine*, December 6, 2019, www.dancemagazine.com/goals-for-the-dance-field-2641527030 .html.

2. Kathleen McGuire, "Why Are We Still So Bad at Addressing Dancers' Mental Health?," *Dance Magazine*, July 27, 2017, www.dancemagazine.com/why-are -we-still-so-bad-at-addressing-dancers-mental-health-2466177083.html; Kathleen McGuire, "Dance Isn't for Everyone," *Dance Magazine*, October 26, 2017, www .dancemagazine.com/dance-mental-health-2501871371.html.

3. Kathleen McGuire, "Experts Talk Mental Health: Four Therapists Sound Off," *Dance Magazine*, November 2, 2018, www.dancemagazine.com/four-dance -psychologists-sound-off-2613604749.html.

4. Abigail Rasminsky, "When Injury Leads to an Identity Crisis," *Dance Magazine*, June 24, 2019, www.dancemagazine.com/injury-depression-2638932468.html.

5. Melinda Barlow, "Abolishing 'Effortless Perfection,'" National Education Association, accessed November 17, 2020, http://ftp.arizonaea.org/home/34818.htm.

6. Tiger Sun, "Duck Syndrome and a Culture of Misery," *Stanford Daily*, January 31, 2018, www.stanforddaily.com/2018/01/31/duck-syndrome-and-a-culture-of-misery/.

7. Harris Green, "Gelsey Kirkland: The Judy Garland of Ballet," in *Reading Dance: A Gathering of Memoirs, Reportage, Criticism, Profiles, Interviews, and Some Uncategorizable Extras*, ed. Robert Gottlieb (New York: Pantheon Books, 2008), 319.

8. Glenna Batson, "Resource Paper: Proprioception," International Association for Dance Medicine and Science, accessed November 17, 2020, www.iadms.org /page/210.

9. Kathleen McGuire, "Perfectionism Is an Epidemic in the Dance World. Here's How to Keep It from Derailing Your Career," *Dance Magazine*, December 18, 2019, www.dancemagazine.com/perfectionism-2641614596.html.

10. McGuire, "Perfectionism Is an Epidemic."

11. McGuire, "Dance Isn't for Everyone."

12. Vera Zorina, "A Masculine Man," in Gottlieb, *Reading Dance*, 142–143.

13. See, for example, Joan Ryan, *Little Girls in Pretty Boxes: The Making and Breaking of Elite Gymnasts and Figure Skaters* (New York: Doubleday, 1995).

14. Gelsey Kirkland, *Dancing on My Grave* (New York: Doubleday, 1986), 56.

15. *Knocked Up*, directed by Judd Apatow (2007; Universal City, CA: Universal Pictures).

16. Garnet Henderson, "What Would It Take to Change Ballet's Aesthetic of Extreme Thinness?," *Dance Magazine*, July 27, 2020, www.dancemagazine.com/ballet -body-2646451850.html.

17. Chloe Angyal, "Kathryn Morgan Returns to the Stage," *Marie Claire*, October 16, 2019, www.marieclaire.com/culture/a29444690/kathryn-morgan -miami-city-ballet/.

18. Kathryn Morgan, "Why I Left Miami City Ballet | #LifeUpdate | Mental Health & Body Image | Kathryn Morgan," YouTube video, 33:40, October 8, 2020, www.youtube.com/watch?v=BjdYTvsPpG4; Chloe Freytag (@chloefreytag), "People are calling out @kathryn_morgan for the illegitimacy of the story she shared of why she left MCB," Instagram post, October 9, 2020, www.instagram.com/p /CGH5k3CA4nC/; Leanna Rinaldi (@leannarinaldi), "I was hesitant in writing this but I realized I was just embarrassed," Instagram post, October 9, 2020, www .instagram.com/p/CGJNW32APhD/.

19. Rachel Rizzuto, "When Social Media Triggers Body Image Issues," *Dance Magazine*, September 23, 2019, www.dancemagazine.com/social-media-body-image-2640309596.html.

20. Lauren Lovette (@laurenlovette), Instagram, February 24, 2020, www.instagram.com/p/B88yc04hyTK/.

21. Marissa DeSantis, "Misty Copeland's 'Fouetté Fail' Is Proof Even the Pros Make Mistakes," *Pointe*, March 28, 2018, www.pointemagazine.com/misty-copeland-fouette-fail-2554122195.html.

22. Chava Lansky, "Meet Shelby Williams, the Real Pro Behind Biscuit Ballerina," *Pointe*, October 17, 2018, www.pointemagazine.com/shelby-williams-biscuit-ballerina-2613111352.html.

23. Stahl, "Our Wish List."

24. Erica N. Goodman-Hughey, "Ballet Dancer Misty Copeland Shares Her Truth Behind the Fairy Tale," *ESPNW*, December 3, 2019, www.espn.com/espnw/culture/story/_/id/28212654/ballet-dancer-misty-copeland-shares-truth-fairy-tale.

25. Courtney E. Martin, *Perfect Girls, Starving Daughters: The Frightening New Normalcy of Hating Your Body* (New York: Free Press, 2007), 207.

26. Martin, *Perfect Girls, Starving Daughters*, 209.

Chapter 5

1. Brenda Dixon Gottschild, *The Black Dancing Body: A Geography from Coon to Cool* (New York: Palgrave Macmillan, 2003), 6.

2. Gottschild, *The Black Dancing Body*, 37.

3. Gottschild, *The Black Dancing Body*, 53.

4. Theresa Ruth Howard, "1846: George Washington Smith Dances Albrecht in the First American Production of 'Giselle,'" MoBBallet.org, https://mobballet.org/index.php/2017/10/23/1846-george-washington-carver-dances-prince-siegfried-in-the-first-american-production-of-giselle/.

5. Melissa Klapper, *Ballet Class: An American History* (New York: Oxford University Press, 2020), 14.

6. Klapper, *Ballet Class*, 14.

7. Patricia Mears, *Ballerina: Fashion's Modern Muse* (New York: Vendome, 2019).

8. Dominique Astorino, "The Royal Ballet Collection from Lululemon Might Be the Most Gorgeous Thing We've Ever Seen," Brit + Co, October 9, 2018, www.brit.co/lululemon-francesca-hayward-collection-2018/.

9. Chloe Angyal, "How Fitness Culture Enlisted Ballerinas to Profit off Our Insecurities," HuffPost, January 26, 2017, www.huffpost.com/entry/how-fitness-culture-barre-class-ballerinas-to-profit-off-our-insecurities_n_588a0259e4b0024605fde868.

10. Jia Tolentino, *Trick Mirror: Reflections on Self-Delusion* (New York: Penguin Random House, 2019), 72.

11. Gottschild, *The Black Dancing Body*, 59.

12. Katherine Davis Fishman, *Attitude! Eight Young Dancers Come of Age at the Ailey School* (New York: Jeremy P. Tarcher/Penguin, 2004), 168.

13. Theresa Ruth Howard, "Is Ballet Brown-Bagging It?," *Dance Magazine*, April 3, 2017, www.dancemagazine.com/is-ballet-brown-bagging-it-2343051742.html.

14. Howard, "Is Ballet Brown-Bagging It?."

15. Gia Kourlas, "A Ballet Hamlet Becomes a God (Apollo, That Is)," *New York Times*, January 17, 2019, www.nytimes.com/2019/01/17/arts/dance/taylor-stanley-apollo.html; Calvin Royal III (@calvinroyaliii), "Me and my girl @MistyonPointe are going LIVE with journalist Budd Mishkin, SUNDAY 4/19 • 5p EST @92nd-streety," Instagram post, April 17, 2020, www.instagram.com/p/B_GFqczgZsH/.

16. Gia Koulas, "Aesha Ash Takes Her Place at the Head of the Class," *New York Times*, August 13, 2020, www.nytimes.com/2020/08/13/arts/dance/aesha-ash-american-ballet-faculty.html.

17. Daniel Applebaum, "Aesha Ash Is Bringing Her Boundary-Defying Spirit to SAB as Its First Black Female Full-Time Teacher," *Dance Teacher*, September 4, 2020, www.dance-teacher.com/aesha-ash-2647438802.html.

18. Lester Tomé, "Black Star, Other Fetishized: Carlos Acosta, Ballet's New Cosmopolitanism, and Desire in the Age of Institutional Diversity," in *The Routledge Companion to Dance Studies*, ed. Helen Thomas and Stacey Prickett (New York: Routledge, 2019), 298–310.

Chapter 6

1. Doug Risner, "Bullying Victimisation and Social Support of Adolescent Male Dance Students: An Analysis of Findings," *Research in Dance Education* 15, no. 2 (2014): 179–201.

2. Risner, "Bullying Victimisation"; Chloe Angyal, "Tights, Tutus and 'Relentless' Teasing: Inside Ballet's Bullying Epidemic," HuffPost, October 5, 2017, www.huffpost.com/entry/ballet-bullying_n_59d5148ce4b0218923e724bf.

3. David Hallberg, *Body of Work: Dancing to the Edge and Back* (New York: Touchstone, 2017), 35.

4. Hallberg, *Body of Work*, 28, 35.

5. Angyal, "Tights, Tutus and 'Relentless' Teasing."

6. Angyal, "Tights, Tutus and 'Relentless' Teasing."

7. Isabel Greenberg, "Princess Charlotte Is Reportedly Taking Weekly Ballet Lessons," *Harper's Bazaar*, December 19, 2018, www.harpersbazaar.com/celebrity/latest/a25628352/princess-charlotte-prince-george-ballet-lessons/.

8. Gia Kourlas, "Hey, Lara Spencer, Ballet Is for Boys," *New York Times*, August 23, 2019, www.nytimes.com/2019/08/23/arts/dance/lara-spencer-ballet.html.

9. Complexions Contemporary Ballet (@complexions_ballet), "In response to the comments @lara.spencer said on @goodmorningamerica today, we wanted to share these words from our dancer, Jared Brunson," Instagram post, August 23, 2019, www.instagram.com/p/B1hol-ZhL_r/; Caitlin O'Kane, "300 Dancers Show Up in Times Square as Lara Spencer Apologizes for Prince George Ballet Comment," CBSNews.com, August 27, 2019, www.cbsnews.com/news/300-dancers-class-in-times-square-as-gma-lara-spencer-apologizes-for-prince-george-ballet-comment-travis-wall/.

10. Washington Ballet (@thewashingtonballet), "Stigmas exist in our society that not only lead to bullying, but keep children from following their dreams," Instagram post, August 23, 2019, www.instagram.com/p/B1go6DEH_8V/.

11. Alexandre Hammoudi (@alexhammoudi), "I will leave it at that . . . ," Instagram photo, August 23, 2019, www.instagram.com/p/B1hdIWcgYsE/; Pacific Northwest Ballet (@pacificnorthwestballet), "Studying ballet takes discipline, focus and determination – this art form requires a high level of physical and mental stamina," Instagram post, August 23, 2019, www.instagram.com/p/B1hoaT0gIEw/.

12. Tiler Peck (@tilerpeck), "#boysdancetoo Here's to all the boys out there who want to dance," Instagram post, August 24, 2019, www.instagram.com/p/B1jJNS OFUES/.

13. Chloe Chomicki and Nathalie Fernbach, "Queensland Ballet Invites Townsville Boy with Autism to Train with Mao's Last Dancer, Li Cunxin," ABC News, March 2, 2020, www.abc.net.au/news/2020-03-03/townsville-ballet-boy-studies -with-li-cunxin-in-brisbane/12015876.

14. Emily McGarvey, "Ballet Stereotypes: 'Male Ballet Dancers Aren't Just There to Look Pretty,'" video, BBC News, March 8, 2020, www.bbc.com /news/av/uk-northern-ireland-51744661/ballet-stereotypes-male-ballet-dancers -aren-t-just-there-to-look-pretty.

15. Angyal, "Tights, Tutus and 'Relentless' Teasing."

16. Angyal, "Tights, Tutus and 'Relentless' Teasing."

17. "About Project B," Royal Academy of Dance, last updated July 29, 2019, www .royalacademyofdance.org/project-b/about-project-b/.

Chapter 7

1. "2 Fired Dancers, Donor Added to Ballet Lawsuit," Associated Press, September 18, 2018, https://apnews.com/1ca527c682da46859cf2c4d6430cd699.

2. Robin Pogrebin and Michael Cooper, "Vulgar Texts and Dancer Turmoil Force City Ballet to Look in the Mirror," *New York Times*, October 3, 2018, www.nytimes .com/2018/10/03/arts/dance/new-york-city-ballet-metoo.html; Joan Acocella, "What Went Wrong at New York City Ballet," *New Yorker*, February 11, 2019, www.new yorker.com/magazine/2019/02/18/what-went-wrong-at-new-york-city-ballet.

3. Michael Cooper and Robin Pogrebin, "City Ballet and Chase Finlay Sued by Woman Who Says Nude Photos of Her Were Shared," September 5, 2018, *New York Times*, www.nytimes.com/2018/09/05/arts/dance/nyc-ballet-alexandra-waterbury .html.

4. Acocella, "What Went Wrong."

5. Priscilla DeGregory, "Lawyer for Ex-ballet Benefactor Calls Client's Lewd Texts 'Obnoxious,'" *New York Post*, January 21, 2020, https://nypost.com/2020/01/21 /lawyer-for-ex-ballet-benefactor-calls-clients-lewd-texts-obnoxious/.

6. Julia Jacobs, "New York City Ballet Dropped from a Woman's Photo-Sharing Lawsuit," *New York Times*, September 28, 2020, www.nytimes.com/2020/09/28/arts /dance/new-york-city-ballet-lawsuit.html; Julia Jacobs, "The Ballet Photo-Sharing Scandal Enters a New Phase in Court," *New York Times*, October 25, 2020, www .nytimes.com/2020/10/25/arts/dance/alexandra-waterbury-chase-finlay-lawsuit.html.

7. Susan Chira and Catrin Einhorn, "Ford Apologizes for Sexual Harassment at Chicago Factories," *New York Times*, December 21, 2017, www.nytimes .com/2017/12/21/us/ford-apology-sexual-harassment.html.

8. Michael Rellahan, "Ballet Teacher on Trial in Chester County for Indecent Assaults," *The Mercury* (PA), January 9, 2020, www.pottsmerc.com/news/ballet -teacher-on-trial-for-indecent-assaults/article_cb0f7d2f-897a-5bce-88fe -990b5ba0b665.html; Chloe Veltman, "Rape Case Against Revered Bay Area Dance Coach Moves Forward," KQED, October 5, 2018, www.kqed.org/news/11696873 /rape-case-against-revered-bay-area-dance-coach-moves-forward; Matthias Gafni, "After a Rape Mistrial in the #MeToo Era, Accusations Fly. What Happened in the Jury Room?," *San Francisco Chronicle*, November 10, 2019, www.sfchronicle.com /bayarea/article/After-a-rape-mistrial-in-the-MeToo-era-14823146.php.

9. Sam Corbishley, "Ex–Royal Ballet Star Jailed for Sexually Abusing Girls During Private Lessons," Metro.co.uk, November 1, 2019, https://metro.co.uk/2019/11/01/ex-royal-ballet-star-jailed-sexually-abusing-girls-private-lessons-11028871/; Alex Marshall, "Royal Ballet Suspends Choreographer Liam Scarlett over Sexual Misconduct Claims," *New York Times*, January 30, 2020, www.nytimes.com/2020/01/30/arts/dance/royal-ballet-liam-scarlett-suspended.html; Alex Marshall, "Royal Ballet and Liam Scarlett Part Ways After an Investigation," *New York Times*, March 23, 2020, www.nytimes.com/2020/03/23/arts/dance/royal-ballet-liam-scarlett.html.

10. "Ex–English National Ballet Principal Faces 14 Counts of Sexual Assault," *Guardian*, January 10, 2020, www.theguardian.com/uk-news/2020/jan/09/ex-english-national-ballet-principal-faces-14-counts-of-sexual-assault-yat-sen-chang; "Argyll's Ballet West Dance School Closes After Sexual Misconduct Claims," BBC News, August 24, 2020, www.bbc.com/news/uk-scotland-glasgow-west-53892375; Peter Smith, "Police Investigation Launched After ITV News Uncovers Allegations of Grooming at Prestigious UK Ballet School," ITV, August 19, 2020, www.itv.com/news/2020-08-17/police-investigation-launched-after-itv-news-uncovers-allegations-of-grooming-at-prestigious-uk-ballet-school.

11. Casey Tolan, Ashley Fantz, and Alessandra Freitas, "Groping, a Nude Photo, a Sex Party Invite: Former Ailey Dancers Say Director Abused Power with Students," CNN, July 25, 2020, https://edition.cnn.com/2020/07/25/us/alvin-ailey-dance-school-troy-powell-investigation-invs/index.html.

12. Ashley Fantz, Casey Tolan, and Alessandra Freitas, "Alvin Ailey Dance Theater Official Fired After Sexual Misconduct Allegations," CNN.com, July 20, 2020, www.cnn.com/2020/07/20/us/alvin-ailey-dance-school-troy-powell-invs/index.html.

13. Robin Pogrebin, "Five Dancers Accuse City Ballet's Peter Martins of Physical Abuse," *New York Times*, December 12, 2017, www.nytimes.com/2017/12/12/arts/dance/peter-martins-ballet-new-york-city-physical-abuse.html.

14. Sarah Kaufman, "New York City Ballet Leader to Take Leave Amid Sexual, Violence Allegations," *Washington Post*, December 7, 2017, www.washingtonpost.com/entertainment/theater_dance/new-york-city-ballet-leader-to-take-leave-amid-sexual-violence-allegations/2017/12/07/9b4e4884-db7a-11e7-b859-fb0995360725_story.html; Wilhelmina Frankfurt, "What's Missing in the Peter Martins Investigation," *Dance Magazine*, December 12, 2017, www.dancemagazine.com/wilhelmina-frankfurt-peter-martins-investigation-2516966253.html; Alyona Minkovski, "Former Peter Martins Dancer Alleges Vicious Pattern of Verbal Abuse and Sexual Misconduct," Salon, January 8, 2018, www.salon.com/2018/01/08/peter-martins-sexual-misconduct-wilhelmina-frankfurt/.

15. Pogrebin, "Five Dancers"; Robin Pogrebin, "Peter Martins Left City Ballet a Year Ago. But He's Not Entirely Gone," *New York Times*, February 22, 2019, www.nytimes.com/2019/02/22/arts/dance/peter-martins-city-ballet.html.

16. Pogrebin, "Peter Martins Left."

17. www.washingtonpost.com/lifestyle/style/ballet-chief-peter-martins-under-investigation-after-sexual-harassment-allegations/2017/12/04/a474eae6-d3a3-11e7-a986-d0a9770d9a3e_story.html.

18. Alexandra Villareal, "'It's Like a Cult': How Sexual Misconduct Permeates the World of Ballet,'" *Guardian*, November 2, 2018, www.theguardian.com/stage/2018/nov/02/ballet-stage-me-too-sexual-abuse-harassment.

19. Villareal, "'It's Like a Cult.'"

20. Alistair Macaulay, "'We, the Dancers': At City Ballet's Gala, Affirming Ballet's Honor," *New York Times*, September 28, 2018, www.nytimes.com/2018/09/28/arts /review-new-york-city-ballet-fashion-gala.html.

21. Macaulay, "'We, the Dancers.'"

22. Michael Cooper, "City Ballet Ordered to Reinstate Male Dancers Fired over Inappropriate Texts," *New York Times*, April 19, 2019, www.nytimes.com/2019/04/19 /arts/dance/city-ballet-amar-ramasar-sexually-explicit-texts.html.

23. Cooper, "City Ballet Ordered."

24. Cooper, "City Ballet Ordered."

25. Cooper, "City Ballet Ordered."

26. Kosta Karakashyan, "What AGMA Got Wrong in Advocating for the NYCB Principals Trading Nude Photos of Ballerinas," *Dance Magazine*, April 24, 2019, www.dancemagazine.com/amar-ramasar-return-to-nycb-2635444405.html.

27. Karakashyan, "What AGMA Got Wrong."

28. "How Much Can You Make in Dance? Here Are More Than 200 Actual Salaries," *Dance Magazine*, July 18, 2018, www.dancemagazine.com/dance-salaries -2587282090.html.

29. Ali Watkins, "Jeffrey Epstein's New York Hunting Ground: Dance Studios," *New York Times*, September 3, 2019, www.nytimes.com/2019/09/03/nyregion/jeffrey -epstein-dance-victims.html.

30. Watkins, "Jeffrey Epstein's New York Hunting Ground."

31. Amy Brandt, "'I Was in Disbelief': Jeffrey Epstein Targeted Dancers at NYC Studios, with Others Acting as Recruiters," *Pointe*, September 3, 2019, www .pointemagazine.com/jeffrey-epstein-dancers-2640183763.html.

32. Jayne Thompson, "The Salaries of Ballet Dancers," Chron, July 1, 2018, https://work.chron.com/salaries-ballet-dancers-5128.html; Madeline Shrock, "Dance Ranked Most Physically Demanding Job in the U.S.," *Dance Magazine*, January 24, 2020, www.dancemagazine.com/dance-most-physically-demanding -job-2644898194.html.

33. "How Much Can You Make In Dance?."

Chapter 8

1. *2018–2019 Season Overview*, Dance Data Project, July 2019, www.dance dataproject.com/wp-content/uploads/2019/07/July-2019-2018-2019-Season-Over view.pdf; Siobhan Burke, "The Choreographer Kyle Abraham Mixes Things Up at City Ballet," *New York Times*, September 21, 2018, www.nytimes.com/2018/09/21 /arts/the-choreographer-kyle-abraham-mixes-things-up-at-city-ballet.html.

2. *Global Resident Choreographer Survey*, Dance Data Project, January 2020, www.dancedataproject.com/wp-content/uploads/2020/01/January-2020-Resident -Choreographers.pdf.

3. Lynn Garafola, *Legacies of Twentieth-Century Dance* (Middletown, CT: Wesleyan University Press, 2005), 216.

4. Garafola, *Legacies of Twentieth-Century Dance*, 216.

5. Chloe Angyal, "Behind the Tutus, Ballet Is a Boys' Club. This Ballerina Wants to Fix That," HuffPost, March 15, 2017, www.huffpost.com/entry/behind-the-tutus -ballet-is-a-boys-club-ashley-bouder-wants-to-fix-that_n_58c9302ee4b01c 029d77a81f.

6. Angyal, "Behind The Tutus."

7. Ashley Bouder, "'He Literally Pat Me on the Head.' Dr. Linda Hamilton and Ashley Bouder Talk Women in Ballet," interview by Dr. Linda Hamilton (video), *Dance Magazine*, September 5, 2019, www.dancemagazine.com/ashley-bouder -feminism-2640197883.html.

8. Bouder, "He Literally Pat Me on the Head"; *Executive & Artistic Leadership Report*, The Dance Data Project, February 2019, www.dancedataproject.com/wp -content/uploads/2019/02/Leadership-Report-2019.pdf.

9. Lauren Wingenroth, "Does NYCB Have a Gambling Problem?," *Dance Magazine*, September 29, 2015, www.dancemagazine.com/does-nycb-have-a -gambling-problem-2306973405.html; Roslyn Sulcas, "New York City Ballet Gambles on Unknown Choreographers," *New York Times*, September 23, 2015, www .nytimes.com/2015/09/27/arts/dance/new-york-city-ballet-gambles-on-unknown -choreographers.html.

10. ABT Women's *Move*ment," American Ballet Theatre, accessed November 17, 2020, www.abt.org/community/diversity-inclusion/abt-womens-movement./.

11. "Creations in Studio K," Tulsa Ballet Theater, accessed November 17, 2020, https://tulsaballet.org/creations-studio-k; Amy Fine Collins, "Female Choreographers Take Center Stage at American Ballet Theater," *Marie Claire*, October 10, 2018, www.marieclaire.com/culture/a23653361/abt-america-ballet-theater -female-choreographers/.

12. "ChoreograpHER Initiative," Boston Ballet, accessed November 17, 2020, www.bostonballet.org/Home/Support/choreograpHER-initiative; Iris Fanger, "Boston Ballet's 'The Nutcracker' Leaps onto TV This Holiday Season," *Patriot Ledger* (MA), September 14, 2020, www.patriotledger.com/entertainmentlife/20200914 /boston-ballets-the-nutcracker-leaps-onto-tv-this-holiday-season.

13. *2018–2019 Season Overview*, Dance Data Project; *2019–2020 Season Overview*, Dance Data Project, July 2020, www.dancedataproject.com/wp-content /uploads/2020/08/July-2020-Season-Report.pdf.

14. Steve Sucato, "Royal New Zealand Ballet's Entire 2020 Season Will Feature Works by Women Choreographers," *Pointe*, October 23, 2019, www.pointemagazine .com/royal-new-zealand-ballet-women-choreographers-2641077060.html.

15. *2019–2020 Season Overview*, Dance Data Project.

16. Roslyn Sulcas, "Dada Masilo Turns Tchaikovsky on His Head in 'Swan Lake,'" *New York Times*, February 1, 2016, www.nytimes.com/2016/02/02/arts/dance/dada -masilo-turnstchaikovsky-on-his-head-in-swan-lake.html.

17. Jennifer Homans, "Akram Khan Remakes 'Giselle,'" *New Yorker*, April 15, 2019, www.newyorker.com/magazine/2019/04/22/akram-khan-remakes-giselle.

18. Chelsea Thomas, "World Premiere: Helen Picketts Full-Length 'Camino Real' Ballet," Dance Informa, n.d., www.danceinforma.com/2015/03/25/world-premiere -helen-picketts-full-length-camino-real-ballet/; Jen Peters, "Female Choreographers Are Reimagining What Stories Ballets Can Be," *Dance Magazine*, April 27, 2020, www.dancemagazine.com/women-choreographers-2645714147.html.

19. "Choreography," Annabelle Lopez Ochoa, accessed November 17, 2020, www .annabellelopezochoa.com/www.annabellelopezochoa.com/Choreography.html.

20. Peters, "Female Choreographers Are Reimagining"; English National Ballet (@englishnationalballet), "Stina Quagebeur's Nora in rehearsal (2019)," Instagram post, May 18, 2020, www.instagram.com/tv/CAVQwAbHyJy/?igshid=1txag8lj8p9ft.

21. Peters, "Female Choreographers."

22. "La Bayadère," American Ballet Theatre, accessed November 17, 2020, www .abt.org/ballet/la-bayadere/.

23. Phil Chan, *Final Bow for Yellowface: Dancing Between Intention and Impact* (n.p.: Yellow Peril Press, 2020).

24. Lynsey Winship, "'Dance Is Not a Museum': How Ballet Is Reimagining Problematic Classics," *Guardian*, January 10, 2020, www.theguardian.com/stage/2020 /jan/09/ballet-reimagining-classics-colonial-politics-dance-race-identity.

25. Sarah Kaufman, "An 18-Year-Old New Ballet Star Salvages an Outmoded Tale of Pirates, Slaves and Stereotypes," *Washington Post*, April 10, 2019, www .washingtonpost.com/entertainment/theater_dance/an-18-year-old-new-ballet-star -salvages-an-outmoded-tale-of-pirates-slaves-and-stereotypes/2019/04/10/c1b685cc -5af9-11e9-b8e3-b03311fbbbfe_story.html.

26. Ellen Dunkel, "Corella Aims to Erase Stereotypes from His Otherwise Familiar 'La Bayadère,'" *Philadelphia Inquirer*, March 24, 2020, www.inquirer.com/arts /pennsylvania-ballet-la-bayadere-angel-corella-stereotypes-diversity-20200304. html; Ellen Dunkel, "Corella's 'Bayadère' for Pennsylvania Ballet Has Merit, but Stereotypes Persist," *Philadelphia Inquirer*, March 6, 2020, www.inquirer.com/arts /pennsylvania-ballet-la-bayadere-dancers-stereotypes-angel-corella-20200306.html.

27. "Moving Stories," American Ballet Theatre, accessed November 17, 2020, www.abt.org/events/moving-stories/.

28. Georgina Pazcoguin, "What's the Tea? with Edwaard Liang," YouTube video, 54:18, May 28, 2020, www.youtube.com/watch?v=xApUFSogie8.

29. *Artistic and Executive Leadership Report*, Dance Data Project, March 2020, www.dancedataproject.com/wp-content/uploads/2020/03/Leadership-Report-2020 .pdf.

30. *Artistic and Executive Leadership Report*, Dance Data Project.

31. Brenda Dixon Gottschild, *The Black Dancing Body: A Geography from Coon to Cool* (New York: Palgrave Macmillan, 2003), 82.

32. Winship, "'Dance Is Not a Museum.'"

Chapter 9

1. Kim Park, Julia Menasce Horowitz, and Monica Anderson, "Amid Protests, Majorities Across Racial and Ethnic Groups Express Support for the Black Lives Matter Movement," Pew Research Center, June 12, 2020, www.pewsocialtrend .org/2020/06/12/amid-protests-majorities-across-racial-and-ethnic-groups-express -support-for-the-black-lives-matter-movement/.

2. Ava Pointe Shoe, Capezio, www.capezio.com/ava-pointe-shoe; Fabric Pointe Paint | Skin Tone, Pointe People, www.pointepeople.com/collections/fabric-pointe -paint-skin-tone; "Freed of London Pointe Shoe Collaboration," Ballet Black, https:// balletblack.co.uk/freed-pointe-shoe-collaboration/.

3. Dan Meyer, "Capezio Vows to Create a Line of Skin Color–Inclusive Pointe Shoes," *Playbill*, June 16, 2020, www.playbill.com/article/capezio-vows-to-create -a-line-of-skin-colorinclusive-pointe-shoes; "We're Listening . . . " Bloch, accessed November 17, 2020, https://us.blochworld.com/pages/were-listening-a-message -from-us-to-you.

4. Claire Cain Miller, "Nearly Half of Men Say They Do Most of the Home Schooling. 3 Percent of Women Agree," *New York Times*, May 6, 2020, www .nytimes.com/2020/05/06/upshot/pandemic-chores-homeschooling-gender. html; Lucy Meakin, "Parents' Chores and Child Care Almost Double During

Pandemic," Bloomberg, May 20, 2020, www.bloomberg.com/news /articles/2020-05-21/coronavirus-almost-doubles-the-housework-for-working -parents; Sarah Chaney, "Women's Job Losses from Pandemic Aren't Good for Economic Recovery," *Wall Street Journal*, June 21, 2020, www.wsj.com/articles /womens-job-losses-from-pandemic-arent-good-for-economic-recovery -11592745164; Patricia Cohen and Tiffany Hsu, "Pandemic Could Scar a Generation of Working Mothers," *New York Times*, June 3, 2020, www.nytimes.com/2020/06/03 /business/economy/coronavirus-working-women.html; Neil Paine and Amelia Thomson-DeVeaux, "How the Pandemic Could Force a Generation of Mothers out of the Workforce," FiveThirtyEight, July 27, 2020, https://fivethirtyeight.com/features /how-the-pandemic-could-force-a-generation-of-mothers-out-of-the-workforce/.

5. Gia Kourlas, "Can Ballet Come Alive Online?," *New York Times*, June 5, 2020, www.nytimes.com/2020/06/05/arts/dance/new-york-city-ballet-american -theater-online-coronavirus.html; Sarah Kaufman, "The Washington Ballet Thought a Virtual Fundraiser Was Safe. But It Still May Have Put Artists at Risk," *Washington Post*, July 13, 2020, www.washingtonpost.com/entertainment/theater_dance /the-washington-ballet-thought-a-virtual-fundraiser-was-safe-but-it-still-may-have -put-artists-at-risk/2020/07/13/a70bf050-c2da-11ea-b4f6-cb39cd8940fb_story.html.

6. Maggie Donahue, "Colorado Ballet Has Furloughed All of Its Dancers," Denverite, September 3, 2020, https://denverite.com/2020/09/03/colorado -ballet-has-furloughed-all-of-its-dancers/; Stephanie Wolf, "Louisville Ballet Furloughs, Cuts Staff and Reduces Salaries," WFPL, April 14, 2020, https://wfpl.org /louisville-ballet-furloughs-cuts-staff-and-reduces-salaries/.

7. "Our Voices," Dancers of NYCB, accessed November 17, 2020, www.dancers ofnycb.com/ourvoices.

8. Theresa Ruth Howard, "Dance Theatre of Harlem Kicks Off Ballet Across America with a New Ballet by Claudia Schreier," *Pointe*, May 28, 2019, www .pointemagazine.com/claudia-schreier-passage-dth-2637913341.html.

Conclusion

1. Several paragraphs of this conclusion appeared in an essay I wrote for *Gay* magazine in 2019: Chloe Angyal, "The Pleasure of Ballet," *Gay*, June 4, 2019, https://gay .medium.com/the-pleasure-of-ballet-83ed8a67e2b2.

INDEX

Vivian Le

Chloe Angyal is a journalist from Sydney, Australia. She is a contributing editor at MarieClaire.com, and her writing about politics and culture has appeared in the *New York Times*, *Washington Post*, *Atlantic*, *Guardian*, and *New York Magazine*. She holds a BA in sociology from Princeton and a PhD in arts and media from the University of New South Wales. She lives in the Iowa City area.